Burn Holy Fire

Religion in Lewes
since the Reformation

Jeremy Goring

The Lutterworth Press

The Lutterworth Press
P.O. Box 60
Cambridge
CB1 2NT

www.lutterworth.com
publishing@lutterworth.com

First Published in 2003

ISBN 0 7188 3040 7

British Library Cataloguing in Publication Data
A catalogue record is available from the British Library

Contents

List of Maps and Tables

The town plan of Lewes on page 150 is taken from W.H. Godfrey, *Lewes: The Official Guide to the Historic County Town* (revised edition, 1977) and reproduced by kind permission of Lewes Town Council.

Preface

I have known and loved Lewes nearly all my life. I first entered the town on foot in 1935 at the age of five, my parents being confident that I was now old and strong enough to walk the seven miles along the Downs from Ditchling. But I was far too tired to appreciate the fine view that greeted us as we skirted the race-course and, passing the new houses then being built on the Nevill estate, made our descent into the town. The only thing that kept me going was the prospect of scrambled eggs on toast at the 'Tatler' tea rooms. Having as yet no taste for history I probably did not notice the ancient churches that I passed on the last lap of the journey down the High Street: St Anne's, with its fine Norman doorway, and St Michael's, with its distinctive thirteenth-century round tower. And I certainly would never have noticed Westgate Chapel, just over the road from St Michael's, and then almost hidden from sight behind an avenue of laurels.

Fifty years later it was an interest in Westgate Chapel that eventually led me to come to live in Lewes and join its historic Protestant Dissenting congregation. It was then that I began to explore the history of a cause that, combining elements of each of the original 'Three Denominations' of Dissent (Baptist, Independent, Presbyterian), may justly claim to be unique in England. I read J.M. Connell's admirable *Story of an Old Meeting House* but was disappointed that, while making much of the ministers, it had little to say about the laity. I particularly wished to find out more about a family named Ridge who had helped to found the congregation in the seventeenth century and remained active well on into the nineteenth: here, it seemed, was a remarkable example of continuity in a period of great religious change. After a chance meeting with Jessie Ridge, the last of a long line of Protestant Dissenters, I decided to pursue the social and religious history of her family. But the project widened when I was invited to give a course of University of the Third Age lectures on the religious history of Lewes. This obliged me to place Westgate Chapel in its wider context and to study the history of all the churches and chapels that had ever existed in the town.

It was at the suggestion of U3A members that I embarked upon the writing of this book.

In the course of doing so I have become indebted to many people. I am especially grateful to my good neighbour Asa Briggs, Lord Briggs of Lewes, for his critical appraisal of the first draft of the text and for kindly agreeing to contribute a Foreword. I also wish to thank Colin Brent, who knows more about the history of Lewes than anyone, for his comments on the early chapters of the book. Other friends who have read sections of the book and made valuable suggestions are John Bleach, Alan Everitt, David Hitchin, William Lamont, Alan Ruston and David Wykes. I have also benefited greatly from conversations with Judith Brent, Christopher Day, Susan Haines, Laurence Keogh, Graham Mayhew, Christopher Whittick and the late Kathleen Vinall. In addition I wish to acknowledge the helpfulness of the staff of the British Library, Dr Williams's Library, Sussex University Library, the Public Record Office, the East and West Sussex Record Offices and the volunteers who look after the library of the Sussex Archaeological Society, of which I have been a member since 1949. I should also like to thank Cliff Bowes, Sarah Greenland and my sons Charlie, George and Danny for assistance with computing, Andy Gammon for designing the cover and illustrations, and Adrian Brink of the Lutterworth Press for making the process of publishing so pleasurable. My greatest debt is to my wife Rosemary, who reads everything I write with a keen eye for clichés, obscurities and hyperbole – and without whose help I should never have been able to embark upon this project, let alone bring it to completion.

Finally I should like to pay a posthumous tribute to two great history teachers. A.E. Wilson first aroused my interest in history – and especially the history of Sussex – when I was a schoolboy. S. T. Bindoff, another of 'Doc' Wilson's former pupils at Brighton Grammar School, supervised my post-graduate studies and, in his best-selling Penguin book *Tudor England,* set a fine (if inimitable) example of how history should be written.

Foreword

Asa Briggs

This absorbing book, which tells many stories and investigates many different situations, speaks for itself. I am privileged, therefore, to have been invited to write a brief Foreword. The author, who has carried out meticulous research, often testing and difficult, invited me to write it for two reasons. First, I am a neighbour in Keere Street, Lewes, and know Lewes over several decades. Second, I am a social and cultural historian, who has always set out to relate local to national and comparative international history – and religious history to social and cultural history.

I also share with Jeremy Goring a sense of delight in time travel, spanning centuries and not, as so many professional historians do, getting caught in one 'period'. I found the pre-Reformation chapter in this book as illuminating as those which dealt with recent history. The detail is as illuminating as the generalisation, and I was gripped at once by one of the first of the many disturbing stories – that of John Hoggesflesh, a largely forgotten early sixteenth-century heretic who for his 'detestable opinions' had his case referred beyond Chichester to the archbishop of Canterbury, to the duke of Norfolk and to King Henry VIII. As Jeremy Goring observes, 'rarely in the history of religious conflict has one obscure individual caused so much trouble to so many important people over such a long period of time'.

There is much in this book about religious conflict, some of it between individuals or groups of people not far separated from each other by their religious convictions, about 'martyrdom', and about the contrast between Lewes and Chichester. Yet these are not the only themes. Others are 'Nonconformist ascendancy' and the role of women in different congregations. One of Jeremy Goring's last stories was about a twentieth-century Hogsflesh (different spelling), the widow of Amos Hogsflesh – a Methodist whose 'spiritual influence sitting quietly in her pew may have been greater than that of a succession of men pounding away in the pulpit'. For Jeremy Goring, 'if continuity and change are the weft and warp of the historical process' – and I believe that they are – 'it seems to be, in religion as in other spheres of life, the women who provide the continuity and the men who produce the change'.

For readers involved in the current life of religion in Lewes the most interesting and in places surprising details concern St Michael's Church and Westgate Chapel, almost directly confronting each other over Lewes High Street. It will surprise many readers that for centuries St Michael's was a stronghold of militant Protestantism. By contrast Westgate illuminates almost every aspect of religious change, and it was a Westgate pastor – Thomas Walker Horsfield, a Yorkshireman and an avowed Unitarian – who wrote what remains the most monumental *History of Lewes* in 1824 and 1827. There are biases, which Jeremy Goring notes, and it was from a hymn by a different Unitarian writer, Frederick Lucian Hosmer, that he took the inspiring title of his book. The pentecostal fire to which it refers has often burned bright in Lewes, and when the great hymn was sung at the close of the service to celebrate the 300th anniversary of Westgate Chapel – on 5 November – the Rector of St Michael's was present and the Roman Catholic parish priest at St Pancras read one of the lessons.

Introduction

In the foreword to his *Carnival in Romans* the distinguished French historian Emmanuel Le Roy Ladurie asked whether the study of the social and cultural history of a particular French town could be of any interest to 'the reader who lives far from south-eastern France, for example in Lancashire, New York or Minnesota'. Most of his readers would probably have replied that, although its compass was confined to developments in a single town, his book threw light on what was happening throughout western Europe. Can something similar be said about a less ambitious study of a particular town in south-eastern England? Can the social and religious history of the Sussex town of Lewes be said to constitute a microcosm of that of England as a whole?[1]

At first sight Lewes seems an unlikely place about which to ask such a question. Only a few nationally known religious figures feature in its story. While Fox, Penn, Doddridge, Whitefield, Spurgeon and J.M. Neale are at one time or another on stage, their appearances are marginal and fleeting. For the most part this book is the record of the thoughts and actions of obscure men and women. However, it does exemplify most of the major themes of the past five centuries of English religious history: the Reformation, the rise of puritanism, the Great Ejection, the emergence of Nonconformity, the Evangelical Revival, the Oxford Movement, Protestant-Catholic conflict, the ecumenical movement and the decline of institutional religion. Moreover, nearly every branch and brand of Christianity is represented here. The roll-call of the denominations that have at one time or another been present in the town is unusually long: besides six Anglican churches the list includes Roman Catholics, Baptists (General, Particular and Strict), Presbyterians (English, Scottish, Irish), Methodists (Calvinistic, Wesleyan and Primitive), Quakers, Independents, Congregationalists, Huntingdonians, Huntingtonians, Salvationists, Unitarians and Free Christians.

The activities of these groupings and their changing fortunes over the

years may be said to constitute the essential fabric of the public religious
life of England. But if such activities are studied out of context, as they
sometimes are in works of purely ecclesiastical history, their true
significance may not always be seen. It is only when events are examined
within the wider social, economic and cultural framework that they can be
placed in their proper perspective. However, setting 500 years of religious
change within the context of the total history of a nation would take up
many stout volumes and test the powers of the greatest polymath. The task
only becomes manageable when undertaken within the confines of a local
community – one small enough to give the work coherence, yet large enough
to give it substance. Lewes, it is here suggested, is one such town. Known
to many merely as a staging post on the way to Glyndebourne, Charleston
or the Newhaven-Dieppe ferry, or as the location of the most spectacular
Fifth of November celebrations in all England, it is a town with a long and
interesting history.[2]

Lewes has almost all the characteristics of what Alan Everitt has called
'the primary towns of England'. Strategically situated on a spur of high
ground overlooking the point where the Ouse cuts through the South Downs,
it has from the earliest times been a place of some importance. Its name is
thought to derive from the *hlaewes* or burial mounds that in the Celtic era
dotted the land on which the town was later built. Whether anyone actually
lived in such a grand necropolis nobody knows for certain, but, standing at
the intersection of a navigable north-south waterway and an ancient east-
west trackway, it was a major route centre and a natural place for people to
settle at. Although there was probably some kind of settlement in Roman
times it was not until the reign of King Alfred that there is evidence of a
burh here. In late Saxon times the town's role as a major administrative
centre is attested by the presence of a royal mint. In the days of Edward the
Confessor the lord of the borough was the great Earl Godwin and no fewer
than 127 burgesses were living here. After the Norman Conquest Lewes
passed into the possession of the Conqueror's friend William de Warenne,
who erected a fine castle within the confines of the Saxon town and began
the building of a great monastery to the south of it in 'Southover'. It was at
this famous Cluniac priory that in 1264 Henry III made his headquarters
on the eve of the Battle of Lewes and, after his defeat by Simon de Montfort,
that the momentous Mise of Lewes was signed. In this century the town
was fortified with walls, which stood the inhabitants in good stead if the
French ever launched attacks upon the Sussex coast, as they did in 1377
when they carried off the prior of Lewes as a prisoner.[3]

It is only from the sixteenth century, however, that enough evidence
survives to enable us to know much in detail about the history of the town.
Henry VIII's reign saw the spoliation of the priory, personally supervised

by his chief minister Thomas Cromwell, who coveted its possessions for his son. Edward VI's brought further destruction of church property and Queen Mary's saw the burning of numerous Protestant martyrs in Lewes High Street. In the age of Elizabeth things became more settled and the town experienced great prosperity. The antiquary William Camden, who toured the Sussex coast at this time, was rather rude about Arundel and Shoreham, but was most impressed by Lewes, which for 'populousness and extent may be ranked among the principal towns in the county'. Lewes, with the new outlet to the sea (the 'new haven') that had been created at Meeching, was now a thriving commercial port which was handling an increasing volume of coastal and overseas trade. Its role as an administrative centre also grew in importance. To it came country gentry from different parts of Sussex to dispense justice, levy taxes, administer the militia or simply to enjoy the social attractions of the town. Some acquired town houses here. Sir John Pelham of Laughton re-modelled the large house in the High Street that later became the White Hart hotel. George Goring of Danny in Hurstpierpoint erected another close by which, after a change of ownership, came to be called Pelham House and finally became the headquarters of the county council. And his elder brother Sir Henry Goring of Burton near Petworth bought the Bull Inn by the west gate and added the substantial back-addition that was later to become Westgate Chapel.[4]

By the seventeenth century Lewes was not only a major marketing centre, full of merchants trading in agricultural produce or in manufactured goods brought up river from Newhaven or down river from the Weald, but also a hive of light industry. Here, in numerous small workshops, craftsmen in leather, cloth and metal wrought the articles and implements to be sold to shoppers from the town or the surrounding countryside. The place teemed with the 'middling sort' of people who, throughout Europe at this time, tended to be attracted to radical forms of religion. Lewes became noted for its puritanism and, when the Civil War broke out, its inhabitants were strongly Parliamentary in sympathy; but there was no fighting in this part of Sussex and the war left the town unscathed. The most serious disruptions occurred after the war was over and the Stuart monarchy had been restored, when the large numbers who had withdrawn from the parish churches were punished for their nonconformity.

In the high Georgian era there was little religious conflict in Lewes. This period, it has been said, saw the 'heyday' of the county town. Colin Brent has recently provided a vivid picture of Lewes at this time, with its 'vibrant intellectual, religious and political life', which stimulated (among others) Tom Paine, Jane Austen and the great geologist Gideon Mantell. People flocked into the place to buy perukes or clay pipes, watch a play or a prize fight, attend the races, witness an execution, vote in an election, sample a sermon or simply meet their friends in one of the town's innumerable hostelries. The prosperity of Lewes was based upon its role as 'the mart of mid-Sussex'. Up the river from Newhaven came the barges loaded with consumer goods and the heavy consignments of coal, iron, and Baltic timber that made its merchants among the richest in Sussex. This wealth led to conspicuous expenditure and the period saw the re-modelling of many of the old timber-framed houses in the High Street, which were re-fronted with bricks or 'mathematical tiles'. Here as elsewhere this was a time of rapid expansion, with the population rising from about 2,500 in 1760 to over 8,500 in 1831. But by the third decade of the nineteenth century, partly owing to growing competition from nearby Brighton, the town's heyday was over.[5]

Although Lewes ceased to be the social and commercial capital of central Sussex its economic advance continued unabated. The Victorian age brought considerable prosperity. The coming of the railways, linking the town to Brighton, Eastbourne, Hastings, Seaford, East Grinstead, Tunbridge Wells and (twice over) to London, strengthened its ancient role as a route centre. It was a time of industrial expansion, with local firms such as the Phoenix Ironworks (owned and managed by the Every family) manufacturing products for a world market. These developments meant that Lewes, with its new and enlarged county gaol, its expanding local government bureaucracy and its continuing role as a major market for agricultural produce, offered plenty of good employment prospects for its inhabitants, whose numbers by the end of the nineteenth century had risen to over 11,000. In the twentieth century, rather surprisingly, the population did not rise as rapidly as that of most English provincial towns: today there are still only about 15,000 people living here. Physical constraints have limited its extension: hemmed in by marsh to the north and south and by downland to the east and west, it has not proved possible to build as many houses as the growing demand has warranted. Nevertheless the years following the first World War did see some westward suburban expansion, some of it necessitated by slum clearances and commercial developments in the older parts of the town.

Since the second World War there have been even more changes in the town. The 'Tatler' tea-rooms have become (inevitably) an Indian restaurant. The butchers, bakers and grocers that once plied their trades in the High Street have also disappeared, their premises now occupied by estate agents, building societies and shops selling souvenirs, antiques or charity clothes. The continued expansion of local government has resulted in the erection of a new and hideously obtrusive County Hall at the top of the town, while commercial development has led to the destruction of many fine buildings at the bottom. Lewes may no longer be what Alice Dudeney, the popular novelist who lived here from 1916 until her death in 1945, called 'the most divine spot in the world', but it continues to attract numerous incomers. The electrification of the railway, enabling people to work in London and live (or at least sleep) in Lewes has brought many long distance commuters and their families into the town. The coming of Sussex University and part of Brighton Polytechnic (now Brighton University) to Falmer, four miles away, has caused a great influx of academics who find Lewes quieter and more congenial than Brighton. Nevertheless, unlike some other Sussex towns, Lewes has not been so swamped by incomers as to lose its identity; many of its residents are genuine 'Lewesians' whose families have lived here for generations.[6]

Among old and new residents alike there is great interest in the town's history, and especially its religious history – as was clearly demonstrated in the summer of 1981 when a grand historical pageant was put on to mark the thirteenth centenary of St Wilfrid's settlement in Sussex. Called 'Tongues of Flame' and directed by Monica Russell, the pageant had a cast of 100 and was performed twice before capacity audiences in the grounds of Lewes Castle. Beginning with the saint's shipwreck on the Sussex coast in 666 and ending with the establishment of Lewes & District Council of Churches in 1957, it gave a dramatic presentation of what the local newspaper called the 'violent story of a religion'. Lewes people take a great pride in their town and its traditions, particularly those associated with Guy Fawkes' Night, when tens of thousands of people flock in to witness the bonfires and street processions that are famed throughout Europe. There is a popular belief that these celebrations are survivals of fire-festivals dating back to the Dark Ages. If Lewes was once a great necropolis is it altogether surprising that such rituals should continue to be practised here in November, the so-called 'month of the dead'?[7]

The first book devoted to the religious history of Lewes was written by J.M. Connell and published in 1931 under the title of *Lewes: Its Religious History*. Some people thought that it paid too much attention to Westgate Chapel, where the author was minister, and not enough to the other places of worship in the town. It may be that similar criticisms will be made of the present work, where the story of this particular congregation again features prominently. This could be due in part to personal bias, but there are other reasons for the imbalance. One has to do with the availability of sources: it so happens that Westgate's records survive in greater abundance than is the case with most other Lewes congregations. The other reason relates to the content of the surviving documents. The records of some churches are so formal that they supply little information about anything but the state of their finances or the condition of their fabric. On the whole the records of Nonconformist congregations are rather more meaty than those of parish churches and provide more evidence of how people thought or acted at a given time. Since the sources for ecclesiastical history so often consist of records of conflicts and disagreements it may be that

Nonconformists, being generally more disputatious than Anglicans, have left more evidence of their activities behind them. When it comes to more recent times, however, there is a more obvious explanation for the prominence of Nonconformity in this book. From the mid nineteenth century onwards it relies heavily upon the evidence of newspapers, and especially the *East Sussex News*, which usually contained more about Lewes than its rival, the *Sussex Express*. While the sympathies of the *Express* were predominantly Conservative and Anglican those of the *News* tended to be Liberal and Nonconformist. The paper was in fact edited for many years by a leading Congregationalist Henry Walston, who was on its staff from 1871 to 1907. He was evidently a man with a mission. At his funeral in 1919 he was described as 'a strong believer in a clean Press', who always 'strove to promote the interests of truth and morality'. Since he clearly considered the Free Churches to be among the greatest forces for good in the world, it was only natural that he was happy to include a great deal about them in his paper. But being a fair-minded man he did not neglect the Church of England: if Anglican clergy provided him with news from their parishes he always seems to have been prepared to publish it.[8]

The unevenness of the sources is not, however, the principal explanation for the prominence of Nonconformity in the pages of this book. The fact is that in Lewes, unlike other Sussex towns, Nonconformists were for a long period more numerous than Anglicans. In the early eighteenth century the congregation of Westgate Meeting was probably larger than the combined congregations of the nearby parish churches of St Michael and St Anne. In the early nineteenth century the number attending Cliffe Chapel and its daughter churches was undoubtedly greater than the total attending Anglican services throughout the town. Ecclesiastically as well as geographically Lewes is the polar opposite of Chichester: in the western county capital, with its great cathedral and its vast array of clergy, it is the Nonconformists who have usually occupied the shadow. In Lewes, throughout the nineteenth century the richest men were almost invariably Nonconformists, with money to spare for the building and endowing of chapels and for the maintenance of their ministries. Their ascendancy persisted into the twentieth century and, although there has been a suffragan bishopric of Lewes since 1909, the established church still has no weighty presence in the town. The absence of an imposing parish church, centrally located like that at Maidstone or Tewkesbury, where a suffragan can feel himself to be seated as in a cathedral, may be a significant factor in the situation. If any building in Lewes ever deserved the designation 'cathedral' it was the Congregational Tabernacle, for long the largest, most prestigious and best situated place of worship in the town, where for a quarter of a century Burgess Wilkinson, known locally as the 'Bishop of Nonconformity', exercised a magisterial ministry.

It has to be admitted that previous accounts of the religious history of Lewes written by Nonconformists have not been free from an element of personal bias. Colin Brent has pointed out how Thomas Walker Horsfield's monumental *History of Lewes* (1824, 1827) reflects the author's own prejudices:

> Horsfield was the pastor at Westgate Chapel, and his Radicalism had a Unitarian edge. He saluted the Marian martyrs who died at Lewes for 'free inquiry in matters of religion'. They left a 'dark damp cell' beneath the Star to confront 'the faggots which blazed before it'. Under Charles II 'the harpies of bigotry' seized the property of Lewes Dissenters whose worship offended 'the minions of a lascivious court'. . . . He denounced (as though pounding a pulpit cushion) 'the poison tree of Rome', the 'haughty, imperious and tyrannical Warennes', the 'arbitrary, bigoted, licentious' Henry VIII. He rejoiced that goats now browsed at Southover where the Cluniac despots had trodden. He admired King Alfred, King Harold and William Wallace, but not De Montfort, promoting instead the Whig paladins of the 1680s, John Locke, Lord William Russell and Algernon Sidney.

Connell, who pounded the same pulpit cushion as Horsfield, was careful not to perpetuate his partisanship. In *Lewes: Its Religious History* he positively leant over backwards to be fair to people with whose churchmanship and theology he disagreed. Although an heir of the puritans, he had good words for Archbishop Laud. 'It is difficult', he wrote, 'not to sympathise with Laud and those who felt as he did nor fail to realise that they were just as sincere in their way of thinking as the puritans were in theirs.' Moving on to the nineteenth century he was full of praise for the High-Church hymn-writer John Mason Neale. 'We should have supposed', he said, 'that the man who did all this fine work and added so much to the spiritual riches of the Church of England and of Christendom generally would have received every encouragement', but 'it has with sorrow to be remembered that a Lewes mob treated him most shamefully.'[9]

What Connell wrote in the preface to *Lewes: Its Religious History* may provide a fitting introduction to this one:

> Lewes may claim to have some special fitness as a starting place for the study of English religious history. Its traditions reach far back into the past. . . . It saw the rise and fall of the great Priory of St Pancras, and the burning of Protestant martyrs in its High Street. It shared in the struggles of episcopalianism and puritanism, orthodoxy and heresy, ritualism and evangelicalism, and these have left their marks upon it, in the variety of its denominational groupings and in the diversity of thought and worship that exist today.

The present work covers, albeit in far greater detail, much the same ground as Connell's pioneering study, considering the same conflicts and exploring the same varieties of religious faith and practice that have existed in the town since the Reformation. However, in order to make sense of the post-Reformation religious history of Lewes, it is first necessary to do as he did and go back even further into the past to the time when Christianity was first planted in this part of England.[10]

I. Religion before the Reformation

Sussex, cut off from the north and east by the dense woodland of the Weald, was the last Saxon kingdom to be converted to Christianity. According to tradition the man responsible for the conversion was St Wilfrid, who first set foot in the shire in 666. It was an involuntary visit, occasioned by a storm that beached the ship in which he was returning to England from Gaul. It is recorded that the local inhabitants gave the intruders a hostile reception: a pagan priest, standing on a high mound, rained down curses on the Christians. It is not known where exactly this incident occurred but, since Wilfrid was travelling to York from Compiègne, it was almost certainly in the eastern part of Sussex, where paganism was most strongly rooted. Might he not have landed near Lewes, then sited on an arm of the sea and conspicuous for the numerous *hlaewes* or mounds, some of great ceremonial significance, that were to be found there?[1]

When eventually Christianity did reach Lewes it may not have come via western Sussex, which Wilfrid had helped to convert, but via Kent, the first kingdom in southern England to embrace the new religion and a natural springboard for missionary enterprise. What is known is that early in the ninth century the king of Kent granted the archbishop of Canterbury a great swathe of lands in east Sussex, stretching from Wadhurst to South Malling. It may have constituted a kind of Christian corridor along which Kentishmen could come to bring the light to Lewes. Was the monastic community that the archbishop established just over the Ouse at South Malling a launching-pad for a spiritual assault on what had once been a great pagan citadel? When churches were eventually built on the downland promontory of 'Hlaewes' over the river it is significant that some of them were erected near one or other of the great mounds. One church dedicated to St Michael and probably erected at the behest of the archbishop of Canterbury, was built at the foot of the biggest mound of all – the one on which the Normans were later to erect their castle keep. Another church, later to be known as

The Diocese of Chichester

The map shows places mentioned in the text and the boundaries of the former rural deaneries within the Archdeaconry of Lewes

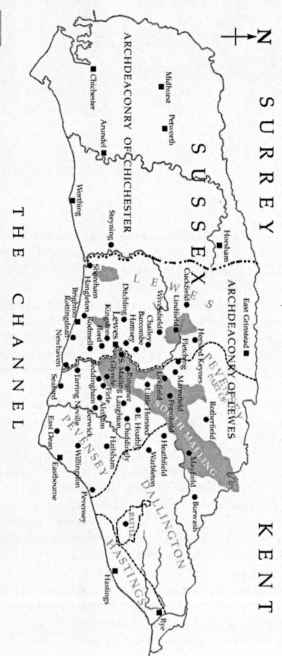

N

SURREY

SUSSEX

KENT

THE CHANNEL

ARCHDEACONRY OF CHICHESTER

ARCHDEACONRY OF LEWES

Deanery of South Malling: Archbishop of Canterbury's Peculiar
Boundary between archdeaconries
Boundary between rural deaneries: Lewes, Pevensey, Dallington, Battle, Hastings.
Major towns

Midhurst
Petworth
Chichester
Arundel
Worthing
Steyning
Horsham
East Grinstead
Cuckfield
Lindfield
Wivelsfield
Chailey
Barcombe
Hamsey
Ditchling
Kingston
Iford
Rodmell
Steyning
Hangleton
Brighton
Rottingdean
Newhaven
Seaford
Plumpton
Lewes
S. Malling
Glynde
Firle
Ringmer
Laughton
Chiddingly
Hailsham
Warbleton
Heathfield
Berwick
Wartling
Wallington
Pevensey
Eastbourne
East Dean
Hurst Keynes
Fletching
Maresfield
Buxted
Framfield
E. Heath
Rotherfield
Mayfield
Burwash
SOUTH MALLING
DALLINGTON
HASTINGS
BATTLE
PEVENSEY
LEWES
PEVENSEY PART OF
Hastings
Rye

St John sub Castro, was built beside two smaller mounds occupying a strategically important site above a crossing-point of the Ouse at South Malling.

The Coming of the Monks

After the coming of the Normans the spiritual conquest of Lewes was finally ensured by the building, to the south of the town, of the great priory of St Pancras, which was founded between 1078 and 1081 by William de Warenne and his wife Gundrada. The first house of the Cluniac order to be established in England, its monks were renowned for the strictness of their rule and the splendour and solemnity of their worship. The original inmates came to Lewes from the mother house at Cluny: at first there were four, later twelve and by 1279 the number had risen to 50. The priory, positioned like a giant siege-engine ready to batter down the walls of Lewes, was a huge structure: its church, a tenth of a mile long with a tower 200ft high, was bigger than Chichester Cathedral. The monks quickly gained control over the religious life of the town and by the middle of the twelfth century they possessed nine out of twelve churches in Lewes. These were the churches of St John sub Castro, St Peter the Less, St Andrew, St Mary in Foro, St Martin, St Nicholas, Holy Trinity, and St Peter and St Mary Westout. In the next century they provided the people of Southover, the new town that had grown up at the monastery gates, with a place of worship: the former *hospitium* of the priory became a parish church. Only St Michael's, St Sepulchre's, All Saints' and the twelfth century church dedicated to St Thomas Becket in Cliffe lay outside the monks' control.

In addition to the parish churches there were other ecclesiastical buildings in and around Lewes. Just over the river in South Malling, not far from the site of the monastery established in the ninth century, was a community of canons founded by Archbishop Theobald in c.1150. South Malling College, with its large church and its extensive living quarters, must have been an imposing structure. To the south and west of the town were two hospitals (or almshouses), one in Southover dedicated to St James and the other in Westout to St Nicholas, situated in what is now Spital Road. Recent excavations at this site have led to the discovery of over a hundred skeletons, some of which are thought to have belonged to soldiers killed in the great battle that took place close by in 1264. Although the Battle of Lewes may have been viewed nationally as a victory of right over wrong, locally it was something of a disaster. Henry III, who arrived in Lewes on 11 May, the eve of the feast of St Pancras, took up his quarters in the priory, where some of his soldiery ran amok and defiled the altars. Later, after the king had lost the battle, Simon de Montfort's troops set fire to the church and did considerable damage to the conventual buildings.

The priory, which was already in financial difficulties, apparently took a long time to recover from the catastrophe. In other English towns situated in close proximity to a powerful but impecunious religious house there was sometimes conflict between monks and townsmen over such matters as the levying of market tolls, but Lewes seems to have escaped this. It is likely that most people welcomed the presence of the monks, who brought custom to merchants and craftsmen and provided employment for servants and retainers.[2]

Whatever they felt about the black-habited monks of St Pancras it is likely that Lewes people were well disposed towards the grey-habited friars, who in the early thirteenth century established a house just outside the town walls to the east. The Lewes Franciscans are first heard of in 1241, when Henry III gave them 10 marks for vestments. They crop up again in the records in 1299, when Henry's son Edward I visited the town and gave them 24s, sufficient to provide food for three days – which indicates that there were then 24 friars. It would be interesting to know if the 'little brothers' of Lewes remained true to the teaching and example of their founder, St Francis of Assisi, whose poverty and simplicity of life-style was in sharp contrast to that of most contemporary churchmen. One thing, however, is clear. They were prepared to show mercy and grant sanctuary to those falling foul of the law, as they did in 1249 when a young man accused of stealing from his father took refuge in the friary, where he remained for ten days.[3]

St Richard and Lewes

In Lewes, as in other towns, rights of sanctuary for criminals were a constant source of friction. There was a particularly serious example of this in the mid-thirteenth century when Richard of Wych, later to be canonised as St Richard, was bishop of Chichester. On one occasion when a thief took refuge in a church some of the townsmen violently forced him out and hanged him. The bishop was outraged and compelled the culprits to dig up the decaying corpse and carry it to the church on their shoulders. Furthermore, those who had aided and abetted them were ordered to be beaten and then to be paraded, with ropes about their necks and only shirts on their backs, through the market-places of Lewes and other nearby towns. It is recorded that the bishop refused the money the men offered in commutation of their punishment 'as if it were excrement'. Another local man who was severely dealt with for infringing the rights of the church was a certain knight who had sacrilegiously imprisoned a priest. The offender was obliged to take the wooden stocks to which he had tied the priest's feet and, 'like a beast of burden carrying its yoke', carry them around the church that the priest had served and through the market-place of Lewes. Once again the bishop refused a great sum of money offered in commutation of this penance.

These stories come from the contemporary *Life of St Richard* and they are immediately followed by this statement:

> He also refused a great sum of money offered on behalf of a new synagogue which the Jews had built, but rejected their requests and bribes and did not rest until it had been pulled down and demolished.

No indication is given of where the synagogue was, but from the context it looks as if it were in Lewes. An important mercantile centre with a considerable population of aliens, Lewes was a likely place for Jews to live. Various people named Isaac and Solomon crop up in the records but it is not certain that any of them were Jews. It has been suggested that the Jews may have lived just outside the town walls in Antioch Street, then a steep street running up the hill from Southover, but there is no documentary or archaeological evidence for this. Only one document refers to Jews: a deed drawn up in c.1240 prohibiting the sale of property in Southover to a religious house also stipulated that it should not be sold to a Jew. If there were Jews in medieval Lewes they would not have remained beyond 1290, when John Peckham, who shared St Richard's strong aversion to Jews, was archbishop of Canterbury. In that year Edward I expelled them from England.

The *Life of St Richard* also records a happier aspect of the saint's association with Lewes and one that provides an interesting insight into the simple piety of the age.

> One day, when he was crossing the bridge at Lewes . . . he saw some fishermen striving hard to catch some fish. One of the archbishop of Canterbury's bailiffs was standing on the bridge supervising the fishermen. He greeted the bishop respectfully and said, 'My lord, we have toiled a long time here, but have caught nothing. If it please you, wait here a short while and, when we have brought in our nets, bless them so that we may let them down once more with your blessing.' The saint stood where he was and smiled. He raised his right hand and blessed both the water and the fishermen and said, 'Now let down the net in the name of the Lord.' And they let down the net and dragged it through the water. When they hauled the net out on to the land they found four extremely fine fish which in English are called 'mullet'; fish like these are not normally caught in that river, for they are sea rather than freshwater fish.

The saint then ordered the fish to be given to the friars whose house stood close by the bridge, 'for he claimed that it was on their account that God had given these fish'.[4]

This may have been the only occasion on which the saint visited Lewes; because it took so long to get here bishops of Chichester rarely came into the eastern part of Sussex. This was one reason why it became necessary to set up another archdeaconry to deal with this end of the diocese. The headquarters of the eastern archdeaconry was in Lewes and its court dealt with probate, tithe disputes and moral offences such as fornication, drunkenness and defamation, and to it were summoned offenders from all over east Sussex. However, those who lived in Cliffe and other places in the deanery of South Malling were subject to the jurisdiction of the archbishop of Canterbury, whose court usually met at St Thomas's. The existence of this 'peculiar' jurisdiction, which accounts for the presence of the archbishop's bailiff on Lewes bridge when St Richard visited the town, may help to explain why the church often had such difficulty in policing the place. Inhabitants of Lewes who were being pursued by the ecclesiastical authorities could escape over the bridge into Cliffe, where the bishop of Chichester's writ did not run, while malefactors in Cliffe could likewise evade punishment by crossing over to Lewes. In the later Middle Ages, when Lollards were being persecuted in Canterbury diocese, Lewes may have offered a safe haven to heretics.[5]

The Later Middle Ages

Because of the lack of documentation it is not easy to discover much about the religious life of Lewes in the later Middle Ages, but what we know about the parish churches indicates a state of decline. By the beginning of the fourteenth century the structures of St Nicholas, Holy Trinity and St Peter the Less were reported to be ruinous and there was a proposal that their parishes be merged with All Saints'. In 1337 All Saints', which was in the patronage of the bishop of Chichester, was said to be impoverished and unserved – as were all the churches in Lewes except those of St Michael and St John sub Castro. Throughout the next century the churches of St Mary in Foro, St Andrew and St Martin continued to stand in a line along the south side of the High Street but they too were not in a good condition and were soon to disappear – as was St Peter Westout. The situation at St Mary Westout, however, may have been rather better: famed for its anchorite who had been walled up there in the thirteenth century and its association with a holy well dedicated to St Anne, it appears to have been a popular place of resort for pilgrims.[6]

The dedications of the parish churches provide some indication of the local popularity of the saints. It is not surprising to find that in Lewes those universally venerated saints, Mary and Peter, each had two churches dedicated to them – as did the ubiquitous John the Baptist with one church just below the castle and another down in Southover. Nor is it surprising to find a church dedicated to St Michael the Archangel, the heavenly contender against evil, standing alongside what may once have been (like other 'St Michael's mounts') a great pagan ceremonial mound. The town's closeness to what was once a great estuary may help to explain the dedication of a church to St Nicholas, the patron saint of sailors, and to St Andrew, who was popular with fishermen. Why St Martin, venerated by soldiers and horsemen, should have found favour is not so clear. Is it merely coincidental that St Martin and St Andrew, like All Saints, had feast-days in November, which – being 'the month of the dead' – may still have had some important cultic significance in Lewes? There is no mystery, however, about the dedication of Cliffe church to St Thomas Becket, assassinated in Canterbury cathedral in 1170. Such dedications were rare in medieval Sussex, but it is understandable that St Thomas's memory should be preserved here in a church belonging to his cathedral and so close to South Malling, where his assassins are alleged to have subsequently taken refuge.

In addition to those commemorated in the dedications of the parish churches some other saints were clearly objects of veneration in Lewes. St Anne, the Blessed Virgin's mother, was honoured not only at St Mary Westout but also at St Mary in Foro, where there was an image of her, for repainting which a parishioner bequeathed money in 1518. Another will, in which the testator requested to be buried 'afore St Christopher within the parish church of St Mary in Lewes', indicates that in St Mary in Foro, as in so many medieval churches adjoining major highways, there was a large mural painting of the 'Christ-bearer': it was probably located opposite the south door, where passers-by would see it and would consequently be safeguarded from accident that day. Two other saints were commemorated in Southover church, where each was honoured with a separate chapel. One was St Erasmus, one of the least well-known of the 14 'auxiliary saints', venerated for the efficacy of their prayers on behalf of human necessities. The other was St Catherine of Alexandria, the fourth century martyr symbolised by the spiked wheel on which she met her death and whose feast-day fell on 25 November. The popularity of this 'auxiliary saint' is attested by the number of late medieval church bells that are inscribed with the words, 'Sancta Katerina, ora pro nobis' – 'St Catherine, pray for us.' Two fifteenth century bells with this inscription survive in Lewes – one at All Saints' and the other at St Mary Westout (now St Anne's).[7]

In the fifteenth century campanology came into its own in England, and in Lewes the sound of church-bells, which was believed to drive away evil spirits, rang out loud and clear, bringing comfort and joy to the hearers. Now wherever a church lacked a bell-tower the parishioners would endeavour to raise funds to build one, as evidently happened with notable success both at All Saints' and at St Thomas's. Apart from these two towers, however, there is no evidence that in the fifteenth century Lewes people were spending money on new church building. In fact there are signs that some of the existing structures continued to be in a bad state of repair. But if this was the case, who was to blame? While the responsibility for the upkeep of the chancels rested with the incumbents, that for the naves lay with the parishioners; but they do not always seem to have been prepared to foot the repair bills. The surviving wills show that, while Lewes people continued to bequeath money for church restoration, the sums tended to be smaller than those left for other works of piety. Thomas Sherman, who in 1494 left 10s for the repair of the church of St Peter Westout, gave much of his wealth (£40 in cash, all his livestock, plus lands and tenements in five parishes) to augment the endowment of the chantry chapel that his brother John had built in St Peter's churchyard, where a priest was to sing masses for the souls of their family in perpetuity. It appears that, at the end of the Middle Ages, piety was becoming privatised. If the rich were worried about the health of their souls, they could take out celestial life insurance policies; but the poor had mostly to rely on whatever the public services – maintained by the parish churches – could provide.[8]

What were the parish churches of Lewes like at this time? Outwardly some of them might have looked much the same as they do today but inwardly they would be very different. The biggest difference would be the complete absence of pews. In those days people normally stood to worship – as they still do in Russia – and only the weakest 'went to the wall', where there would probably be a few benches to sit on. The nave of the church was an open space which served as a parish hall, used for 'church ales' and other seasonal festivities. Its walls would probably have been decorated with colourful frescoes, like those of the 'Lewes school' still to be seen at Plumpton and Clayton: these pictures, telling the story of man's creation, fall and redemption, were 'visual aids to salvation' in a largely unlettered age. The nave would have been cut off from the chancel, which the priest entered by a private door from the churchyard, by a tall screen similar to the one now standing in the back of the church at Rodmell near Lewes. The screen was surmounted by a beam on which stood the rood or crucifix, flanked by statues of St Mary and St John – such as those at Southover referred to in Agnes Morley's will of 1511, in which she bequeathed money for the maintenance of lights to stand before these images in perpetuity. In the chancel stood the great stone altar, where on Sundays and feast days the priest re-enacted the sacrifice of Christ. When he sang mass the laity were merely spectators of the drama: only once a year at Easter, having made their annual confessions during Lent, were they bidden to receive communion; and then, since the wine was reserved for the priest, they were only given the wafer. Services were in Latin and, except on rare occasions, when there was a visiting preacher, few words of English would have been spoken.[9]

In the first half of the sixteenth century, however, all this was to change. England experienced the great religious transformation that has come to be called 'the Reformation' and, in Lewes as elsewhere, many old and familiar structures and practices were to disappear.

II. Reformation, Reaction and the Roots of Conflict

The first indications that England was about to experience a great religious upheaval came in 1534, when the authority of the Pope was formally repudiated and the Royal Supremacy established. Although the high constables of Lewes soon learned to date their accounts by the regnal years of a sovereign now to be acknowledged as 'in earth of the Church of England and Ireland only supreme head', it is unlikely that many in the town would have understood all the implications of the change. When the clergy were required to remove the Pope's name from their service books, all those in Lewes seem to have done so. None followed the example of Richard Boord, vicar of Pevensey and Westham, who said that he 'would rather be torn with wild horses than to assent or consent to the diminishing of one iota of the bishop of Rome his authority'. Boord had allegedly tried to persuade John Senock, a monk of Lewes priory, to flee the realm with him, but to no avail. In Lewes the monks evidently remained loyal to the Crown – as did the friars, in spite of later accusations that they had been circulating treasonable rumours that the king was dead.[1]

There was certainly one man in Lewes for whom the prospect of religious change would have been welcome. He was John Hoggesflesh, who lived in the parish of St Mary Westout. Evidently a keen reader of the Bible, he looked forward, as others did secretly at this time, to the overthrow of the Church of Rome and its replacement by one whose polity and practice accorded with New Testament teachings. In October 1534 he was charged with refusing to 'give any honour or worship' to the Blessed Virgin and with affirming that 'it is not necessary to be confessed to a priest, but only to God'. He was also alleged to have said that the sacrament of the altar was not the body of Christ but 'a thing lift up in the figure of the lifting up of our Lord on the cross'. After a preliminary hearing before six JPs he

was despatched from Lewes to Chichester, where he was arraigned before
a court composed of the diocesan chancellor, the dean, two canons, the
mayor of the city and other dignitaries. After a lengthy trial, in which he
defended his position vigorously with numerous biblical texts, his judges
appear to have been confounded. Uncertain about the seriousness of his
errors, they referred the case to Archbishop Cranmer, who in turn referred
it to the duke of Norfolk, who in his turn referred it to the king in his new
capacity of Supreme Head of the Church in England. In due course King
Henry confirmed that the opinions were erroneous and the bishop of
Chichester was accordingly instructed to have Hoggesflesh condemned.
Eventually this 'famous heretic' (as Bishop Sherborne called him) was
forced to recant his 'detestable opinions', do public penance in the cathedral
and read out a declaration of his errors in the market-places of Chichester,
Midhurst and Lewes. Rarely in the history of religious conflict has one
obscure individual caused so much trouble to so many important people
over such a long period of time.[2]

How had Hoggesflesh acquired his impressive knowledge of Scripture?
Before the publication of Miles Coverdale's edition in 1535 the Bible in
English was a prohibited book and to be caught reading it was a crime. And
before 1538 when, in accordance with the Second Royal Injunctions, the
churchwardens of St Andrew's (and probably other Lewes parishes as well)
bought a Bible to be set up (chained) in the church for the use of
parishioners, it was difficult for the laity to lay hands on one. In 1534
there were in fact only two (strictly illegal) vernacular versions available.
One was the New Testament newly translated into English by William
Tyndale and printed clandestinely in the Netherlands, copies of which were
being shipped to England from 1526 onwards. They were smuggled into
the country, chiefly through ports along the south coast, and it is not
impossible that some may have arrived in Lewes, where (as contemporary
subsidy rolls record) a number of Dutchmen were then living. But if
Tyndale's New Testament was not the source of Hoggesflesh's extensive
biblical knowledge it would almost certainly have been the much earlier
translation made by John Wycliffe, manuscript copies of which were still
being secretly circulated in southern England in the early years of the
sixteenth century. Some of those charged with possessing them, whom the
authorities branded as Lollards, are known to have congregated close to
the boundary of the dioceses of Canterbury and Chichester. Since, owing
to the existence of the peculiar deanery of South Malling, Lewes in fact
lay on this boundary it is possible that there was a bunch of these heretics
in the neighbourhood and Hoggesflesh, who was accused of the stock
Lollard offence of denying the validity of the Holy Sacrament, may have
been one of them.[3]

The Departure of the Monks

A year after Hoggesflesh's indictment the practical significance of the establishment of the Royal Supremacy was to become apparent. In 1535 the king's chief minister Thomas Cromwell sent round a team of inspectors to visit the monasteries and in due course Richard Layton, the one appointed to investigate the situation in Sussex, arrived in Lewes. Not surprisingly he found the evidence of what he was looking for, which was 'corruption'. The sins of the monks of St Pancras, like those of so many houses, were allegedly legion: they included fornication, sodomy and – 'what is worse' – treason. In fact the sub-prior confessed to preaching treason with the full knowledge of John Peterson, the prior. In due course Layton reported that he had interviewed Peterson, who had fallen to his knees and asked for mercy, and that he had commanded the two alleged traitors to appear before Cromwell at Court. There were probably no foundations for the charges of treason, but they provided the king's minister with an excuse for a speedy suppression of the priory. Cromwell took a particular interest in the Lewes house, the largest and wealthiest monastery in Sussex, because he himself planned to acquire its property to give a landed base to his son Gregory, whom he wanted to set up as a Sussex squire. Given such corruption in high places it is not surprising that the priory of St Pancras became the first of the greater English monasteries to be suppressed. After much pressure had been brought to bear upon him Prior Peterson surrendered his house 'voluntarily' on 2 November 1537.[4]

Cromwell, who had lived in Italy and knew that country's areas of expertise, thereupon called in an Italian military engineer called Portinari to demolish the great priory church. His gang of 17 men used the sapping and mining techniques employed in continental siege warfare to raze the huge edifice to the ground. Few of the conventual buildings survived. The lead and bell-metal, the most valuable materials, were bought by local purchasers. The stone, a rare commodity in Sussex, was either sold or stolen and put to new use: quantities of it were used in house building in Lewes, Southover, Kingston, Barcombe, Hangleton and Wivelsfield. Timber and glass also had value and local people were quick to join in the plunder. In December 1537 one of the four men whom Cromwell had appointed to guard his newly-acquired property gave a graphic account of their difficulties in preventing theft. 'When we be at the one end', he complained, 'they steal the glass out of the windows, bear away doors and pluck down ceilings at the other ends, nor will walls nor doors keep them out.'[5]

For those able to take advantage of the opportunities for lining their own pockets the dissolution of the priory was a boon. For others, like the 80 monastic servants who had lost their employment and the 14 'poor beadmen' of St James's hospital 'nigh the gate of the priory' who feared that they would lose 'all their living', it may have looked like a disaster. The dissolution may also have been regretted by local gentry like the Thatchers of Ringmer who had looked to the priory to provide banking facilities. But the paucity of bequests to the priory in the wills of local people suggests that, on the eve of the Reformation, the monks were not particularly popular. It seems, however, that the Lewes friars were better liked. Local people left them money not only to pay for funeral masses, which they were often prepared to perform more cheaply than parish priests, but also in some cases they made them bequests with no strings attached. Margaret Apsley of Buxted, who in 1511 bequeathed to the brethren 'one of my greatest brass pots' and a 'plain table cloth' but did not ask for masses, seems to have been more concerned about the present state of the men's living accommodation than the future state of her soul. If the friars were well liked locally there may have been some regrets when the house at Lewes – one of the last friaries in England to be dissolved – finally closed its doors in December 1538.[6]

What became of the monks and friars who were compelled to leave the cloister? The 24 monks in the priory all received life pensions and many gained new employment in the Church. Prior Peterson became treasurer of Chichester cathedral and absentee rector of Shere in Surrey, holding the two appointments in plurality until his death in 1555; he was also dean of South Malling College until its dissolution in 1548, when he received generous compensation for loss of office. Of the other monks eight are known to have been given livings, two of which were in Lewes: John Peverel became rector of Southover and later of St John sub Castro, while John Sympson went to St Mary Westout. The friars were less fortunate: they received no pensions and none appears to have obtained fresh employment in the Church.[7]

Although some believed that Henry VIII, having dissolved the monasteries, would go on to destroy the parish churches, such fears proved to be groundless. But towards the end of his reign an Act was passed empowering parishes to dispose of redundant churches – whereupon three in Lewes, all in a bad state of repair, were pulled down and their parishes merged with those of neighbouring churches. In 1538 the parish of St Mary in Foro was absorbed by that of St John sub Castro, and St Peter's by that of St Mary Westout: this was apparently a great help to the parishioners of St Mary's who, so it is said, were now able to re-roof their nave. In 1545 St Andrew's merged with St Michael's, whereupon large quantities of St Andrew's redundant stone were sold at a knock-down price to local people, among whom were the rector and churchwardens.[8]

Edwardine Upheavals

It was only after Henry's death in January 1547, however, that the parishes were to feel the full impact of the Reformation. With the accession of the boy King Edward VI the reins of government passed to royal councillors bent on a more radical reform of the Church. Orders were issued for the removal from parish churches of everything that smacked of superstition – roods, statues of saints, wall paintings and redundant vestments such as chasubles, copes and albs. Then, after the abolition of the Latin mass and the introduction of an English communion service in 1549, orders were issued for the destruction of altars. At St Michael's the churchwardens responded positively and promptly. In 1548 they paid John Harman, a Lewes glazier, 2s.6d. for 'defacing' stained glass images. Because it was unusual for glass — an expensive commodity – to be destroyed at this date, it appears that the people of St Michael's were exceptionally iconoclastic in outlook. Furthermore, their removal of three altars in 1548 – some months before they were ordered to do so – suggests that they were more than willing to participate in the destruction. Nowhere else in Sussex, except at Rye, did local people display such destructive enthusiasm.[9]

In the following year the churchwardens were ordered to prepare inventories of all their plate, jewels, ornaments and other valuables, prior to placing them at the Crown's disposal. Each parish was to be allowed to retain only the minimum needed for Protestant worship – one chalice (or two in large parishes) and a surplice or two for the clergy. However, because commissioners were not appointed to collect the loot until 1553, most parishes seem to have had time to take avoiding action by selling off their surplus stuff. The only evidence about what happened in Lewes comes from the churchwardens' accounts of St Michael's, which show that they had sold off a large quantity of surplus church goods after the merger with the parish of St Andrew in 1546. It is therefore possible that there was little left to dispose of, apart from an 'old cope' which was passed to the parish clerk's wife to be made into a carpet. The decision to turn a now useless ecclesiastical garment into a floor-covering indicates a very practical, down-to-earth approach to life. Long before the word came into the language it appears that Lewes people were committed to recycling.[10]

The plunder of the parish churches was accompanied by that of the gilds and chantries, whose property had been declared forfeit to the Crown by statutes of 1545 and 1547. This meant the end of South Malling College, whose great church was pulled down and the residential accommodation for its dean and canons turned into a private house, and of Sherman's more modest chantry in Westout. The 1547 Act also decreed the confiscation of the property of religious gilds – a measure that had serious consequences for some Sussex towns where a gild constituted a kind of friendly society for the living as well as a support group for the dead. In Lewes, however, such gilds seem to have played a very small part in the life of the community. On the eve of the Reformation there appears to have been none within the town's walls. In Southover, however, there was a 'Brotherhood of Cologne', mentioned in a 1521 will requesting masses for the souls of its members both living and dead. And in Cliffe there was a Brotherhood of St Thomas, which owned a house in the parish bequeathed to it in 1513 by William Batnor. The bequest was intended to augment the income of a priest, who would sing for the souls of the 'brethren and sistern' of the fraternity. After 1547 all that was left in Lewes of the charitable institutions of the pre-Reformation church were the two former monastic hospitals of St Nicholas and St James, which survived as parish almshouses.[11]

The Crown's confiscation of the endowments of masses for the dead was justified by the contention that belief in purgatory was a thing of the past, but the evidence suggests that this was not the case in Lewes. 21 of the 33 inhabitants who made wills in the period 1530-46 endowed masses for their souls and some of them requested them to be said annually for a number of years after death. In January 1544 Katherine Parker, a rich widow living in St Andrew's parish, directed that at her death 30 masses should be said in Southover church and ten a year for ten years thereafter for the souls of herself and her late husband. And in July of that year George Morley, clerk, requested that six priests should 'sing and say dirges and masses for my soul and all Christian souls' in the same church at his burial, his 'month's mind' and on the anniversary of his death. But for some years after 1544 there were no more bequests for masses from Lewes people. This does not mean that everyone had suddenly abandoned belief in purgatory but that, after the passing of the 1545 Chantries Act, they knew that money left for the endowment of masses was likely to be appropriated.[12]

Wills and Opinions

Since religion is an intensely personal matter it is always difficult to ascertain what people actually believed. In an attempt to do this historians of Tudor England have devoted a good deal of attention to the language people used in the 'soul clauses' of their wills. If they bequeathed their souls to 'Almighty God, the Blessed Virgin Mary and the whole company of Heaven' their religious attitude has been classified as 'traditional' and, if they left their souls simply to 'Almighty God', it has been classified as 'non-traditional'. If we adopt this system of classification for wills made by Lewes people what do we discover? Up to the mid-1540s the great majority of testators use the 'traditional' language, but thereafter the proportion decreases dramatically, so that by the end of Edward's reign all references to the Blessed Virgin or to the whole company of Heaven have disappeared. In this respect Lewes was no different from anywhere else in east Sussex at this date, where (as Graham Mayhew has shown) those using 'traditional' language amounted to about 60% of the testators in 1547 and only 10% in 1553. But the analysis of wills does not end there, for historians have gone on to make a further distinction between wills that were simply 'non-traditional' and those that were positively 'Protestant', in that they expressed a distinctively Lutheran view of justification by faith alone. In east Sussex, throughout the 1550s the latter are rare, never accounting for more than 10% of the testators. In Lewes at this period the proportion was even smaller, for only two testators used language that can confidently be classified as Protestant. One was Ralph Becheley, who in January 1552 bequeathed his soul to God, 'most surely trusting through the merits of his dear son Jesus Christ to be a partaker of everlasting life'. The other was Thomas Sampton, who in November 1556 made an unusually fulsome affirmation: 'My hope is my soul to be among the elect and chosen of God through faith in Jesus Christ our Lord, as Holy Scripture teacheth all men, above all things, to love our heavenly Father.'[13]

The evidence of soul-clauses, however, should not be pressed too far. Sometimes the language was not that of the person who made the will but of the scribe who wrote it or the priest who witnessed it; and in any case the terminology may reflect cultural conventions rather than deeply-held convictions. The difficulty in using such evidence to determine someone's deepest beliefs is shown by the example of Peter Flussher of St Andrew's, who made his will in January 1539. He made no mention of the Virgin or the saints, bequeathing his soul simply to 'Almighty God my Redeemer'. He gave thanks for the soundness of his mind to 'my only Saviour Jesus Christ'. And he then went on to do something that no other local testator did in this period: he endowed a series of eight sermons to be preached in Lewes soon after his death 'to the setting forth of God's holy word and to the furtherance of the Christian people hearing the same'. Although he sounds like a man firmly in favour of reform, he was evidently still old-fashioned enough to believe in purgatory, for he provided for five masses to be said for his soul at his funeral and at his 'month's mind'.[14]

In Lewes, as in other towns at this time, it is noticeable that, while fewer people left money for masses to ease the pains of the dead, more were leaving it to relieve the poverty of the living. In Henry VIII's reign less than a quarter of local testators had bequeathed money for poor relief, but in Edward's the proportion rose to two-thirds. In the parishes of St Mary Westout, St Michael and Southover some testators made bequests to the 'poor men's box' that every church was now supposed to possess. But only one of them left more than 3s. 4d. He was John Batnor who bequeathed 40s to be distributed to the poor 'in time of sickness or need'. Like his uncle William, who had endowed the Brotherhood of St Thomas in Cliffe, he was evidently mindful of the needs of those less fortunate than himself; but the 'brethren and sistern' that he was supporting were on earth, not in heaven. However, for a rich man 40s was but a modest sum to give to charity. In Lewes there were not many signs of what one historian, seeking to show that the Reformation benefited the poor, has described as 'the rise of the Protestant charitable impulse'.[15]

There is also no evidence that the Reformation brought with it the kind of material benefits that it often did elsewhere. The dissolution of the monasteries and chantries enabled many towns to extend their holdings and increase their institutional authority. This certainly happened at Chichester, where the corporation's acquisitions included the extensive possessions of the Gild of St George and the great church of the Grey Friars, which thenceforward became the city's guildhall. However, nothing comparable took place in Lewes, which was not an incorporated borough. Unlike Arundel, Hastings and Seaford, which all received charters of incorporation in the Tudor period, Lewes remained a 'mesne' borough, nominally subordinate to the lords of the town. Its government was in the hands of the jury of the court leet, which by the sixteenth century had come to have a semi-autonomous existence as the 'Fellowship of the Twelve'. And although in practice it enjoyed many of the privileges of ruling bodies in corporate towns, the lack of a charter entitling it to acquire and hold lands in mortmain prevented the borough from benefiting substantially from the ecclesiastical changes of Henry VIII's and Edward VI's reigns. The situation might have been different had Lewes possessed a major religious confraternity, such as the Gild of St George in Chichester: then the townsmen would have had an incentive to seek incorporation as a step towards acquiring property at a moderate price.[16]

The Marian Reaction

In July 1553, with the death of Edward VI and the accession of his fervently Catholic half-sister Mary, the process of religious change was brought to an abrupt halt and a strenuous effort was made to unmake the English Reformation. Although, since their buildings had been destroyed and their properties sold, it proved impossible to restore the religious houses, much could be done to put the clock back in the parishes. Soon orders went out to the churchwardens to re-erect the altars, restore the roods and make the churches fully fit for Catholic worship. How swift were the people of Lewes to obey? Because of the lack of churchwardens' accounts we only know what happened at St Michael's, where the response was predictably slow. The rood was evidently not restored until 1556, when 3s 8d was paid for making it and a further sum for painting it. Because the accounts for Mary's reign are incomplete there is no knowing if and when the parishioners restored the altar. They had acquired a wooden communion table in 1548 but it is not known for how long after the Queen's accession they obstinately continued to use it. But if the Marian restoration of Catholicism was unpopular at St Michael's there is no doubt that in some quarters it would have been warmly welcomed. Gabriel Fowle of Southover, who in January 1555 bequeathed to his parish church his 'written mass book' (evidently hidden away in the hope of better times), doubtless rejoiced at the restoration of the old religion. Fowle was one of a substantial minority of Lewes testators, amounting to 30% of the total, who now revived the old custom of endowing masses for their souls. But he was clearly aware that there might be difficulty in finding priests to sing them: he asked that masses be sung by ten priests, 'if they can be got'.[17]

The aspect of Mary's ecclesiastical policy that probably affected Lewes most profoundly was her attempt to root out doctrinal errors. Although there is no firm evidence of any inhabitant of the town at this time being accused of heresy it was to Lewes, the capital of eastern Sussex, that most of the condemned heretics in the county were brought for execution. The public burnings were staged in the High Street just outside the Star Inn, which stood on the site of the present Town Hall. According to the Tudor martyrologist John Foxe the first took place on 22 July 1555, when Dirck Carver was put to death. He was a native of Flanders who had migrated to Brighton to set up in business as a brewer and had been arrested for holding illegal prayer-meetings in that town. Imprisoned in Newgate, he was examined by the bishop of London, who charged him with denying the validity of the mass and of auricular confession – the very same offences that had got John Hoggesflesh into trouble twenty years before. Carver horrified Bishop Bonner by saying that Catholic doctrine was 'poison and sorcery' and that 'if Christ were here you would put him to a worse death than he was put before'. Foxe goes on to relate that, 'at his coming into the town of Lewes to be burned, the people called upon him, beseeching God to strengthen him in the faith of Jesus Christ'. After his Bible had been taken from him and thrown into the 'barrel' prepared for the burning, Carver went into it himself and, having retrieved the book, threw it into the crowd. Then, in a 'joyful voice', he addressed the assembled company:

> Dear brethren and sistern, witness to you all that I am come to seal with my blood Christ's Gospel, for because I know that it is true; it is not unknown unto all you, but that it hath been truly preached here in Lewes and in all places in England, and now is not. And for because that I will not deny here God's Gospel and be obedient to man's laws, I am condemned to die. Dear brethren and sistern, as many of you as do believe upon the Father, the Son and the Holy Ghost unto everlasting life, see you do the works appertaining to the same. And as many of you as do believe upon the Pope of Rome or any of his laws, which he sets forth in these days, you do believe to your utter condemnation and, except the great mercy of God,

you shall burn in Hell perpetually.
At this point the sheriff interrupted him angrily. 'Speak to thy God that he
may deliver thee now', he said, 'or else to strike me down to the example
of this people.' To this Carver replied, 'The Lord forgive you your sayings',
and continued speaking to the people in a loud voice:

> Dear brethren, and all you whom I have offended in words or in
> deed, I ask you for the Lord's sake to forgive me, and I heartily
> forgive all you which have offended me in thought, word or deed.
> Lord have mercy upon me, for unto thee I commend my spirit, and
> my soul doth rejoice in thee.

These, according to Foxe, were 'the last words of that faithful member of
Christ before the fire was put to him'. It is not known for certain whether
Carver actually spoke them. Was this account really based on the evidence of
bystanders? Or was it a pious reconstruction, consciously or unconsciously
influenced by the biblical account of Christ's crucifixion, of what Carver might
have said in the circumstances? Whatever the truth of the matter it is significant
that this is the only place in Foxe's account of the sufferings of the Sussex
martyrs where he records the actual words reportedly spoken on the scaffold.[18]

In the summer of 1556 six more Protestant martyrs, including a
'minister' named Thomas Wood who may have been serving a cure in Lewes,
were burned at the stake outside the Star Inn. However, the execution that
probably made the strongest impression on the townspeople was the last
one, which occurred on 22 June 1557. On this occasion ten people – six
men and four women – perished in a single fire. As in the previous year,
most of them came from the High Weald. They included the most
celebrated of the Sussex martyrs, Richard Woodman, a prosperous
ironmaster from Warbleton whose exploits are recounted in the *Dictionary
of National Biography*, but the rest were obscure folk like Margery Morris
of Heathfield and her son James, and a young man from Rotherfield called
Alexander Hosmer. Hosmer's name, which Foxe wrongly records as
'Hosman', has not been entirely forgotten. In the early years of the
seventeenth century members of his family, seeking greater freedom in
religion, migrated from the Weald to America, where one of their
descendants, Frederick Lucian Hosmer, a Unitarian minister, was to write
the hymn that provides the title of this book.[19]

The Elizabethan Religious Settlement

Because of what they had seen and heard of the sufferings of the Protestant
martyrs it is likely that many in Lewes rejoiced at the news of Mary's death,
which took place on 17 November 1558, but it is not known if there were
any public celebrations. The surviving town accounts throw no light on the
matter: the payment made early in the new reign 'for men to watch when

the great fire was in Westout' clearly refers to something more serious than a celebratory bonfire. However, the reference to 'our most gracious sovereign lady Elizabeth by the grace of God of England, France and Ireland, Queen, Defender of the Faith, etc.' – a fulsome style omitted in the less gracious reign of Philip and Mary – suggests that those responsible for the government of the town rejoiced at the news of Elizabeth's accession. It would be a mistake, however, to say that everyone welcomed it. Alice Copland of St Michael's parish, who made her will on the second day of the new reign and provided for masses and dirges at her burial, would no doubt have been distressed at the prospect of a Protestant regime that would make such ceremonies once more unlawful. So too presumably would Richard Russall of All Saints', who made his will in the following February and was apparently the last Lewes testator to request a funeral mass. 'I will to have mass and dirge at my burial according to the laudable custom of the realm', he said. How aware was he that the customs that had been 'laudable' under Mary would soon become inadmissible under her sister?[20]

As it transpired, the Crown lost no time in countermanding all the measures that Mary had taken to ensure the establishment of Roman Catholicism. When the instructions arrived to purge the churches of what Protestants called 'popery' the churchwardens of St Michael's promptly disposed of their altars and Latin books. But at Southover the wardens were apparently not quite so quick off the mark. It was not until Elizabeth had been on the throne for over a year that they recorded the sale of a 'great wooden cross', the stone from two altars, an altar frontal of red and black Bruges satin, a cope of green damask and vestments of 'crimson purple' velvet. Part of the money raised was used to pay a carpenter and his boy for 'boarding up the high altar' and to purchase a copy of the newly published English Prayer Book. Henceforward all was to be politically and ecclesiastically correct, but after the loss of such colourful fixtures and fittings the church interior must have seemed rather bare and drab.[21]

In numerous Sussex parishes, even if the wardens proved compliant, the clergy refused to co-operate with the Crown's ecclesiastical programme and were subsequently deprived, but in Lewes none seems to have reacted in this way. The only man who might have made a stand for the old religion was Thomas Brown, appointed rector of St John sub Castro in 1556, but he died soon after Elizabeth's accession – possibly in the great influenza epidemic that carried off so many clergy at this time. Because of so many deaths and deprivations there was a chronic shortage of clergy at this period and in Lewes a number of parishes long lacked incumbents. A diocesan survey of 1563 revealed that there were resident parsons only at St John sub Castro and St Mary Westout, that St Michael's was served by a curate and that All Saints' and Southover had neither parson nor curate. The survey did not cover Cliffe, but it is known that the living was vacant at that time.[22]

In the early years of Elizabeth's reign the lack of clergymen able and willing to plant Protestantism firmly in Sussex brought the ecclesiastical authorities almost to the point of despair. A report made in 1569 stated that the whole diocese of Chichester was 'very blind and superstitious for want of teaching': in fact almost the only bright spot was said to be 'about Lewes'. Concern was also expressed in the report about the number of deprived clergy of Romish persuasion who were still lurking in the shire and maintaining the old religion under the protection of Catholic gentry. One of these was David Michell, a former monk of Lewes priory, who after the dissolution had served as rector of Horsted Keynes until his deprivation in 1560 and was now living in the household of the Gage family not far from Lewes at Firle.[23]

The 'Hotter sort of Protesatants'

In the next decade the authorities became worried about the activities not only of Catholics but of people at the other end of the ecclesiastical spectrum – those who were reluctant to accept the Elizabethan settlement of religion on the grounds that it was not radical enough. They were the 'hotter sort of Protestants', who looked to Calvin's Geneva as the very model of a godly commonwealth and thought that the Church of England was 'but halfly reformed': their programme was to purge it of all surviving ceremonies that to them smacked of 'popery'. Because of their wish to purify church and society such people eventually came to be known as 'puritans', but if they attached any label to themselves it would most likely have been 'the godly'. Apparently the first clergyman of this stamp in Lewes was a native of Monkwearmouth and father of five children named David Thickpenny. He had earlier served at Brighton, where he was accused of conducting worship without a surplice, not using the Prayer Book and omitting 'divers things' from the service of baptism. Furthermore, it was alleged, he 'preacheth and inveigheth against such as have troubled him'. So outrageous was his preaching that he was suspected of belonging to the Family of Love, a radical sect that denied the validity of the sacraments and the authority of bishops. Suspended from his living by the bishop of Chichester in 1576, he complained to the Privy Council, who referred the matter to Archbishop Grindal, who appears to have listened sympathetically to his side of the story. He soon afterwards moved to Lewes to become curate of St Michael's, where people evidently responded positively to his preaching.[24]

In the same year another zealous Protestant divine arrived in the town to take up a much more important position. He was Thomas Underdowne, a Cambridge graduate with a reputation for classical scholarship, who become rector of St Mary Westout and St John sub Castro. Early in 1583, preaching in St Michael's before a mixed gathering of clergy and laity, he is alleged to have said that

> there was no cause why the people should fear any danger to fall
> upon them for having any doctrine from a man not outwardly called,
> for it was not a few collects or imposition of hands that maketh a
> preacher but, if he had an inward assurance and persuasion that he
> was called by God, he might lawfully preach.

Such radical notions gave great offence to some of his more conservative
hearers and especially to Henry Shales, rector of Hangleton. Soon
afterwards he is reported to have delivered a sermon in the same church
denouncing Underdowne and the other 'godly ministers' in the diocese as
'the new brotherhood, the brotherhood of separation, the separated
brethren, private spirits, this new faction and such like'. He also said that
every one of them 'claimeth to be bishop in his own charge' and that they
would not 'stay for the magistrates in reformation'. The ensuing dispute
came to trial in the Lewes archdeaconry court, where the judge ruled in
favour of Underdowne and his fellow puritans. Shales promptly appealed
against the decision and the matter was eventually brought to the notice of
the Privy Council in London: the outcome is not known but it is unlikely
that the government would have regarded the puritans' activities as
subversive. In other parts of England at this time, to the dismay of the
authorities, radical puritans were setting up *classes* or ministers'
conferences to regulate the affairs of local churches, but there is no evidence
that Underdowne and his 'new faction' planned to do this. It is likely that the
'Lewes *classis*' referred to by one historian never in fact existed. There does
not appear to have been a 'Lewes group of puritans' campaigning vigorously
for ecclesiastical reform. The survey of the Sussex ministry made in 1585,
black-listing those incumbents who were 'impossible to be framed to any
good', was not the work of Underdowne and his associates but of another
group of ministers in the far east of the county.[25]

Nevertheless, the activities of some puritans in the Lewes area did cause
alarm in high places. In the autumn of 1583 Underdowne was one of the
leaders of the resistance to the attempts being made by John Whitgift, the
newly elevated archbishop of Canterbury, to stamp out puritan
nonconformity. When his commissary summoned the clergy in the
deaneries of Lewes and Pevensey to appear before him in St Michael's
church and asked them to sign an undertaking that they would adhere strictly
to everything in the Prayer Book, Underdowne was among a small number that
refused to do so. As a result he and the other non-subscribers, including Samuel
Norden, the newly instituted rector of Hamsey near Lewes, were suspended
from their livings. Unwilling to accept the commissary's ruling, the two men
joined a deputation of eight Sussex ministers who went up to Lambeth Palace
to argue their case with the primate. Underdowne, who was the group's chief
spokesman, disputed vigorously with Whitgift and, since he kept his composure

while the archbishop lost his, seems to have had the better of the argument. In the end some sort of compromise was arrived at and the ministers duly had their suspensions lifted. Underdowne was apparently able to continue his nonconformist practices without fear of being hauled before the Lewes archdeaconry court. Indeed, as deputy to the official principal, he himself often presided over the court – which sometimes sat not (as was customary) in St Michael's church, but in his own parsonage house.[26]

In Lewes the position of the puritan ministers was greatly strengthened by the support that they received from the laity. When Thickpenny was in trouble for preaching without his bishop's licence in 1580 his cause was championed by powerful friends within the town's ruling elite, the Fellowship of the Twelve. John Stempe, the Fellowship's most influential member, described the curate as 'an honest man and zealous in good religion', who 'led his life so that it might be a spectacle of honest living to others'. Additional tributes to his honesty came from two of Stempe's colleagues, Laurence Newton and John Brode. Doubtless Thickpenny would also have had the strong approval of John Batnor, then serving his third term as high constable of Lewes, whose son of the same name was a noted puritan divine. And a fifth member of the Twelve, Robert Aware, who died that year after requesting a 'godly sermon' at his burial and stipulating that his children should be brought up to 'godly exercises', would almost certainly have been a supporter. Stempe therefore had no difficulty in procuring a 'testimonial' to Thickpenny's character under the town seal of Lewes, 'subscribed with the hands of the Twelve of the said town'. Except perhaps in Rye, where the corporation appointed and maintained a preacher to supplement the meagre spiritual fare provided by the vicar, nowhere did a Sussex puritan minister receive such unanimous official approval.[27]

The puritan ministers were also patronised by some of the country gentry who, at a time when Lewes was the administrative capital not merely of eastern Sussex but of the whole county, were building themselves town houses there. Although Underdowne was evidently on bad terms with George Goring, who in 1583 not only refused to pay him tithes but also questioned the legality of his institution into the church of St John sub Castro, he is likely to have enjoyed the support of a more influential county family – the Pelhams. Sir John Pelham, whose fine house stood in a prominent position in the heart of the town and who had, as a young man in Mary's reign, fled abroad and taken up residence in Geneva, was a fervent Calvinist. In his will (1580) he made a vigorous profession of his faith:

> Acknowledging myself to have grievously and many ways offended
> Almighty God, for the which I am heartily sorry and do earnestly
> repent the same, not doubting in the mercy of God but that he will
> receive me, a penitent sinner, into . . . the holy company of heaven,
> a place prepared of God for all his elect.

Here he was expressing a Calvinistic predestinarian conviction, which in theory was orthodox Anglican doctrine but in practice was embraced mainly by the 'hotter sort of Protestants' whom posterity has labelled puritans.[28]

Pelham died at about the time Underdowne arrived in Lewes, but the minister was fortunate to have the backing of someone even more influential. Growing up in the Wealden parish of Chiddingly, where the Sackvilles were major landowners, he had early enjoyed the patronage of this important family: it was to Thomas Sackville, Lord Buckhurst that as a young man he had dedicated his translation of Ovid's *Invective against Ibis*. Buckhurst who, as patron of the living, had presented Underdowne to the church of St John sub Castro, was a cousin of the queen and a prominent member of the Privy Council. In 1583, when Underdowne absented himself from the Lambeth negotiations in order to go to court 'to speak with a very honourable personage', it was probably Buckhurst whom he went to see; and it may have been because he had his backing that he spoke so boldly to the archbishop. Buckhurst was not well disposed towards Whitgift and did not share his strong aversion to puritanism: in his view the main danger to the realm came not from zealous Protestants but from potentially subversive Catholics who, in the event of a Spanish invasion, might constitute a kind of fifth column within the realm. In 1586, when the fear of invasion reached fever-pitch, he was appointed joint Lord Lieutenant of Sussex and Surrey, with special responsibility for coastal defence. Lewes became his headquarters and he himself took up residence at the Vine, the fine house (now Shelley's Hotel) that he had bought at the top end of the High Street – just over the road from Underdowne's rectory. For a time the church of St Mary Westout had one of the most powerful men in England as a parishioner, and Underdowne and other Lewes puritans could rejoice at having in their midst someone so strongly sympathetic to their cause.[29]

After the Armada crisis was over and Buckhurst had ceased to reside in the town, however, there is evidence that the Lewes puritans, who for a decade seem to have been in the ascendancy, suffered a setback. Underdowne ceased to preside over the archdeaconry court and in 1589 his curate at St John sub Castro, a man named Freeman, was in trouble for not wearing a surplice and not reading all the service in the Prayer Book. In the following year Underdowne himself was charged with the same offences, and also with omitting the sign of the cross in baptism. In addition he was accused of two other standard puritan misdemeanours – not holding the appointed services on Wednesdays and Fridays, and not offering prayers for the bishops and archbishops. In April 1591 he was summoned again to the archdeaconry court and given until September to comply, but by that time he had resigned his living. Probably in poor health, he retired to his native Chiddingly, where he died in 1593.[30]

Godly Discipline and Social Control

In view of the puritans' emphasis upon the authority of the Bible it comes as a surprise to discover that in 1586 St John sub Castro was among the small number of churches in the Lewes archdeaconry where it was reported that no 'sentences of Scripture' had been painted on the walls. Instructions to 'beautify' them in this way had been issued earlier in Elizabeth's reign, and for two reasons. One was in order to obliterate any idolatrous medieval frescoes that might reappear if the lime-wash peeled off. The other, and more important, reason was to ensure that, since the church was the chief agency for the enforcement of morality, the words of the Ten Commandments and other biblical injunctions were kept constantly in sight and mind. Although St Michael's, another Lewes parish in puritan custody, did not appear on the 1586 list of defaulters, it probably should have done; it was not until 1595 that the churchwardens there eventually got round to paying a painter to adorn their walls with sentences. Since the work was done in the body of the church it was naturally paid for by the churchwardens, who were the legal owners of the nave, while the chancel remained the property of the rector. It is said that in 1587 the chancel of St John sub Castro, which it was Underdowne's responsibility to keep in repair, was in such a ruinous state that it had to be pulled down. Here was a sign that chancels in Lewes and elsewhere had become virtually redundant, it now being the standard practice for the communion table to be placed in an east-west position in the nave.[31]

Now that the word had taken priority over the sacrament the main focus of parishioners' attention was not the communion table but the pulpit. And now that long sermons had become the order of the day people could no longer be expected to stand during services and so were provided with seating. Filling the church with pews also made life easier for the churchwardens. After the 1559 Act of Uniformity had made church attendance compulsory on pain of a fine of a shilling a Sunday, they had the responsibility of reporting defaulters; and if people sat in orderly rows it was easy to spot absentees. At this period the parish churches were becoming part of the machinery of social control and where people sat now became of the utmost importance. As a rule the rich sat in the best seats at the front and the poor on benches at the back – so that the social hierarchy, upon whose maintenance the good order of society was thought to depend, was publicly displayed. In the later years of Elizabeth's reign, when St Michael's was filled up with pews, no-one could be in any doubt that the leading men in the parish were John Stempe, William Darell and Peter Pemell, who in 1581 had, at their own expense, 'builded the foremost seat in the chancel'. Since the parishioners' social status was so closely related to where they sat in church it is little wonder that there was often a dispute over a pew, as at Southover in 1595 when Agnes Dickner was punished 'for not sitting in the seat assigned to her by the churchwardens'. In 1609 there was such a serious contention about the seating arrangements in this church that the matter had to be referred to the Fellowship of the Twelve for arbitration. However, no Lewes dispute seems to have been as bitter as the one at nearby Little Horsted, where in 1586 one parishioner, finding another occupying his pew, 'threw him over the seat and the first that came to the ground was his head'. The privatisation of what had once been regarded as public – a characteristic feature of Tudor England – was causing conflicts in church of a kind never before experienced.[32]

To deal with such disputes and other disorders puritans wished there to be in every parish a minister willing and able to dispense 'godly discipline', but in Elizabeth's reign few Lewes ones were in this situation. Resident incumbents were rare. At St Thomas`s there was apparently no rector until 1575, when Christopher Holford was instituted, only to depart a year later. There was then an interregnum until 1590, after which there was a series of four incumbents, each of whom stayed for only a year or two before resigning, probably because the stipend was insufficient to keep body and soul together. It appears that none of them was a graduate, which to puritans (who placed a high value on a university education) might have been seen as a drawback. But the situation changed in 1599 with the appointment of John Bracegirdle, newly ordained with a BD as well as an MA from Cambridge. He was clearly better off financially than his predecessors, because for a time he held the living in plurality with that of St John sub Castro, but he only stayed until 1605, when he moved to a more profitable charge at Rye. In the absence of resident incumbents most parishes had to rely on the services of curates, few of whom appear to have been men as dedicated and devout as David Thickpenny. For some years Southover was served by Henry Paley, who in 1586 was accused of neglecting his duty of catechising the youth of the parish and also of being 'a common brawler and haunter of ale houses'. However, for a third offence – beating his wife – there were apparently mitigating circumstances. A neighbour testified that 'they found her all bloody with a blow he had given her on the nose, but she then confessed that she did first strike him'.[33]

By the end of Elizabeth's reign, primarily because of the shortage of ministers who could preach the Word and serve as 'a spectacle of godly living to others', the process of Reformation was clearly far from complete. Unlike Rye and many other provincial towns, Lewes lacked a municipal corporation that could appoint and fund a 'common preacher' or 'lecturer' to advance the Protestant cause. From time to time gifted and dedicated divines like Underdowne and Thickpenny occupied one or other of the town's pulpits, but they did not stay long enough in post to make the same impact as a continuous succession of official preachers. Furthermore, with

its population divided into six parishes, each with a modest sized church,
Lewes lacked a building large enough to hold the kind of numbers to whom
Richard Fletcher or Richard Greenwood regularly lectured at Rye. When it
came to the maintenance of moral discipline throughout the town Lewes may
also have been at a disadvantage when compared with Rye. Without a borough
court before which offenders could be brought the town's rulers' control
of the situation was limited. This became clear in 1595 when the Fellowship
of the Twelve drew up new articles 'for the better ordering and government' of
the town and 'for the better increase and continuance of perfect peace and
unity'. At a time when the peace of Lewes, like that of other towns, was
threatened by an increasing number of vagrants, beggars and other 'disordered
persons', they wished to give particular attention to the inns and alehouses.
Unlike the godly governors of sixteenth century Geneva they did not aim to
close these places completely, but they did arrange for them to be visited
regularly by the constables for the purpose of 'finding out lewd persons'
and ensuring that they were 'duly punished according to the quality of the
fault'. However, since they had no judicial powers, it appears that the
punishment of drunkenness and similar disorders continued to be a matter
for the church courts. Thus the likes of John Beard, a Lewes man accused
in the archdeaconry court in 1594 of being 'overtaken with drink' and –
perhaps in a vain attempt to justify his behaviour – for saying that 'Christ
was drunk', would continue to get away with little more than a reprimand.[34]

At the beginning of Elizabeth's reign, William Barlow, bishop of
Chichester, had informed the Privy Council that Lewes, along with Rye,
Hastings and Brighton, was 'governed with such officers as be faithful
followers of God's word and earnestly given to maintain godly orders';
and for those then in authority, anxious to see the extinction of the old
religion, this could only be good news. By the end of the reign, however,
things were rather different. If Anthony Watson, who had succeeded to the
see of Chichester in 1596, had taken enough interest in the affairs of his
diocese to investigate the situation in the eastern part of it, he might have
been alarmed rather than reassured to discover that such an important town
as Lewes was in the hands of men 'earnestly given to maintain godly orders'.
By this time 'godly order' had come to be associated primarily with the
'hotter sort' of Protestants termed puritans, who were thought to be planning
to reform the church in ways not altogether pleasing to those wielding
authority within it.[35]

III. Puritans, Laudians and the Great Civil War

When James I came to the throne many puritans hoped that this devoutly Protestant monarch would be willing to listen to their pleas for further reformation of the English Church. With this in view, throughout the summer of 1603 godly ministers and laymen in divers English shires were hard at work drawing up petitions to be presented to the king. In Sussex the ministers' petition was drafted by Samuel Norden, whose house at Offham just outside Lewes became the headquarters for the operation. One of the two named as 'penners' of the gentry's petition was his kinsman William Newton, a lawyer noted for his piety and the owner of a fine house in Southover which his father had built out of Lewes priory stone. And one of those responsible for obtaining signatures to a third petition drawn up on behalf of the 'commonalty' of Sussex was a Lewes tradesman named William Pemell. All the petitioners urged the king to establish 'a learned, resident and godly ministry', while the ministers requested that he would also remove the burden of 'those ceremonies which press the conscience of many of God's servants'.[1]

Norden led the delegation of four Sussex ministers who went to Hampton Court at the time of the famous Conference, called by the king to consider the puritan demands. But he did not grant the hoped for reforms. No heed was given to the request, dear to the hearts of the more militant puritans who had long been in trouble for nonconformity, that 'ceremonies' such as the wearing of the surplice and the giving of the ring in marriage be deemed unlawful. In fact, after Richard Bancroft became archbishop of Canterbury in 1605 all those ministers who persisted in their nonconformity were deprived of their livings. Among them was the redoubtable Norden who died, a deeply disappointed man, in 1609. In his will, of which his 'loving cousin' William Newton was an overseer, he described himself as 'minister of the gospel, though (to my great grief) debarred to serve the Lord Jesus and his church'. In some respects his death, followed by that of Archbishop Bancroft a year later (and the subsequent elevation to the primacy of the more moderate George Abbott) marked the end of an era. The non-conforming puritans may have lost a battle but they had won the war. No longer were they to be hauled before the church courts for refusing to observe the rubrics of the Book of Common Prayer. For the next twenty years or so they (and the more moderate puritans who had not made a stand over ceremonies) were to be free to get on with what they regarded as their principal task – that of purifying a society corrupted by sin. To quote the words of the petition signed by nearly 1300 members of the 'commonalty' of Sussex, many of whom almost certainly lived in Lewes, what most concerned puritans of every hue was the need to shut up 'the gulf which was wont to swallow up sin and defile the land with the loathsome smoke thereof'. And this necessitated the planting of a godly minister in every parish in the land.[2]

It is not always possible to discover the names of the parish clergy of Lewes at this period, but those who were graduates of Cambridge, where the influence of the eminent Elizabethan puritan teacher William Perkins remained strong, may well have been among the 'hotter sort' who favoured further reform of the Church. William Innians, who served St Mary Westout from 1598 to 1628 and St John sub Castro from 1602 to 1617, was an MA from an unspecified university, almost certainly Cambridge, where his son James (who was to succeed him as rector of St Mary's) later graduated. Leonard Stalman, the young Yorkshireman who ministered at St Michael's from 1622 and at Southover from 1624 until his departure for Steyning in 1630, was also a Cambridge man. When he signed St Michael's registers he invariably referred to himself as 'minister' – the title by which puritan divines always preferred to be known. Others who used this appellation were Alexander Reason (an alumnus of that noted 'puritan seminary', Emmanuel College, Cambridge) who succeeded Stalman at Southover, and Richard Russell, who followed him at St Michael's. Russell in turn was succeeded by another 'minister', George Bunyard, a Cambridge graduate, who had previously been rector of Norden's old parish of Hamsey. In addition to the parish ministers there was also, from the late 1620s onwards, an extra-parochial preacher or 'lecturer' in the town. His duty was to supplement the spiritual fare on offer on Sundays with additional sermons on weekdays, when hearers would be drawn not only from the local population but from people coming into town for business or pleasure. Many market towns at this period had such lectureships, which were often established by puritan laymen wanting to maintain a preaching ministry free from episcopal control. In the case of Lewes it was funded by a group of local gentry headed by Sir Thomas Pelham of Halland in East Hoathly (nephew of the Marian exile), who had a house in the town, and Anthony Stapley of Patcham near Brighton. The man appointed to the post was Anthony Lapthorne, who apparently held to the doctrine, which must have been deeply satisfying to someone in his position, that 'preaching was the only means to salvation'. He was evidently a powerful preacher: Richard Baxter, who likened him to Bishop Latimer, was to call him a 'rustic thunderer'. What impression he made and how long he stayed is not known, but it seems that some kind of extra-parochial lectureship was maintained in the town until the late 1650s. Thus Lewes now possessed what it had so long lacked – a 'common preacher' who was able to devote all his energies into turning the place into what could properly be described as a 'puritan town'.[3]

If the puritans had things more or less their own way in Lewes proper, the same evidently did not apply over the bridge down in Cliffe. Cliffe, being in South Malling deanery, lay outside the jurisdiction of the Lewes archdeaconry court, where William Innians (like Underdowne before him) frequently sat as surrogate. The man who often presided over the deanery court meeting in St Thomas's church was evidently a person of very different temper – Anthony Hugget, rector of Cliffe from 1611 to 1642. Hugget, who combined the benefice with the vicarage of Glynde, was apparently not a university graduate but, judging by a rather verbose sermon he delivered at St Paul's Cross in 1615, prided himself on being a Greek scholar. And according to one of his friends, he was 'a sincere and painful preacher of the word of God'. Nevertheless he evidently had little sympathy with the 'hotter sort' among his parishioners. In 1623 William Pemell, who was probably the same man who had campaigned so vigorously for ecclesiastical reform 20 years earlier, was hauled before the deanery court 'for most unreverend sitting with his hat upon his head upon Easter Day and before and since in time of divine service'. By failing to take off his hat he was demonstrating the conviction, common among the godly, that a church was no different from any other building, and to treat it as specially sacred smacked of popery. Pemell's defiance was matched by that of another independent-minded Cliffe parishioner Thomas Prior, who took exception to Hugget's habit of haranguing his congregation from the pulpit: in 1623 he was accused of 'laughing at Mr Hugget' and giving him 'unfitting speeches' during the catechism.[4]

In the light of the accusations that were later to be made against him it is likely that one of the things that caused Hugget to harangue his parishioners was their failure to attend church regularly. Some, like the men accused of drinking in Widow Roson's house in Cliffe in service time one Sunday in January 1621, may have had an aversion not only to St Thomas's but to any kind of church-going. But others may have gone off to worship elsewhere in the town where the preaching was more to their liking. Such 'gadding to sermons' was a common puritan practice and it was probably especially so in Lewes, where there were so many churches in close proximity to one another and so many good sermons on offer. In the absence of churchwardens' presentments for Malling deanery or (prior to 1638) for Lewes archdeaconry it is not known how many were formally charged with non-attendance at their parish churches, but a sampling of the diocesan Act books suggests that those Lewes people who were accused of this offence were not classifiable as puritans. The otherwise unknown Richard Smith of Lewes, who came up before the archdeaconry court in 1608 for 'not coming to church nor receiving holy communion this three or four years', was also in trouble on account of 'other grievous faults that he hath' and does not sound like one of the godly.[5]

Who constituted the 'godly' in Lewes at this time? As Patrick Collinson discovered when asking the same question about Cranbrook, surviving wills provide disappointingly few clues. Only a handful of 175 Lewes wills drawn up between 1600 and 1640 give any indication of the testator's personal beliefs. Most bequeathed their souls simply to 'Almighty God', with only a minority making any reference to Jesus Christ. One who did so was William Pemell's brother John, who used an unusually pious form of words: 'I do willingly and with a free heart render and give again into the hands of my Lord God and Creator my spirit, which he of his fatherly goodness gave unto me when he first fashioned me in my mother's womb, hoping most assuredly through the only merits of Jesus Christ my Saviour to be made partaker of life everlasting.' But further investigation reveals that exactly the same words were used in 17 other Lewes wills and that the formula was supplied by the scribe employed to write it. He was George Seager, a prominent St Michael's parishioner who from 1625 until his death in 1647 was a member of the Fellowship of the Twelve; but it is not clear whether he devised the wording himself or borrowed it from a formulary. Only six Lewes testators entertained the Calvinistic hope that in the afterlife they would be numbered among 'the elect'. And only one, William Hollingdale, gave what appears to have been a strong personal affirmation. He adapted Seager's formula, adding 'love and compassion' to the divine attributes, and concluded with a ringing declaration of faith in the Father and the Son, 'unto whom with the Holy Ghost my Comforter, three persons but one true, eternal and ever-living God, be ascribed all dominion, power and glory now and forever more. Amen.' Since Hollingdale, unlike many testators, was not making his will on his death-bed, he presumably had time to consider carefully what words to use in composing it.[6]

Opposing Popery and Prelacy

What is impossible to discover, from wills or any other source, is the strength of people's *negative* religious feelings. In the later years of the sixteenth century Protestants in Lewes, as in other parts of the country faced with the threat of a Spanish attack, had generally been strongly anti-

Catholic in sentiment. But after the 1599 invasion scare had proved to be unfounded such feelings may have abated. In 1600 when an Irish labourer in Cliffe was found guilty of sedition for saying, 'I love not the Queen nor yet her laws, but I love the Pope and his laws with my heart', he was merely ordered to be pilloried and whipped. The authorities could afford to be lenient in a situation where such noxious opinions were unlikely to be infectious. In 1603 the rector of St Mary Westout with St John sub Castro reported that there were no 'papists' in either of his parishes and the same probably applied to other Lewes parishes for which no returns survive. But there were pockets of disaffection in the nearby villages. In that same year Lewis Bennett, a clergyman resident in Barcombe, was indicted for saying that 'Catholics were the true Protestants and that the puritans and Brownists were but dissemblers'. He had gone on to suggest that, in dealing with the ignorant and unlearned, images were preferable to sermons, 'for that sermons went in at one ear and out at the other'. This in fact may have happened to his own words, since no-one seems to have taken them seriously. The only local group of people known to have remained consistently loyal to the old religion was the small community ruled over by the Gages at Firle. It was here in 1619 that a man, who had probably been drinking deeply in the local hostelry, was overheard to say that in the event of a Spanish invasion 'he would sooner take the part of the Pope or the King of Spain than of the King of England'. Subsequent to this a rumour that the Gage family had 'six or seven cartloads of arms in their house in a secret place' was carried along the coast to Hastings by a Lewes butcher, who was promptly arrested and despatched to the Privy Council in London.[7]

Although, after peace was made with Spain in 1604, there may no longer have been real expectations that a foreign force, supported by a Catholic 'fifth column' within the county, would attempt an invasion of Sussex, widespread alarm was caused in the following year by the discovery of the Gunpowder Plot. When news of Guy Fawkes' failure to blow up the Houses of Parliament reached Lewes it would certainly have been received with rejoicing. Townsmen would have agreed with their new diocesan bishop Lancelot Andrewes, who had been consecrated two days previously, that November the Fifth should for ever be observed as a Holy Day. It is not known, however, whether all parishes complied immediately with the statutory requirement that the day should be marked by the ringing of church bells. The first mention in the churchwardens' accounts of St Michael's of a payment (of one shilling) for 'ringing the 5th of November' occurs in 1622; a less generous sum of 4d was expended two years later, but none for many years thereafter. There was evidently more enthusiasm for the commemoration down in Cliffe, where the churchwardens are found paying two shillings to bell-ringers on 5 November each year from 1621, when their surviving accounts begin. In 1634 they bought 'a Book of Prayer for our great deliverance from the Gunpowder Treason' and in 1653 they recorded that the bells had been rung 'in remembrance of the great deliverance which ought never to be forgotten'. If in Lewes, as in Dorchester at this time, the day was marked by special sermons reminding people of the continuing Catholic menace, it is most likely that they were preached in the principal parish church of St Michael's.[8]

In Lewes as elsewhere anti-Catholic feelings probably became more pronounced after the accession of Charles I in 1625. The new king, who had a Catholic queen and was believed to have Romanist leanings himself, was a supporter of those in the Church of England who, so the puritans believed, were intent on unmaking the English Reformation. Confirmation of their fears came in 1628 when Richard Montagu became bishop of Chichester. He was a man of very different temper from his predecessor George Carleton, who had occupied the see from 1619. Montagu was what contemporaries termed an 'Arminian', one strongly opposed to the Calvinism that had been so prevalent in the Jacobean Church that it had virtually amounted to orthodoxy. He shared the sentiments of the bishop of London, William Laud, who wanted to restore the beauty and dignity that, he believed, had been lost to the church at the Reformation. The impact of the new conservatism, however, was probably not felt in Lewes until 1630 when George Thatcher, a young man recently ordained by Montagu, was instituted as rector of St John sub Castro. He was presented by the patron of the living, Edward Sackville, earl of Dorset, who was Lord Chamberlain to Queen Henrietta Maria and (in contrast to his grandfather Lord Buckurst) was evidently a man of conservative religious views. It is also significant that, unlike all the other university-educated clergy who had come to Lewes since the beginning of the century, Thatcher came not from Cambridge but from Oxford, which had become a bastion of Arminianism. Thatcher died prematurely in 1632 and was succeeded by another Oxford graduate Thomas Russell, who had been ordained by the strongly anti-puritan bishop of Oxford, Richard Corbet. But any attempts he may have made to persuade his parishioners to show reverence towards the 'sacrament of the altar' were evidently not altogether successful. In 1637 one of them, a widow named Devereux, was charged with 'unreverently abusing the holy sacrament' at a service at St John's. On receiving communion she had, 'as common fame and report goeth' exclaimed in a loud voice, 'Here is dry bread indeed!' And, to make it more palatable, she had proceeded to eat it with cheese.[9]

In the 1630s the restoration of the 'sacrament of the altar', which meant moving back the communion tables to their pre-Reformation positions, became a major cause of conflict in the parishes. In Sussex as elsewhere the placing of the communion tables altar-wise, behind rails at the east end of the churches, became what Anthony Fletcher has termed 'the touchstone of Arminianism'. Inevitably it tended to be the parishes closest to Chichester that were first affected by the new regime and it took time for the tide of change to reach Lewes. Significantly it was Cliffe, which lay within the direct jurisdiction of Laud (now archbishop of Canterbury) that first felt its impact. Like the early Christian missionaries, the Arminian reformers evidently came to Lewes along the ancient corridor from Kent. The standard-bearer was Sir Nathaniel Brent, Laud's vicar-general, who arrived in Cliffe in July 1635 and promptly ordered the communion table to be placed in a north-south position and 'railed in with a decent rail to keep off dogs and to free it from pollutions'. He also ordered the churchwardens in all other parishes to take Cliffe's altar-rails as 'their pattern' and to ensure that parishioners knelt when taking the sacrament. His instructions would doubtless have met with approval from Hugget, who was later to be criticised by his parishioners for making even the lame to kneel at communion. Hugget would also have been pleased by the injunction that priests should henceforth be provided with suitable garb. The Cliffe churchwardens, however, were probably not so happy. Soon after Brent's visitation they were obliged to spend £1 10s for two and a half yards of purple broadcloth for the communion table and £3 4s for a new surplice of 'fine holland' for their rector. Even if they had no conscientious objections to the Laudian reforms they might have jibbed at spending nearly a quarter of their annual income on restoring the 'beauty of holiness' to their church. When compared with the total of 4s paid that year 'to poor travellers at several times', £4 14s would have been considered a very substantial sum.[10]

While the Cliffe churchwardens apparently complied with Brent's instructions, it is not known how many of those in other Lewes parishes were prepared to do so. What is clear is that two years later the churchwardens of St Michael's had still not done as they had been bidden. When the archdeaconry court was held in the church on 19 July 1637 William Nevill, the diocesan chancellor, was horrified to see that the table was still in its east-west position and proceeded to move it 'with his own hands' into a north-south one. A week later, however, John Parmely, one of the churchwardens, who doubtless thought that setting the table altar-wise was popish, went into the church one evening and moved it back again. He was promptly summoned to attend the archdeaconry court held at St Michael's on 1 August and in the following month the parish had to pay 7s for his absolution. How many parishioners supported his action it is impossible to say, but it is clear that not everyone approved of Parmely as a person and some were apparently prepared to blacken his reputation. In the following year, after he had ceased to be a churchwarden, he and his wife were accused of something that, among puritans, was regarded as a very serious offence – 'living in incontinency before their marriage'. But since the only evidence offered was the birth of a baby 'within one or two and thirty weeks next after their marriage' (indicating that it was only about one month premature) the charge was apparently rejected.[11]

The Laudian insistence upon uniformity in the church also led to a systematic attempt to stamp out nonconformist practices among the clergy. In July 1635, when Brent came to Lewes, Richard Russell (minister at St Michael's) and George Bunyard (minister at Hamsey) were castigated for failing to bow at the name of Jesus and, threatened with suspension, promised that they would henceforth conform to the law of the church. In 1638, following the issue of visitation articles by Brian Duppa, the newly-appointed bishop of Chichester, Bunyard (now minister at St Michael's and Southover) again got into trouble. To the question, 'Doth he use the prescribed form of prayer before his sermon to prevent the indiscreet flying out of some in their extemporary prayers?', the St Michael's churchwardens replied that their minister 'useth an extemporary prayer, as we conceive it to be'. They also reported that 'we never hear him read the canons'. By this time, however, the Arminian offensive was on the wane and, after the calling of the Long Parliament in 1640, it soon came to an end.[12]

   With the overthrow of the ecclesiastical hierarchy came the destruction of its judicial machinery, and puritan ministers were no longer to be troubled by the presence of spies in the pews. Now they were free to give up reading from the Prayer Book, to abandon their surplices and to behave as they believed that Scripture directed. Nor would the laity any longer get into trouble if they sat rather than knelt at communion or kept their hats on in church. And the churchwardens of St Michael's, who from 1638 had dutifully recorded their payments for bread for 'the sacrament', could revert to their old practice of describing it as 'the communion'. Now it was the non-puritans who were in trouble with the authorities. In the autumn of 1642, shortly after the outbreak of war between King and Parliament, orders were issued requiring ministers to give or loan money to support the parliamentary cause. Among those sent for by the House of Commons for refusing to do so was Thomas Russell of St John's but, unlike other defaulters, he was quickly discharged. If he did have strong Arminian principles he was evidently unwilling to make an issue of them.[13]

   A worse fate befell Anthony Hugget, the rector of Cliffe, a much more controversial figure who never seems to have been popular with his parishioners. Soon after his arrival in Lewes he had been publicly denounced as a 'rascally priest', a 'drunken fellow' and a 'lying knave'. In 1619 he had incurred the wrath of John Holter, a Cliffe butcher, who complained to the Court of Requests that the rector was refusing to pay his meat bills and 'doth threaten and give out speeches' – unjustly, so he contended – that this was in retaliation for the non-payment of tithes. In 1643 the charges against him included 'incontinency', wife-beating and excessive severity towards those of his parishioners who had been unwilling to kneel at communion or had attended worship in other churches. And, to crown all, it was reported that he had been 'seen in the royal army'. Whatever the truth of the allegations, Hugget was driven from his benefices. According to John Walker, author of *The Sufferings of the Clergy*, the 'puritan party' pursued Hugget 'with the utmost fury and rage' and 'hunted and pressed him so close that he was secured by a neighbour in the next parish who hid him under a bed'. The boot that had for so long been kicking the godly into conformity was now on the other foot and in due course the disgraced rector was formally deprived of his livings and not long afterwards died.[14]

The Civil War and its Aftermath

The report that Hugget had been 'seen in the royal army' may have been a fabrication, since no such army ever came within marching distance of Lewes. Throughout the war eastern Sussex witnessed no fighting, although once in 1643 the Parliamentarian general Sir William Waller and his troops passed through the town and the church bells of Cliffe rang out a greeting. The main signs that there was a war on were the victims of the conflict from different parts of the country who came to Lewes in search of succour. In 1644 the churchwardens of Cliffe were kept busy paying out shillings and sixpences to itinerant refugees and, like the good shopkeepers that they were, they recorded their payments with meticulous attention to detail. The recipients of relief included a widow 'whose husband was plundered of £400 in goods near Bristow', a widow and four children from a town near York 'which Sir Thomas Glenham burnt to the ground' and Robert Brasegirdle, 'a plundered man of Ireland who had a certificate from the Speaker of Parliament for relief'. The horrors of war seem to have made the Cliffe wardens, whose predecessors 20 years earlier had been accused of robbing the poor box to pay for the communion wine, more responsive to the needs of the less fortunate members of society.[15]

Throughout the Civil War Lewes townsmen appear to have been staunchly Parliamentarian in sympathy. It was here that the Grand Committee, administering the county on Parliament's behalf, held its meetings. After the collapse of the diocesan administration this committee, which was dominated by the puritan magnates Sir Thomas Pelham of Halland and Herbert Morley of Glynde, took control of religious affairs throughout Sussex. In effect Lewes now replaced Chichester as the ecclesiastical capital of the county. In the rapes of Lewes and Pevensey the administration of church affairs was delegated to the 'Committee at Lewes', on which sat lesser gentry like Herbert Hay of Glyndebourne and William Newton of Southover. Newton, living in the house now known as Southover Grange just five minute's walk from the Bull Inn, where the committee's meetings often seem to have been held, probably did much of the donkey work. This venerable puritan who, as a young man, had witnessed the persecution of godly ministers, now had the task of supervising the removal of ungodly ones. By all accounts Newton was not a vindictive man, but such a remarkable turning of the ecclesiastical tables must have given him a certain amount of quiet satisfaction. After the end of the Civil War the Committee at Lewes continued to play an important part in the religious affairs of eastern Sussex, but it could no longer call on the services of Newton, who died in 1648 at the age of 84. Not long before his death the old man, whom his step-grandson John Evelyn (who had stayed with him while a schoolboy in Southover) remembered as 'a learned and most religious gentleman', made this solemn profession of his faith:

> There be three things that hath greatly humbled me, first the guilt of my sins, secondly the promise of my nature to commit sin and thirdly the grievances of this life which follow upon the former; but, after my dissolution by God's mercy in Christ apprehended by faith, I shall be freed from them all, so that the combat between the flesh and the spirit will cease and be no more and all traces shall be wiped from my eyes.[16]

Like other puritans Newton hoped that, now that the Civil War – the outward struggle between Christ and Antichrist that mirrored the 'combat' within – was successfully over, the outcome would be the complete purification of the Church of England. On a material level this would mean, among other things, the removal of the last vestiges of 'popery' from the parish churches. Although the frescoes had been lime-washed over and the statues destroyed in Tudor times there probably still remained in the churches a large amount of stained glass which, because it contained examples of the 'graven images' condemned in the Bible, the puritans regarded as idolatrous. At St Michael's, where some medieval glass is known to have been removed in Henry VIII's time, there may not have been much left. In 1641 the churchwardens there paid a glazier 5s 3d for 'mending the windows', but there is no knowing whether the breakages had been deliberate or accidental; and there is also uncertainty about a further payment of 3s 6d in 1643 for 'glazing the church'. In the same year £1 14s ld was paid at St Thomas's for 'mending the church windows and the leads': the size of the sum indicates that a great number of windows had been broken and that as a consequence most of the church had had to be reglazed. This certainly suggests that the destruction was deliberate. It may be significant that this year saw the presence in the town of numerous Parliamentarian soldiers – men notorious for their iconoclasm.[17]

The process of purification of the church, of course, meant much more than ridding its buildings of their coloured glass and letting in the clear light of day. The most important task was to get rid of unfit clergymen and put godly ministers in their place. How far was this achieved in Lewes? Apparently only Hugget, the unsatisfactory rector of Cliffe, had been expelled from his living. Thomas Russell, rector of St John sub Castro, in spite of his Arminian leanings and his initial unwillingness to help finance the Parliamentarian army, was not forced out; but he evidently agreed to a transfer to Berwick (eight miles away to the east) in 1647. This happened after the committee responsible for ecclesiastical affairs decided to merge St John sub Castro with St Michael's, a parish then described as 'destitute'. The other ministers in the town, who were probably all men of puritan sympathies, appear to have carried on until death or resignation removed them. In the immediate post-war years, in the absence of ecclesiastical records, it is not always easy to say who came to replace them. But it is known that the minister appointed in 1646 to serve St Mary Westout (which by this date was often referred to as St Anne's) and Southover was Benjamin Pickering, a 'godly, learned and orthodox divine' whose undergraduate studies had overlapped with Oliver Cromwell's at Sidney Sussex College, Cambridge. Pickering had previously ministered at East Hoathly, where he had enjoyed the patronage of Sir Thomas Pelham, who had helped to ensure his appointment as a member of the Westminster Assembly of Divines set up by Parliament in 1643 to reform the Church of England. It was in this capacity that in the following year he had preached a 'fast sermon' before the House of Commons, in which he spoke of the 'glorious days' that were in store for Christ's church. It would have suited Pelham's book to have his protegé moved from the country to the county town, where his gifts as a preacher could be put to better use. He continued to minister in Lewes, living at Southover until his death in 1657, when he was succeeded by his son-in-law Edward Newton.[18]

Prebyterians and Independents *versus* Quakers

The new minister, who was apparently no relation of William Newton of Southover, was a Cambridge man who had later migrated to Oxford, where he had become a Fellow of Balliol. Before coming to Lewes he had ministered for five years at Kingston Buci near Shoreham where, although the parish had only three houses, 'so many attended his ministry from neighbouring parishes that he had a good auditory'. Like his father-in-law he belonged to the majority party within puritanism which by this time had come to be designated Presbyterian – as opposed to those in the next largest party, who were known as Independents. But in Lewes these labels seem to have had little significance, for what united the two groups was more important than what divided them. What united them was a determination to ensure that the practices and structures of the English church conformed as closely as possible to the New Testament model. What divided them were relatively minor differences of opinion about who precisely should exercise authority in the church. Generally speaking the English Presbyterians, unlike their better-known Scottish counterparts, did not advocate a hierarchy of church courts composed of ministers and lay elders: they believed that authority was vested in local bodies of ministers, such as the 'presbytery of Sarum' that had ordained Newton in 1652. The Independents, on the other hand, had a less exalted view of the ministry, believing in the independence of the local congregation of 'saints' or true believers, who were deemed to constitute the 'visible church of Christ'. They were also more tolerant of diversity, being willing to welcome people to their pulpits whom the Presbyterians would have regarded as extremists.[19]

In Lewes the bastion of Independency was St Michael's, that old-established centre of radical religion, where since 1647 the incumbent had been Walter Postlethwaite, a fiery young man who had been Edward Newton's contemporary at Emmanuel College and who seems to have come to Lewes straight from Cambridge. At St Michael's he ministered to a congregation which, by all accounts, was the largest in the town. As with David Thickpenny in Elizabethan times his high standards attracted favourable comments from his contemporaries. He is reported to have been 'a sound preacher, holy liver and strict governor of the flock that was his charge'. Although serving as a parish minister he belonged to an extremist group known as the Fifth Monarchy Men, who were eagerly expecting the Second Coming of Christ. He personally held the view that things were so bad in England that God would soon abandon this country and set up the government of Christ in America or the East Indies. Understandably Cromwell's government distrusted such alarmists and tried to keep a careful eye on them. However, when William Goffe, the Major-General who had been put in charge of Sussex, visited Lewes in November 1655, he heard Postlethwaite preach twice at St Michael's and was impressed by the moderation of his views. This bears out a contemporary testimony that 'his private opinions affected not his ordinary preaching' – which, on the face of it, seems a bit difficult to believe.[20]

Like all puritan divines Newton and Postlethwaite wished to see the purification not only of the church but of the whole of society. Both were insistent on the necessity of orderliness, sobriety and a strict observance of the sabbath. Postlethwaite would therefore have drawn some solemn conclusions from the 'sad accident' that occurred in the town one Sunday morning not long after his arrival. On 18 April 1648 a group of children and apprentices, fooling around while their parents and masters were in church, started a fire that got out of hand and destroyed nearly a whole street. Significantly the houses that were burnt 'were observed to be the most profane in all the town', whereas a nearby house that was 'very famous for religion' escaped unharmed. The incident was regarded as a 'warning for all profane and licentious livers to take heed how they profane the Lord's day'. While puritans laid great emphasis on keeping Sundays sacred they insisted that all other days, even those that had traditionally been called 'holy', should be treated like ordinary weekdays. This applied especially to Christmas Day, observance of which in England had been officially abolished by a decree of 1646. While this decree was unpopular and widely disregarded throughout the land it was evidently acceptable in Lewes, where many tradesmen doubtless disliked the disruptions of 'holy days' and welcomed the opportunity to carry on business as usual. Even after 1660, which saw the restoration of this and other popular festivals, Lewes people continued to ignore the traditional holidays. In 1663 a visitor to the town was astonished to find 20 shops open on Christmas Day.[21]

Among those in Lewes most strongly opposed to Christmas (and indeed to the whole Christian calendar, which they regarded as pagan) were the Friends of Truth, the most vigorous and well- organised of the various sects to emerge in the aftermath of the Civil War. Popularly known as Quakers, because they quaked with fervour as they prayed, the Friends shunned all outward forms of religion and urged people to listen only to 'the Spirit of Truth in the inward parts'. In March 1655 Thomas Robinson of Westmorland, one of the first 'Publishers of Truth', came to the town and visited the house of John Russell in Southover, where he met a group of 'Seekers' – spiritually-minded men and women who had withdrawn from all organised worship. Here the visitor declared the truth 'to the convincement of Ambrose Galloway and Elizabeth his wife and Stephen Eager, who were then members of the said meeting', whereupon the three of them decided to join up with the Friends. Soon afterwards George Fox, the movement's principal founder, came to Lewes and attended a meeting at Southover before walking on to Warbleton, 16 miles away in the Weald. Not everyone in Lewes was receptive to the Friends' message and from 1656 onwards there are numerous reports of people throwing dirt and dung at them and even attempting to set fire to the house where they met. On one occasion the sons of some of the local Independents, armed with swords, guns and pikes, attacked a group of Friends who were holding an open-air meeting on Castle Green. In their turn the Friends, who were much less quiescent than the Quakers of today, sometimes responded vociferously. It was their custom to interrupt the services held in the parish churches, which they referred to contemptuously as 'steeple-houses'. In 1659 one of their number, Mary Akehurst of Cliffe, went into St Michael's at sermon time and put a question to the preacher, who was probably Postlethwaite.Her action infuriated the congregation, who threw her out of the church and made a strong complaint to her husband, a prominent merchant and former churchwarden at Cliffe, who beat her and put her in chains.[22]

It is clear that by 1659 the godly party in Lewes had gone a long way towards achieving their aims. Godly ministers occupied the pulpits and exercised godly discipline in their parishes. Men 'earnestly given to maintain godly orders' made up the membership of the Fellowship of the Twelve, the self-perpetuating oligarchy that, in the absence of a borough corporation, administered the affairs of the town. The 21 drapers, haberdashers, saddlers, apothecaries and other prosperous tradesmen listed as being 'of the Twelve' in 1659 were drawn exclusively from the town's 'hotter sort' of Protestants. This can be said with certainty since all but one of those that lived on long enough to fall foul of the restored ecclesiastical establishment were in due course to be branded 'Dissenters'. As godly rulers their primary task was to promote good order in the town – which meant dealing first and foremost with the exceptionally disorderly behaviour that occurred in and around the town's alehouses. In 1651 an earlier order for the 'repressing of the great number of alehouses in Lewes' was re-issued by the county magistrates at the request of the Twelve. But this time there was an additional instruction that licences should only be given to those whom 'the Company of the Twelve or the major part of them shall present and certify to be fit persons'. If Lewes was to be, like Rye, a 'city set on a hill' setting a shining example to the surrounding countryside, it clearly had to be a place where godly discipline was strictly enforced, even if this aroused opposition. It has in fact been suggested that in Lewes, Rye, Dorchester, Newbury and other towns where the rulers tried to establish 'New Jerusalems' attempts to carry through such a programme of reform 'invariably proved deeply divisive and met with determined and persistent opposition'. This certainly happened in Rye but, in the absence of meaty municipal records, there is no knowing whether this was also the case in Lewes. All that can be said is that it is *likely* to have been so. The sabbath-breakers and others who were denounced as 'profane and licentious livers' on the occasion of the great fire of 1648 and who may have constituted a sizeable proportion of the populace, were probably glad to see the end of the rule of the godly in Lewes. When the Commonwealth collapsed in 1660 and Richard Cromwell escaped to France via Newhaven in a ship provided by a sympathetic Lewes merchant, many in the town were doubtless pleased at the prospect of a restored monarchy and a re-established church.[23]

IV. Ejection, Schism and the Long Persecution

The puritans knew that the restoration of Charles II in 1660 would mean the restoration of episcopal government and many other features of the old ecclesiastical order that had been swept away in the Civil War. But they had been encouraged by the king's promise of 'liberty to tender consciences' and toleration of 'differences of opinion in matters of religion which do not disturb the peace of the kingdom'. Many hoped that they would be able to come to an accommodation with the king that would permit them to remain with a good conscience within the restored church. These hopes, however, were soon to be dashed. In 1662 Parliament passed an Act of Uniformity ordering the re-ordination of all who had not been ordained by a bishop and requiring the 'assent and consent' of the clergy to everything in a Prayer Book which, although it had recently been revised, still enforced practices that the puritans regarded as 'popish'. The clergy were still required to wear surplices, to make the sign of the cross in baptism, to use the ring in marriage and to administer the communion to people kneeling. More offensive to many than the revival of such 'ceremonies' was the restoration of the church courts, which effectively deprived ministers like Newton and Postlethwaite of the right to administer 'godly discipline' in their own parishes.[1]

The Act of Uniformity stipulated that those who refused to conform should resign their livings by St Bartholomew's day, 24 August 1662 – a date deliberately chosen to ensure that non-conforming ministers would be deprived of the half-yearly tithes due at Michaelmas. As a consequence over a thousand clergymen, subsequently described as the 'Bartholomeans', withdrew from the Church of England. Many years later Edmund Calamy published an *Account* of their lives, which ranks among the most readable yet least read of the English classics. Although Calamy, himself the son and grandson of ejected ministers, was clearly concerned to present these men in the most favourable light, defending them against charges of religious radicalism and emphasising their moderation, it is likely that by and large his *Account* is trustworthy. For the most part he was making use of reports from local correspondents with first hand knowledge of the people they were writing about. Much of the information about the ministers deprived in east Sussex was evidently supplied by Thomas Barnard of Lewes, who had known many of them personally. They included the town's two best-known clergymen: Walter Postlethwaite of St Michael's and Edward Newton of St Anne's and Southover.[2]

On Sunday, 17 August Newton preached for the last time from the fine Jacobean pulpit at St Anne's, taking his text from 2 Timothy 2.7: 'Consider what I say; and the Lord give thee understanding in all things.' The meat of the message was evidently in the passage that followed, where Christians are exhorted to endure all things 'for the elect's sake', so that they 'may obtain the salvation which is in Christ Jesus with eternal glory'. What Postlethwaite said to his people at St Michael's is not recorded, but he probably spoke in similar vein. For both men the decision to resign their livings and go out into the world without a home or a regular income was a momentous one that would inevitably involve hardship for themselves and their families. Things were made even harder for them after the passing of the Five Mile Act in 1665, which forbade ministers who refused to take the oath of non-resistance 'to come or be' within five miles of any corporate town or parliamentary borough or of any place where they had preached since the Act of Oblivion of 1661. Calamy said that after the passing of the Act Newton 'was forced to be a stranger to his own house and family, and could not have the satisfaction of conversing with them but by stealth and in disguise'. Warrants were often issued for his arrest, but 'Providence so far hid him that he was never taken, though his own house and the houses of his friends were often searched for him'.[3]

Newton continued to exercise his ministry clandestinely, preaching 'privately' and continuing his 'endeavour to promote practical religion' in and around Lewes. In this he was for a time assisted by two other ejected Presbyterian ministers – James Bricknell from Beddingham and John Earl from Tarring Neville – and by two Lewes-born students for the ministry, the cousins John Brett and William Staninough, both of whom had been obliged to leave Oxford. Similarly Postlethwaite, who also continued to minister secretly in Lewes, was supported by another ejected Independent divine, Henry Godman from Rodmell, and by a former ministerial candidate evicted from Oxford, John Crouch, the son of a Lewes tailor. Some of these men had secular occupations. Brett, the son of a prosperous Lewes grocer who had been a member of the Twelve under the Commonwealth, helped to support himself by practising 'physic', while Bricknell took up another occupation favoured by ejected ministers and kept a school. Also working as a schoolmaster in Lewes was Edward Beecher, who had been displaced as an 'intruder' from the vicarage of Kingston-juxta-Lewes on the restoration of the lawful incumbent in 1660. In Calamy's *Account* of these men the story of John Earl is the most memorable and moving:

His beginning was very small, but his latter end exceeding great. His books, household stuff and other expenses kept him in debt till he was ejected; upon which he would sometimes pleasantly say that he could never get out of debt till he was out of his living. His concern was more for work than maintenance; saying if God provided the former, he would trust him as to the latter. When he was ejected he removed with his increasing family to Lewes, where he exercised and improved his ministerial talent and was a great instrument in bringing meetings to be public. He had a great memory, as well as a sound judgment, and was a very useful preacher and expositor. . . . He was in labours abundant, going about doing good. He frequently travelled on foot as far as Maidstone, Chichester, London, &c. and, wherever he came and had opportunity, he preached the word of God. As his courage was great, so his sufferings were many. He was prosecuted in the bishop's court and indicted at sessions and assizes. His house was often beset and searched for meetings. The officers, once searching for him, entered every room of the house except that to which Mr Earl was withdrawn, which was as easy to be discovered as any of the rest, and they more than once passed by the chamber-door. At another time and place in Lewes a justice and other officers came into the very room filled with auditors where Mr Earl at that instant was; but while some designedly held discourse with the justice, a crowd went out and Mr Earl, stooping down, passed with them and retired to some private part of the house, and was ready to preach in the very same place in the afternoon. . . . Warrants were often out against him and once he suffered imprisonment, which he underwent joyfully. No part of his sufferings went nearer his heart than those occasioned by the Five Mile Act, which made ministers hide like the worst of criminals. But afterwards he said, he knew some ministers who, had it not been for that Act, had wanted bread for their families. Being scattered about, they fed many, who fed them and theirs; thus, according to Sampson's riddle, the eater yielded meat and sweetness. . . He frequently discovered great satisfaction in his nonconformity and at his death signified his firm belief that God would provide for his family, as he accordingly did. He died March 20, 1669 [1670], about the 35th year of his age. He lived much, though not long. He left behind him a widow and 6 small children, and his wife big of a 7th. Mr Newton preached his funeral sermon on the Lord's day after from Zech. 1.5.[4]

Lewes, according to Calamy, was 'a town that hath been blessed with more than an equal share of these good ministers'. In addition to those

already mentioned there was a Scotsman named William Wallace, who had
been ejected from East Dean near Eastbourne and who (like Earl) made
Lewes his base for operations further afield. He was described by Calamy
as 'a bold, faithful and laborious man', evidently more of a pastor than a
preacher, for 'he spoke English very ill'. He too had some narrow escapes.

> Once at Brighthelmstone, when the officers of the place broke in
> upon the meeting and made search for the minister, several women
> big with child stood about him . . . and the officers not attempting
> to remove any of them, Mr Wallace escaped, whereas putting any
> of them aside would have discovered him. At another time, at the
> same house, the officers of the town set a guard, and kept those
> that were met prisoners while they sent to Lewes (which was six
> miles) for a justice's warrant.

Yet another incomer was John Stonestreet, an Independent minister of
some distinction who had previously served at Lindfield. Described by Calamy
as 'an eminently gracious and holy man', he remained in his parish for some
time after his ejection, preaching in private. But after an unpleasant encounter
with a 'violent justice', he decided to move to Lewes, which was in fact his
native place. Here he had several relatives who would have been able to give
him support, including his brother George, a prosperous mercer, and his
brother-in-law Richard Russell, a wealthy apothecary of St Michael's parish.
However, unlike many ejected ministers, he evidently had ample means of
his own, for when he came to make his will in 1668 he left property in
Hailsham and over £400 in cash.[5]

The Dissenting Laity

It is likely that one reason for the influx of ejected ministers into Lewes
was the presence in the town of large numbers of lay people able and willing
to succour them. Although it is impossible to discover exactly how many
withdrew from the parish churches along with their ministers in 1662, it
certainly constituted a substantial proportion of the town's inhabitants. An
episcopal survey of 1669, which may have erred on the side of caution,
stated that the Lewes Presbyterians numbered 'about 500'; and on this basis
it has been suggested that, after deducting worshippers who came into the
town from surrounding villages, the total body of resident Presbyterian
'hearers' (including babes in arms) numbered about 450. The Independents
were merely reported to be 'numerous', but a recent estimate puts their
number at about 135. Having added in the Quakers meeting in Cliffe, whose
numbers were put at 60 (which, after deducting the out-of-town adherents,
should probably be reduced to 40), the total number of Dissenters living in
Lewes was probably in the region of 640. This represents about a third of
the total population of the town – a higher proportion than in any other

town in Sussex with the possible exception of Rye. Significantly the Dissenters were thickest on the ground in that old hotbed of nonconformity, the parish of St Michael, where they constituted 45% of those assessed for the 1665 hearth tax.[6]

The episcopal survey makes no mention of the presence in Lewes of a fourth body of Dissenters – the Baptists. Commonly called 'Anabaptists' (because they insisted on re-baptising those who wished to join them) or 'Antipaedobaptists' (because they were opposed to infant baptism), they represented the oldest and most radical strand of nonconformity in England. Their origins may have lain in the Lollard movement, which from the mid-fifteenth century had flourished in the Kent and Sussex Weald and which in Mary Tudor's time produced most of the martyrs burned at the stake in Lewes. Like the Lollards these early Baptists insisted that Christian belief and practice had to be strictly in accordance with New Testament teaching. Apart from practising adult baptism by total immersion, which the main body of Dissenters thought to be unscriptural and unnecessary, they differed from the Presbyterians and Independents on several points of doctrine. The Lewes congregation, like most of those in Kent and Sussex at this time, were not Calvinists. They were 'General' as distinct from 'Particular' Baptists, believing that Christ had died for the generality of mankind and not just for the 'elect' who had been predestined to salvation. At the time of the episcopal survey it is probable that the Baptists had no conventicle in Lewes. The nearest one seems to have been seven miles away at Ditchling, where in 1669 'about 10' Anabaptists were said to assemble on a Sunday. It is likely that this number included some from Lewes, for in 1674 three townsmen – Thomas Brad, a tailor with a copyhold on Keere Street, and the brothers John and Joshua Coles, both glovers – were charged with attending an illegal conventicle at Ditchling. On the whole, however, prosecutions of Baptists were rare, not only because they were few in number but also because, being for the most part humble folk of limited means, they may not have been thought worth prosecuting.[7]

On the other hand the main body of Dissenters in Lewes, as a recent analysis by Colin Brent shows, included many of the more prosperous people in the community.

> They . . . enjoyed economic vigour and social weight, permeating
> every sector of the town's commercial life except the drink
> trade. . . . They were especially drawn to the manufacture and sale
> of textiles and clothing; 30 shearmen, weavers, felt- makers, dyers,
> tailors, hosiers, hatmakers, glovers and collar- makers, 24 drapers and
> haberdashers, and 15 cordwainers and shoemakers, accounted for
> a third of the 199 male nonconfor-mists known to have been resident
> between 1663 and 1686.

Quite a number were also merchants engaged in the import and export business, of great importance in a major marketing centre like Lewes. The Quakers Ralph and Thomas Akehurst, sons of the Mary Akehurst who had been chained up by her husband, imported wine, brandy, grain, glasses and pantiles through the port of Newhaven; while Ambrose Galloway the younger exported cannon cast in the Weald. Most Quakers, like the Presbyterians and Independents, belonged to what the 1669 survey called the 'middle sort' – that is, the self-employed tradesmen and craftsmen who, according to sociologists of religion, are always the people most likely to embrace radical opinions. Few of those prosecuted for nonconformity were designated 'labourers', partly perhaps because, if such people had been brought before the authorities, they would probably have been too poor to pay the fines.[8]

The Prosecution of Dissenters

In Lewes those responsible for prosecuting Dissenters were the two constables, who from time immemorial had been chosen annually from within their own ranks by the members of the Fellowship of the Twelve. After 1662, however, the system became unworkable since the overwhelming majority of this body of substantial citizens were themselves Dissenters: only three of the 23 members of the Fellowship appear to have been Anglicans willing to enforce the requirement that all were to attend their parish churches every Sunday. As a consequence the magistrates were obliged to dissolve the old constitution and impose upon the town high constables chosen annually by themselves. Between 1663 and 1665 these loyal officials duly presented to Quarter Sessions a total of 99 people in the parishes of All Saints, St Anne, St John sub Castro and St Michael for non-attendance at church. In 1670 they referred no fewer than 133 to the Horsham Assizes for the same offence: it is not surprising that 60% of them lived in St Michael's parish, for so long a great stronghold of puritanism. Dissenters living in the suburban parishes of Cliffe and Southover, being outside the Lewes high constables' jurisdiction, largely escaped prosecution at this time, although a few non-attenders were brought before the ecclesiastical courts, which had been restored in 1660 after a 20-year hiatus. But in the suburbs, as in Lewes proper, the churchwardens appear to have been reluctant to present their neighbours for non-attendance: in fact on one occasion the two Southover wardens, one of whom was himself a non-attender, were cited for failing to make any presentments at all.[9]

While in the eyes of the authorities absence from church was a serious enough matter, it became much more so when compounded by attendance at rival meetings for worship, which contemporaries called 'conventicles'. In the autumn of 1663 a visitor to Lewes reported that these flourished 'as much as in Oliver's time', which sounds like an understatement. In Cromwell's day all the Presbyterians and most of the Independents would have attended the services in the parish churches; now that the majority had seceded it was likely that the numbers meeting on private premises had increased greatly. To put an end to such meetings a Conventicle Act was passed in 1664, making it unlawful for a group of five or more adults to come together 'under colour of religion', and in 1670 a second (much harsher) Act extended the prohibition to outdoor meetings for worship. One such conventicle was held at Henge Lane (below Mount Caburn) on 29 May 1670, which, to compound the offence, was the king's birthday. It was said to have been attended by about 500 people, including two professional informers who reported it to the authorities. The preacher on this occasion was the Independent divine Henry Godman and his text from the Epistle to the Ephesians, which included the words, 'because the days are evil', was thought to be particularly seditious. The informers duly handed in the names of 53 attenders, most of whom were ordered to pay substantial fines. Almost all refused to pay and as a consequence had their goods distrained: Richard White, a brazier, forfeited kettles and other brassware to the value of £10 13s; Thomas and Richard Barnard, drapers, had to part with six cows from the farm that they jointly owned with their mother at Northease; Walter Brett the younger, a grocer, was deprived of two barrels of sugar after a butt of currants had proved too heavy to shift. Apparently the only person to pay a fine was the wife of Benjamin Wood, a mason, who preferred to part with 5s rather than let the bailiffs confiscate her best bedclothes.[10]

In March 1672, on the issue of Charles II's Declaration of Indulgence, the penal laws were temporarily suspended and the Dissenters were free to worship openly, provided that licences were obtained both for their 'teachers' and for the houses where they met for worship. Newton obtained a licence as a Presbyterian teacher and also one for the houses of William Harris and Frances Pickering, his sister-in-law. Postlethwaite, however, did not live long enough to get a licence: he made his will on 1 January 1672 and died soon afterwards, his body being buried in St Michael's churchyard on 11 January. For those who were of the 'Congregational' persuasion the licensed teachers were John Lever and John Crouch, and the approved buildings were Lever's own house and the 'back house' of the apothecary Thomas Fissenden. But the Dissenters did not enjoy their freedom for long, for in the following year, after Parliament had obliged the king to recall his Indulgence, the penal laws were back in force. On 7 September 1673 informers infiltrated an illegal conventicle of about 150 'hearers' meeting in Fissenden's barn in All Saints' parish and reported 28 of them to the authorities. After that the Independents and Presbyterians appear to have attracted little adverse attention from the authorities until

1685 when, in the aftermath of Monmouth's rebellion (which had been strongly supported by Dissenters), 52 townsfolk were branded as 'ill affected'.[11]

Those who undoubtedly suffered most at this period were the Quakers, whose refusal to worship in their local 'steeple houses' continued to get them into trouble. Among the most outspoken of these conscientious objectors was Stephen Eager who, when called before the magistrates at Lewes in 1663, replied that 'he did go to the true church, which was in God'. But Friends were also punished for continuing to resist payment of church taxes and tithes. Their intransigence infuriated the rector of All Saints', William Snatt, who in August 1675, accompanied by the high constables and a posse of soldiers, entered their meeting-house at Puddle Wharf and, 'abusing many with blows and cruel punches', threw them out into the street. On this and on other occasions the Friends were heavily fined. Once when the tailor Ambrose Galloway refused to pay a fine, the bailiffs broke into his shop and took away 'men's coats and breeches and children's coats and other goods' worth over £20. In addition the Quakers were often punished for their refusal to pay the militia tax. In 1680 Thomas Robinson, a Cliffe feltmaker, was taken to court for not paying twopence, 'the tax for maintenance of drums and colours, which for conscience sake he refused to pay them', whereupon he had to forfeit 3 lbs of hemp worth 3s 6d. Sometimes their refusal to co-operate with the authorities caused them to be imprisoned in Horsham gaol, one of the last to suffer this fate being the aged Mary Akehurst. In July 1687, although in a very weak condition, she was taken to Horsham on horseback, 'one of the bailiffs . . . threatening that if she could not hold on he would have her dragged at the horse's tail'. It was such people that William Penn, who had visited Lewes in 1672 and had lodged at Mary Akehurst's house, had in mind when he wrote:

> The Lord blessed their labours with an exceeding great increase, notwithstanding all the opposition made to their blessed progress by false rumours, calumnies and bitter persecutions, not only from the powers of earth but from everyone that listed to injure and abuse them.[12]

Continuing Conformists

Because so much information survives about the lives of the Dissenters at this period there is a risk that scant attention will be given to those who continued to conform. What was the effect upon the Church of England of the Great Ejection of 1662? How did it manage to carry on after the loss of about a fifth of its clergy, among whom were many of the most learned and dedicated men in its service? There are some indications that in Lewes, as elsewhere, there was a serious shortage of clerical manpower. From

1663 to 1669 Henry Thurman served both St Michael's and St Anne's, two populous parishes that had not hitherto been combined. From 1675 to 1681 William Snatt had the oversight of St Michael's as well as All Saints' and St Thomas's; to add to his responsibilities (and his emoluments) he also occupied a prebendal stall in Chichester cathedral and (from 1679) was simultaneously vicar of Seaford. Pluralism on such an unprecedented scale was now a practical possibility since so many people had withdrawn from the parish churches and no longer required the clergy's services. Lewes Dissenters even performed their own clandestine funerals, often after dark: in 1663, when Thurman interrupted a midnight burial in St Anne's churchyard, it was reported that the mourners 'grew so insolent that they were very like to throw him into the grave'.[13]

Because information about Lewes clergy at this period so often comes from those opposed to them it is not always easy to reach an objective assessment of their calibre. William Snatt's reputation has suffered severely at the hands of the Quakers, with whom he was so often in conflict. They described him as a drunkard who stayed up 'unseasonable hours', whose 'conversation was with the wickedest men' and who was 'much hated by his own hearers for his wickedness'. What is not clear from their account of his character is that Snatt, the son of a master of the Free School at Southover who numbered John Evelyn among his pupils, was an Oxford graduate who had been ordained to the priesthood in 1669 by Bishop Henry King. He was evidently held in high esteem by Guy Carleton, bishop of Chichester 1678-85, who said that 'Lewes is such a factious place that the good that Mr Snatt has done is remarkable'. Thanks to his efforts, he said, the parishes of St Michael and All Saints, which had formerly been 'deeply infected with fanaticism', had become 'conformable to the discipline of the Church of England'. Perhaps in response to a report that the rector was not a great preacher Carleton described his 'good example' as the equivalent of 'the best sermon every day in the week and all the year through'. That Snatt, who moved to Cuckfield in 1681, was a man of unshakeable High Church principles is shown by his decision in 1689 to resign from his benefice rather than take the oath of allegiance to William and Mary. Much of our information about his successor at All Saints' and Cliffe, John Eresby, also comes from Quaker accounts of how 'wickedly and maliciously' he had treated them. In addition he was the subject of adverse criticism from a local magistrate Henry Shelley, who once reproached him for the brevity of his Sunday services. In a town where long sermons had become almost de rigueur it was not thought good enough for a clergyman simply to read a few prayers and a short homily and then dismiss the people with a blessing. Like Snatt, Eresby also resigned his livings soon after the accession of William and Mary but he was evidently not a Non-Juror.[14]

In the years after 1662 the clergy in Lewes, as elsewhere in the realm, were faced with the formidable task of trying to restore all that the long years of political and ecclesiastical upheaval had swept away. One of their most important duties was therefore to ensure that fit and proper persons were appointed as churchwardens. This, however, proved particularly difficult in a town where so many men of substance, from whose ranks churchwardens were normally appointed, were now Dissenters. Matters came to a head at St Michael's, the parish most tainted with Dissent, in April 1663, after 25 householders (most of whom were non-attenders) proposed John Geary (a Presbyterian) and John Crouch (an Independent) for election as churchwardens. Thurman, the new incumbent, promptly declared the nominations invalid and the crisis passed; but this did not prevent the two serving their term in 1665-6.

There were similar irregularities at Cliffe, which lay within the hundred of Ringmer where the former Parliamentarian families of Spence, Morley and Hay continued to exercise influence: no-one was able to prevent Presbyterians being elected as churchwardens of St Thomas's in 1669, 1670 and 1674. The appointment of Dissenters to these posts was not as incongruous as it may seem since, with the increasing secularisation of the parish, some of their major responsibilities (such as the administration of the Poor Law and the maintenance of highways) could not properly be called ecclesiastical.[15]

The churchwardens, nevertheless, still had important ecclesiastical functions and at this period one of the most burdensome was the maintenance of church fabric, a task made the more difficult by the unwillingness of some Dissenters to pay their church taxes. Dilapidation appears to have been a particular problem at Southover, where in 1677 it was reported that the belfry stairs were 'out of repair' and that 'the healing and covering of the said church is in decay'. The churchwardens were also supposed to maintain the spiritual structures of the church by ensuring that worship was in accordance with the Prayer Book authorised by the 1662 Act of Uniformity. This may have been difficult at Southover, where 15 years after the passing of the Act the church evidently still lacked a copy of the book. At Cliffe, however, the wardens appear to have done their duty in this respect, 7s having been paid for a Prayer Book in September 1662. But it is unlikely that all the book's appointed services were regularly used, since it was not until 1667 that there is any record of payments for bread and wine for holy communion; thenceforward, however, the eucharist was celebrated three times a year – at Easter, Whitsun and Christmas. These accounts, the only Lewes ones surviving from this period, also provide further indications of compliance with governmental instructions. In 1681 a large sum was paid to a 'Mr Jones' for 'painting and writing' the Commandments on the wall of the nave, for 'beautifying the chancel' and also for 'drawing and painting the King's Arms' on cloth. In 1682 the wardens dutifully arranged for a special peal of bells to be rung on Charles II's birthday – a reminder to all Dissenters within earshot that the Head of State was also Supreme Governor of the English Church and in both capacities demanded their total obedience.[16]

That Lewes people needed such a reminder is clear from a letter written to Bishop Carleton in 1683 by his deputy registrar at Lewes, Thomas Barrett:

> This part of your diocese, as it is far remote from your palace, so is filled with a sort of men who are further remote from loyal principles than perhaps any other diocese. . . . For here is contempt of the king's command and all Acts of Parliament. We still have conventicles held, schism maintained, and the preachers of it defended by those pretended officers of justice who, for fear of being thought too active in prosecution, have totally neglected what lay in their own way for promoting the loyal cause.

One of these negligent 'officers of justice' was Henry Shelley, who from 1673 until his removal from the bench in 1683 for promoting 'faction and schism and disobedience to the government', was the sole resident magistrate in Lewes. Shelley, although nominally an Anglican, had close family ties with local Independents and was inclined to protect Dissenters from the severest rigours of the law.[17]

When it came to dealing with the threat posed by religious dissidents at the other end of the ecclesiastical spectrum, however, the king had no more loyal subjects than the people of Lewes. As was to be expected, the so-called Popish Plot of 1678 aroused strong anti-Catholic feelings in the town. On 5 November in the following year there was much burning of bonfires and parading of banners depicting 'bloody Jesuits', 'wanton friars' and 'devils dancing attendance on the Pope'. In the procession were boys with painted faces, one of whom 'carried holy water in a tin pot, sprinkling the people with a bottle brush', and at the head of it marched 'Guy Faux with his dark lanthorn'. Such frolickings, which culminated in the ritual burning of the Pope in effigy, would have had particular significance down in Cliffe, where (according to the not altogether reliable testimony of local Quakers) the rector, William Snatt, 'did keep in his house a crucifix and other popish relics'. It is not known whether anti-Catholic demonstrations of this kind were held in succeeding years, nor what the reactions were in 1685 when, after the accession of the crypto-Catholic James II, the lighting of bonfires on 5 November was declared illegal.[18]

In 1687 King James, seeking to protect Catholics and curry favour with Dissenters, issued a Declaration of Indulgence, which suspended all the laws passed against both parties. So strong was their belief that this time, unlike 1672, the penal code would not be reinstated, the Lewes Presbyterians and Independents proceeded to follow the example of the

Quakers and provide themselves with permanent places of worship. According to Calamy's account Edward Newton now for the first time 'publicly exercised his ministry in a house fitted up for the purpose'. And Joseph Whiston, an ejected minister from Maidstone who had succeeded Postlethwaite as pastor of the Lewes Independents in 1672, now began to preach openly in a meeting- house in All Saints' parish, which may have been Thomas Fissenden's old barn newly converted for the purpose. The expectation that such freedom of worship might be lasting was soon to be confirmed with the accession of William and Mary in 1688 and the passing of the Toleration Act in the following year. Protestant Dissent was now to become a permanent feature of the religious scene – and in Lewes a particularly prominent one.[19]

V. Dissensions within Dissent

The Toleration Act of 1689 granted freedom of worship to everyone except two groups of people who were regarded as being morally and theologically beyond the pale: Roman Catholics and disbelievers in the doctrine of the Trinity. Since there appears to have been no-one in either category in Lewes at this time the Act's exemptions had little local significance. The nearest Catholics were still the Gages at Firle, but nobody now suggested that they were storing supplies of arms and ammunition in the hope of a Spanish invasion. The only threat they posed was ideological: as rich and powerful landowners they were in a good position to exercise an undesirable influence on the minds of local Protestants, but there is no evidence that anyone in Lewes was affected in this way. There was once a popular story about the widow of a Presbyterian wine cooper of Lewes named Challoner who, left almost penniless after her husband's premature death in the early 1690s, found a refuge for herself and her young son in the Gages' hospitable household and became a convert to Catholicism. The tale had an interesting twist because, so it was alleged, she was the mother of a bright youngster named Richard who, having been trained at Douai as a missionary priest, returned to England in 1730 and engaged in a famous controversy with Dissenters, the very people among whom his early years had supposedly been spent. Recent research, however, indicates that the future Bishop Challoner was not born in Lewes and that his parents were almost certainly not Dissenters.[1]

While Roman Catholics would have to wait over a century before they were allowed to worship openly, Protestant Dissenters could now enjoy a large measure of toleration. How permanent this would prove to be only time would tell; there was always the possibility that a statute passed by one Parliament might one day be repealed by another. But the Act's passing was generally an occasion for rejoicing among all the Dissenters except the Presbyterians. Unwilling to be categorised as 'separatists' most of them would probably still have preferred 'comprehension' within the church (provided it had been properly reformed and broadened) to permission to operate outside it.

Baptists, Quakers and the Limits of Toleration

The Lewes Baptists, some of whom had previously been in the habit of travelling on Sundays to Ditchling (where the chances of prosecution were probably smaller), were now free to worship nearer home. In 1697 a licence was granted under the terms of the Toleration Act for 'a meeting for Anabaptists at the house of John Henty near the Free School in Southover'. The house was in fact situated on the north side of Eastport Lane and had a garden stretching down to the Winterbourne. Nowadays the stream often consists of little more than a trickle, but 300 years ago it is likely to have provided a sufficient supply of 'living water' not only for baptisms by total immersion but also for the ritual washing of the feet of the faithful – a practice that was prevalent among General Baptists at this time. How numerous the Lewes Baptists then were, it is difficult to say. The episcopal survey of 1724 records the existence of six 'Anabaptist' families in Lewes and others in places in easy reach of the town – one in Alciston, two in Barcombe, one in Beddingham, two in Chailey, four in Firle and one in Hamsey. To these should be added those recorded in the South Malling deanery survey of 1717: one family in Cliffe, another in Glynde, and 'one preaching Anabaptist that is an inmate' at Ringmer. Unfortunately the 'Evans List', a survey of Dissenting congregations made in 1717 by a Chichester Presbyterian minister who was only interested in counting Presbyterians and Independents, provides no information about Lewes Baptists. Its compiler even managed to overlook the existence of Baptists at Ditchling, which had the largest congregation of this persuasion in east Sussex. Even after 1741, when they opened their own purpose-built meeting-house in Eastport Lane, the Lewes Baptists remained a branch of 'the Church of our Lord Jesus Christ meeting in and about Ditchling'. It was to Ditchling that they went for the formal 'church meetings' held once or twice a year for the purpose of administering finances, admitting members, ordaining deacons and admonishing those found guilty of drunkenness, fornication, 'disorderly walking' or some other breach of good Christian behaviour. It was not until 1803 that the Lewes congregation became fully independent.[2]

Throughout the eighteenth century the General Baptists of Sussex and Kent continued to be a predominantly rural sect set apart from the main body of Protestant Dissenters, who were normally of a higher social standing and who flourished mainly in the towns. As the diocesan surveys indicate, some of those who attended the Lewes Baptist meeting probably lived in nearby villages. Unlike the Presbyterians and the Independents they had no professional ministers but were served by self-taught lay preachers. One such was William Evershed, born into a 'humble but virtuous' family at Fletching in 1717, who early in life was employed as a ploughboy on a local farm. He is said to have had a great thirst for knowledge and continued to acquire it as he followed the plough, 'having his task transcribed and fixed to his sleeve, he performed the duty of his master and improved his mind at the same time'. He often stayed up late reading theology or history and from the age of 19 was preaching regularly at Lewes, Ditchling and elsewhere. He later moved to West Sussex, where he acquired his own farm and became pastor of the flourishing General Baptist congregation at Horsham.[3]

In the early years of the eighteenth century some of these Horsham Baptists had come to hold theological opinions which, in the eyes of orthodox Dissenters, represented an even more serious departure from the truth than their denial of Predestination. Prior to his death in 1714 the pastor of the Horsham congregation was Matthew Caffyn, a controversial figure known as 'the Battle Axe of Sussex', whose denial of the deity of Christ (using arguments similar to those of the Italian heretic Faustus Socinus) had led to his being dubbed a 'Socinian'. It was because of Caffyn's known heretical reputation that the Lewes Presbyterian minister Thomas Barnard became so alarmed when news reached him in 1705 that a young woman from Horsham, whose parents were Baptists, was lodging temporarily in Cliffe. He promptly went to see her and 'interrogated her whether she did believe the Lord Jesus Christ to be God, and did believe in him with all her heart', recording that he did this because he 'feared that the Anabaptists she had been conversant with were Socinian'. His anxiety was understandable. Denial of the doctrine of the Trinity at this time was not merely a heresy but, under the terms of the 1698 Blasphemy Act, a crime. If Caffyn's opinions were beginning to infect people in Lewes this would have been a serious matter and Barnard was clearly taking no chances.[4]

Heretical though they may have been, the Baptists at this period were not being persecuted for their beliefs or practices. But it was a different matter with the Quakers. Although after the 1687 Declaration of Indulgence they enjoyed complete freedom of assembly, the Friends' refusal to conform to the ways of the world continued for a time to get them into trouble. Several Lewes tradesmen suffered for their convictions. Benjamin Moseley's insistence on keeping his shop open on 14 December 1688, 'the thanksgiving day for the Prince of Orange', led to some of his drapery ware to be thrown into the street and trampled in the dirt. Again in the following year Richard Stephens, a grocer, had his windows broken and much of his goods despoiled because he perpetuated the old puritan custom of opening for business on Christmas Day. But the Quakers' most serious offence in the eyes of the authorities was their continued resistance to the militia tax. In May 1690 Ambrose Galloway, who had refused to pay seven shillings, had his house invaded by a troop of soldiers and suffered the confiscation of pewter and brassware – a large part of which was never returned – to the value of £5.[5]

After 1690, however, there are fewer references to Quakers suffering persecution. One of the few Lewes Friends known to have been punished for disobedience was the brewer Thomas Beard, who had hops to the value of £4.10s confiscated by the constables in 1713 for non-payment of tithes owed to the rector of Cliffe and who suffered again in 1725 and 1726 for like offences at Southover. The last Lewes Quaker to be named in the minutes of the Sussex 'Meeting for Sufferings' was Elizabeth Rigge, widow, arraigned in 1735 for her refusal to pay tithes due to the rector of St Michael's. It is noteworthy that in these years the names of Friends from Lewes feature less prominently in the lists of tithe-refusers than their co-religionists in other Sussex towns and villages. Was this because Lewes clergy were more lax or because Lewes Quakers were more law-abiding? Whatever the truth of the matter it seems to have been the case that, as the eighteenth century proceeded, the Society of Friends generally became less refractory and more 'conformed to the world'. It gained respectability and at the same time, as one of its own historians has put it, experienced 'a diminished effusion of the Holy Spirit'. It is also likely that the Society, in Lewes as elsewhere, was diminishing in numbers. In the 1720s the families attending Lewes Friends' Meeting were far fewer than they had been 50 years earlier. The 1724 diocesan survey recorded the presence of only four Quaker families in Lewes – plus one in nearby Tarring Neville. Even after adding the four in Cliffe and the one at Glynde recorded in the South Malling deanery survey of 1717, the total only comes to ten. But it is arguable that ten families of committed Quakers exercised a greater influence on the spiritual life of the community than a much larger number of nominal Anglicans or, for that matter, Presbyterians or Independents.[6]

Presbyterians, Independents and the Happy Union

The people about whom most information survives for this period are the Presbyterians, thanks to the detailed autobiographical account kept by Edmund Calamy's correspondent Thomas Barnard. Barnard, one of those punished for attendance at the famous Henge Lane conventicle in 1670, was born in 1643, the son of a prosperous Lewes draper who was a member of the Twelve under the Commonwealth. He had originally followed his father's trade but from 1673, 'having from the first an eye to that solemn ordination which I intended in due time to receive', he had devoted most of his energies to acting as an unofficial assistant to Edward Newton. In

February 1688, following the issue of the Declaration of Indulgence, he had been ordained at a gathering held at Glyndebourne by the laying on of the hands of Newton and two other ejected Sussex ministers. Henceforth he regarded himself as being properly 'authorised for the performance of all ministerial acts as God in his providence should administer occasion'. By his own account the ministerial duty that he performed most frequently and assiduously was that of baptism. Between 1688 and 1699 he baptised nearly 150 children, 24 of whom lived in Brighton. Sometimes he was prepared to travel even greater distances to christen children in their own homes, particularly if they belonged to important families like the Faggs of Glynleigh near Pevensey, where boys were baptised in 1696 and 1699. In May 1691 he even went as far as Hastings to perform an adult baptism by total immersion in the sea – something about which he may have had some misgivings, since he took the precaution of recording the event in his register in Latin.[7]

Barnard records that on 21 August 1695, 'which was solemnly observed as a day of fasting and prayer', he was formally installed 'by the unanimous election of the church' as Newton's co-pastor. At the same time he listed the names of all those who at that date were communicant members of the congregation. Apart from the two ministers there were exactly 50 people, of whom 31 were women: they included Mary, widow of the ejected Scottish minister William Wallace, and Newton's sister-in-law Frances. She was the daughter of the celebrated Benjamin Pickering and widow of Elias D'Aranda, a former curate of Mayfield who after his ejection had served as minister of the French church at Canterbury. Barnard later added the names of those who joined the congregation after August 1695. By the end of 1699, 54 names had been added, of whom 37 were women. The 54 included five living outside Lewes who were subsequently recorded as having been 'dismissed to Brighton' in April 1700, when a daughter church was established there and a Lewes member, John Duke, was appointed as its first minister. Although by 1700 the communicant members of the Lewes congregation still numbered well under a hundred Barnard relates that the 'auditory' (which included non-members) had greatly increased and was continuing to do so. He therefore felt that the congregation should abandon their Watergate Lane meeting-house and move to more commodious premises in a better location higher up the town, but his senior colleague opposed him.[8]

This led to a major crisis, as Barnard recorded in his register:

Upon the unreasonably obstinate opposition made and persisted in by Mr Newton, my brother-pastor, unto that necessary and most inoffensive enlargement which was a matter of conscience with me, for enlarging the gospel interest of our Lord Jesus Christ, the church stood like a tottering house ready to drop on our heads. For

a year and a quarter many stood looking on, but not one offered to
enter into our communion.

Barnard, who evidently had ample private means, was undeterred by
Newton's opposition and went ahead with the purchase of what he referred
to as a 'useful place' – the old Bull Inn (formerly known as Goring House)
situated hard by the town's crumbling West Gate. The building's large
Elizabethan back-addition was gutted and turned into a meeting-house with
seats for 250 people, which was formally opened for worship in 1700 on 5
November, a date of some significance in such a Protestant town as Lewes.
Although invited to share the use of these spacious premises – known
variously as 'Bull Meeting', 'Westgate Meeting' or 'Upper Meeting' –
Newton rejected the offer and 'sealed the schism with an opposite
sacrament' on 6 April 1701. A substantial minority of the congregation
remained behind with him in the old meeting-house in Watergate Lane,
which was henceforth called the 'Lower Meeting'; and here he continued
to officiate until 1709, when old age and infirmity obliged him to resign.
He died three years later, just 50 years after his forced departure from St
Anne's: then aged about 85, he was the last survivor of the Bartholomeans
in this locality. Newton, according to Calamy, 'studied to be as inoffensive
as he could with a good conscience, and he had the general good opinion
both of the ministers and people of the Established Church'. But he did not
record that latterly Newton had been in conflict with some of those in his
own communion, and especially with Barnard. It may be that Barnard, in
corresponding with Calamy, had withheld this information out of respect
for the memory of his senior colleague – or that Calamy, who could be
described as more a hagiographer than a historian, had known about the
conflict and had simply chosen not to mention it.[9]

One of the things that may have prompted Barnard's decision to move to
the Bull was the hope that the Presbyterians would have a meeting-house
large enough to share with the next largest body of Dissenters – the
Independents. The Independents, in spite of their attachment to a different
form of church government, had always enjoyed a good relationship with
the Presbyterians. This is clear from the evidence of wills such as that of
the locksmith Alexander Owden who, although evidently a Presbyterian, in
1688 left money to be distributed among the poor members of both the
Dissenting congregations – that of 'Parson Newton of Southover' and that
of 'Parson Whettstone of Lewes'. The latter was Joseph Whiston, minister
of the Independent congregation from 1672 to his death in 1691, who was
a strong supporter of the idea – then in vogue in London and elsewhere –
of a 'Happy Union' between the two denominations. According to Calamy,
he had 'had a considerable hand in promoting an association of ministers
of both sorts' in east Sussex. This information had almost certainly come
from Barnard, whose respect and affection for Whiston, described as a

man of 'great wisdom and moderation', shines through the account of his life. However, the further information that the inter-denominational association of ministers had 'died with him' suggests that others in Lewes were less keen on such co-operation. Barnard relates that in 1694 there had been 'an hopeful prospect of a union between the two congregations of Dissenters', but that 'after long consideration' it did not take effect, 'God's time for it not being yet come'. Opposition to the union may have come either from Newton or from Comfort Star, who had succeeded Whiston as pastor of the Independent congregation in 1691.[10]

Star seems to have been a more deeply committed Independent than his predecessor. He was the son of an Ashford physician who had emigrated (along with the Hosmers and other Wealden separatists) to New England in 1635 and had gained an MA at Harvard, the new university that his father had helped to endow. Having returned to England to serve a church in Carlisle, he was ejected in 1662 and thereafter ministered to a number of Dissenting congregations in his native Kent before moving to Lewes. Here he remained as pastor of the Independents until his retirement, at the ripe age of 84, in 1708. The brevity of Calamy's account of his life, bereft of the personal details and favourable comments contained in. his account of Whiston's, may be an indication that his Lewes correspondent did not have a close relationship with him. Be that as it may, Barnard clearly got on very well with Star's successor, a much younger man named John Olive, who took up his post in 1709 and who almost immediately accepted his suggestion that the Independents should join the Presbyterians at Westgate. Accordingly the union of the two congregations was effected on 6 November 1711, which 'was observed as a day of solemn prayer and fasting with laying aside of ornaments'.[11]

The list of communicant members drawn up in 1711 puts the combined strength of the two congregations at 169, of whom 112 were Presbyterians and 57 Independents. In both cases the women greatly outnumbered the men: 71:41 with the Presbyterians and 35:22 with the Independents. Prominent in both groups were members of the family of Ridge, who had farmed at Iford just outside Lewes since the mid-sixteenth century and had been among the first supporters of the Dissenting cause in the town. Two had been present at the Henge Lane open-air service in 1670: Thomas Ridge of Cliffe, draper, and his brother William Ridge of Iford, yeoman – the latter living long enough to witness the opening of Westgate Meeting in 1700. Their eldest brother Stephen, a prosperous farmer whose former home at Westmeston had been licensed for Independent worship in 1672, had been present at the illegal conventicle held the following year in Thomas Fissenden's barn. It is likely that Stephen, who after his retirement lived on in Lewes until 1715, and his son Richard took an important part in the negotiations leading up to the union of 1711. This was a highly satisfactory arrangement for members of the widely extended Ridge family who, in spite of their differing denominational allegiances, were henceforth able to worship under one roof.[12]

Evidence of the strength of the Westgate congregation, jointly ministered to by John Olive and (after Barnard's retirement in 1715) by Joseph Beach, is provided by the 'Evans List' of 1717. The total number of 'hearers' is given as 425, of whom 50 were electors for the county (45 for Sussex and five for Kent) and 42 for the borough. Of the hearers 120 (33 gentlemen, 18 yeomen, 50 tradesmen and 19 labourers) were also subscribers. Similar details are given for the congregation presided over by Newton's successor at the Lower Meeting, Thomas Force. Of his 170 hearers 18 were electors for the county (17 for Sussex and one for Kent) and twelve for the borough; and the subscribers were made up of 16 gentlemen, 10 yeomen, 19 tradesmen and 15 labourers. Some of these people lived not in Lewes itself but in outlying parishes and came into the town to worship on Sundays. Such, for example, were 'the Presbyterian family lately come into the parish' at Ringmer and the 'two farmers who are Dissenters with their wives and several of their servants' at South Malling referred to in the 1717 survey of Malling Deanery. The reference to wives is a reminder that women probably continued to constitute the majority of communicant members of both Upper and Lower meetings – but about them little information survives. All that is known about Anne Ridge, who was doubtless one of the Dissenting wives mentioned in the 1717 survey, was that she was born Anne Peckham at Framfield in 1682, married Richard Ridge in 1707, bore three sons and three daughters (one of whom eventually married Westgate's minister Ebenezer Johnston), outlived her husband and was buried at St Michael's in 1764. Throughout her long life, as the wife, mother and mother-in-law of men prominent in the affairs of Westgate, her role, although never formally recognised, was doubtless a decisive one; but, whatever they may have been, her achievements remained unsung.[13]

One most important sphere of service at Westgate, then restricted to the men, was that of acting as trustees of the meeting-house. For some years after its opening for worship in 1700 the building remained the private property of Thomas Barnard, but in 1719 he finally agreed to vest it in a body of thirteen trustees. Five of them had been members of his own congregation, five of John Olive's and three had joined since the union of 1711. Apart from William David, a glover from Willingdon, and Richard Ridge, who farmed at Upper Stoneham in South Malling, all lived in Lewes or Cliffe. Without exception they were men of some substance. William Attersoll, Richard Ridge's brother-in-law, 'carried on a great business' as a carpenter and builder, eventually in partnership with his son John (appointed a Westgate trustee in 1755). Thomas Barrett, a clockmaker, 'made lantern and long case clocks of distinction' that were much in demand throughout Sussex. Richard Button and John Chatfield were prominent residents of Cliffe, the one a schoolmaster respectable enough to be styled 'gentleman' and the other a 'yeoman' rich enough by the time of his death in 1725 to be able to bequeath the then princely sum of £25 to his friend and minister John Olive. The venerable Thomas Fissenden carried on his father's successful practice as an apothecary with a 'physic garden' whose site is now commemorated by Garden Street, while the youthful Stephen Jackson, described in the trust deed as an 'upholder', was soon to leave Lewes to prosper himself in London. Thomas Norman was a leading seller and binder of books, while John Peckham was a master dyer with a fulling-mill at Fletching. Three others were in the forefront of local trade: the 'haberdasher of hats' William Read, the currier James Reeve and the tallow-chandler Stephen Weller. Many of the trustees took an active part in public affairs: from 1719 to 1720 Reeve and Weller served together as borough constables, an office held previously by Barrett, Fissenden and Read and subsequently by Attersoll. At this period the trustees and other leading Westgate members played such a prominent part in the government of the town that it could be said that in Lewes, as nowhere else in Sussex, Dissent was virtually part of 'the establishment'.[14]

This favourable state of affairs was not to last. By 1730 throughout southern England both Presbyterians and Independents were expressing concern about a reported decline in their numbers and influence. Economic recession was affecting the fortunes of the laity and, perhaps as a consequence, some Dissenting ministers were conforming to the Church of England. The situation was apparently especially serious in Wiltshire and Hampshire, but it is likely that Sussex Dissenters were faring no better. At Westgate Meeting the number of subscribers was certainly falling in the 1720s; as people died or withdrew their support few came to replace them. Among those who left was Richard Russell, a third generation Dissenter who, having married an Anglican and qualified as a doctor, had built up a fashionable practice and was on his way to achieving fame as the 'founder of Brighton'. Among those who died was Thomas Barnard's brother Richard, whose annual subscription of £5 had been the highest on the list; his son's subsequent failure to continue the subscription must have caused great disappointment. Things were probably similar at the Lower Meeting, which in 1723 was reported to be 'upon the decline by reason of the death and removal of many'. Among Dissenters in Lewes as elsewhere a new generation had grown up whose faith, untested in the fires of persecution, had grown weak and cold. The eighteenth century saw a reaction against the excesses of the seventeenth: rationality was the order of the day and in matters of religion it now became customary to keep things cool. 'Tolerance', once a synonym for the endurance of suffering, took on a new meaning: increasingly it came to signify 'toleration' – a readiness to take a dispassionate, detached attitude to one's own and other people's beliefs and practices. Lewes people, it seems, had even lost some of their old hostility towards Roman Catholicism: after 1727 there was no more celebratory bell-ringing on 5 November at St Michael's nor after 1736 at St Anne's.[15]

Dissenters Divided

The tolerance of Lewes Dissenters was to be sorely tested in the early Georgian period, which saw growing divisions within their ranks. While persecution reigned Presbyterians and Independents had worked closely together, united in their resistance to a common foe. In Lewes the spirit of co-operation had continued long enough to produce the union of the two congregations at Westgate in 1711 and the appointment of a united body of trustees in 1719. But although they met in a single jointly-owned building the two congregations apparently continued to hold separate services: it is likely that one normally met in the morning and the other in the afternoon. With seating for over 250 this may not have been a physical necessity but, because of growing differences of opinion, it may have become a theological one.

Throughout England at this time Presbyterians and Independents were beginning to be divided not only over matters of church government but also over doctrine. In February 1719 a conference of the 'Three Denominations' (Presbyterian, Independent, Baptist) was held at Salters' Hall in London to consider an issue that had arisen in the west of England. Should ministers, on their appointment, be required to make a declaration of their belief in the doctrine of the Trinity? Most of the Presbyterians present at Salters' Hall, while orthodox in doctrine, were opposed on principle to subscription to creeds and voted against the proposal to introduce it. On the other hand most Independents voted for the motion, which was lost by four votes. John Olive was present at the meeting and is known to have voted with the conservative minority; his colleague Joseph Beach did not attend, but had he done so he would almost certainly have voted with the majority. Be that as it may, there is no doubt that at this time fundamental issues divided the two congregations at Westgate.[16]

The point of contention probably had less to do with the Trinity than with another doctrine that was causing dissension in mixed Presbyterian-Independent congregations all over the country. The problem was that while the Independents for the most part remained strictly Calvinistic, maintaining that Christ had died only for the elect, the Presbyterians were moving closer to the position held by the General Baptists in affirming that he had died for the generality of mankind. The picture was more complicated in Lewes, where there were two Presbyterian ministers – Beach at Westgate and Force at the Lower Meeting – who appear to have been on opposite sides of the divide. This is indicated by the discussions that took place in 1723 when

Olive's adherents were said to be 'in danger to be broken to pieces by the divisions occasioned by Mr Beach and his party'. The situation was so serious that at one time they were considering withdrawing from Westgate and uniting with Force's people at the Lower Meeting. Such a move, some thought, would be 'the most proper and effectual way to preserve and strengthen the common interest of religion in the town' which, they feared, was 'like to be brought very low, if not utterly destroyed'. After a lengthy consideration of the pros and cons of the proposal someone pointed out that it might 'cause grief to Mr Barnard', now nearing 80 and likely soon to die. It was also feared that it would 'give disgust to Madam Spence' who, as lady of the manor of South Malling, was probably Westgate's richest and most socially prestigious supporter. The dissidents may have sensed that, being a woman, she would have not wished to give credence to the conflicts that were so exciting to the men. A more practical objection was that, once Olive's people had vacated Westgate, it might be difficult for them ever to return. The counter-proposal was then made that they should remain at Westgate, 'shut Mr Beach out of the pulpit by putting a lock thereon' and 'set a guard at the pulpit door'. To lock this door was in fact quite feasible at Westgate, where the minister ascended to the pulpit by a special staircase from the stable-yard at the rear of the meeting-house. In the end, however, less militant counsels prevailed and the Independents decided that the best policy would be to stay put.[17]

How did Lewes avoid the kind of schism that took place at this time in other provincial towns where there were united congregations of Protestant Dissenters? Part of the explanation has to do with the composition of the body of trustees who were the legal proprietors of the meeting-house. It was unusual for trustees to be chosen in such a way that there was an even balance between denominations. In other mixed congregations it was common for the wealthier members, who were the trustees and subscribers, to be Presbyterian and the less prosperous ones to be Independent. Consequently, if there was a conflict over doctrine or practice and the two parties decided to go their separate ways, it was often the Independents who were obliged to vacate the meeting-house and seek alternative accommodation. Had the Lewes Independents implemented their plan to join Force's congregation the Lewes religious scene might have come to resemble that at Sheffield. Here, following a disagreement over the appointment of a new minister in 1714, a formerly united congregation of Dissenters had split into a Presbyterian 'Upper Meeting' and an Independent 'Nether Meeting'. The situation at Westgate, however, was rather different. Many of the Independents were evidently as affluent as the Presbyterians and, thanks to Barnard's wisdom and foresight, they were joint proprietors of the building and thus had every right to remain in it. Also, as William Attersoll was quick to point out, it would be inappropriate and inexpedient for Olive's people to withdraw from Westgate since he and the other Independent trustees would still be legally bound to bear their share of 'the burden of taxes and repairs'. This point would not have been lost on Richard Ridge, the wealthiest and most influential of the Independent trustees who, when asked his opinion about the proposed schism, evidently spoke against it. He probably thought that maintaining the status quo would be the best way of preserving not only 'the common interest of religion in the town' but also the particular interests of his widely extended family, who doubtless wanted to continue to have an opportunity to meet together at Westgate on Sundays.[18]

At the conclusion of the matter the Independents stated that they had decided to remain at Westgate 'for the sake of offering up a more pure service, the preserving mutual charity, and not giving the enemy the occasion to blaspheme'. The good reputation of Protestant Dissent in Lewes was thought to be at stake. And so, 'after humbly spreading the case before the Lord in prayer and begging his direction and assistance', they concluded that 'the most direct and proper way in which to follow after the things that make for peace' was to lay aside 'carnal reasonings' and to leave everything to 'the ordering and disposal of Him who walketh in the midst of the Golden Candlesticks'. Their faith was duly rewarded. For nearly 20 years Olive and Beach continued to serve as joint pastors at Westgate and together to further the 'common interest of religion' by working in harmony with Force at the Lower Meeting. On occasion all three ministers would preach at a single combined service, as a diary entry for 9 January 1740 made by Richard and Anne Ridge's son William shows:

> A Fast kept on account of war with Spain, kept at Lewes in the Upper Meeting House in following manner: Mr Beach prayed a short prayer, then he read a psalm and chapter and then prayed again, then he preached a sermon on Revelation 3.2, then sung a psalm, and then Mr Olive prayed and then he preach a sermon on Jeremiah 14.8, and then Mr Force went up and preach a sermon on the 3 chapter of Jonah, and then he prayed, and then sung another psalm, and then made a short exhortation for a collection for the poor.
> The service began about eleven a clock and continued till about 3.

This may have been the last occasion on which the three ministers came together for an act of worship at Westgate, for in the following year Olive died and Beach retired. Force carried on for a little longer, but early in 1742 his 33-year long ministry at the Lower Meeting eventually came to an end.[19]

Dissenters Reunited

That year the two Westgate congregations finally became one with the joint appointment as minister of Ebenezer Johnston, a native of Dumfries, who had probably been acting as a kind of probationary minister since his arrival in Lewes in the summer of 1741. He was only about 23 years old but he was evidently well equipped for his task, having recently completed a rigorous four-year course of study at Northampton academy, where the celebrated Philip Doddridge was principal. Here the curriculum was exceptionally broad, including not only Latin, Greek, Hebrew, logic and philosophy but also mathematics, physics, anatomy, astronomy, history, geography and other subjects not regularly taught at universities. However, although he had acquired a great fund of knowledge, it remained to be seen whether he had enough wisdom to tackle the formidable task that lay ahead of him.[20]

Johnston's ordination took place at Westgate on 21 July 1742. Descriptions of such events are rare for this period but fortunately an account of this one survives. It is in the commonplace book of William Ridge, who was so impressed by the occasion that he recorded all the details of it 'as near as I could call to mind' after returning home that evening. The service, which began at 10.45 am and continued, apparently without a break, until 3.15 pm, was unusual in that it represented a combination of the practices of both Presbyterians and Independents. At the beginning of the service, in accordance with Independent custom, members of the congregation were asked to indicate, by a show of hands, 'whether they did not allow of the invitation' to Johnston. Then the new minister was asked to 'read his belief' and make public his 'resolutions to keep his belief'. Such a requirement, standard among Independents, was not normal among Presbyterians, who were now not in favour of creeds. But when it came to the climax of the service, Presbyterian practice prevailed. When Johnston knelt down before the seat where the visiting ministers (from Battle, Brighton, Burwash, Rye and elsewhere) were sitting most of them stood up and laid their hands on the young man's head while Samuel Snashall of Stoke Newington prayed over him. This is a clear example of ordination by the 'presbytery', which in England (unlike Scotland) was an exclusively ministerial body. Its status was not normally recognised by the Independents, who believed that the highest authority was vested in the whole body of believers, who were seen to constitute the 'visible church of Christ'. It is significant that on his ordination certificate a reference to the 'imposition of hands' was added later in the margin.[21]

Some elements in the ordination service, however, were common to both denominational traditions. There were hymns (which were probably by Isaac Watts) and long extempore prayers. There were readings from Scripture: two passages from the New Testament and the whole of the 34th chapter of Ezekiel, containing the statement – so appropriate for this hitherto divided congregation – that 'I will set up one shepherd over them, and he shall feed them'. There was a sermon, which would probably have gone on for well over an hour. And then, following the act of ordination, there was a second sermon – the 'charge' to the new minister, given on this occasion by the great Dr Doddridge, who had come down specially from Northampton for the ceremony. At the conclusion of the four and half hour service all the participating ministers walked to the nearby house of William Ridge's brother-in-law Cruttenden Weller, where they received much needed refreshment. It is likely that Lewes High Street had never before witnessed such a great convocation of Dissenting divines.[22]

Among the 15 ministers who sat down to dine that afternoon was David Jennings, who had preached the principal sermon, taking as his text 2 Cor. 4, 5: 'For we preach not ourselves but Christ Jesus the Lord.' He was by this date the most influential of the London Independent ministers and was famous both for his orthodoxy and for his fondness for fostering divisions. What was he hoping to achieve? Did he really hope that this attempt to unite two apparently disparate congregations would succeed? Some years previously, commenting on the situation in a mixed Presbyterian-Independent congregation not unlike Westgate, Jennings had told Doddridge that the members were 'too far divided already ever to be comfortably united under one minister'. He had therefore suggested that they would do better to 'split rather than unite, like Jeremy's two figs, one very good and one very bad, which may be squeezed together but will never incorporate'. But Doddridge took a different line. While agreeing that in big cities it was sometimes desirable that orthodox and unorthodox should meet in different places, he opposed divisions in small provincial towns.[23]

It is interesting to speculate about Johnston's feelings as he embarked upon his ministry at Westgate. His ordination certificate, which Jennings was the first to sign, refers to him as the successor to John Olive and there was clearly an expectation that he would stand firmly in the Independent tradition. At his inauguration he had dutifully read out a statement of his beliefs and had publicly proclaimed his resolution to 'keep' them. But what precisely were his beliefs? Was he, as Jennings doubtless hoped, a sound Calvinist who would 'preach not himself but Jesus Christ'? Or was he, like his mentor Doddridge, a 'Middle Way man' – one who tried to steer a middle course between Calvinism and Arminianism? While at Northampton Johnston would have experienced an approach to theological study not normally found in Independent academies, for John Locke's *Essay concerning Human Understanding*, with its avant garde common-sense psychology, was on the syllabus and students were taught to think for themselves. Doddridge's method was to present them with both sides of a controversy and then leave it to their own judgment to decide which side to take. The consequence was that most of his former pupils eventually abandoned Calvinism and, ceasing to feel at home among the Independents, threw in their lot with the Presbyterians.[24]

The situation at Westgate in Johnston's day may well have resembled that at Kidderminster, where Benjamin Fawcett ministered from 1745 to 1780 and where the congregation was said to have been 'very much mixed as to doctrinal opinions'. It was reported that Fawcett, a near contemporary of Johnston's at Northampton academy, was not only Arminian but also 'Arian' in doctrine, indicating that he denied the full divinity of Christ, but he 'managed so far to conceal his opinions as to be very popular with his hearers'. Such a stratagem may sound disingenuous but it was in fact one that Doddridge himself would have commended. 'With a prudent eye for congregational majorities,' writes Robert Webb, 'Doddridge offered a message of hope that the skilful minister might command his flock and, in time by subtly calculated preaching, educate them.' In his addresses to the Westgate congregation Johnston, who in 1749 purchased Doddridge's *Christ's Invitation to Thirsty Souls* and his *Rise and Progress of Religion in the Soul*, may have followed his mentor in maintaining a stance that was at once both rational and evangelical. It may be that, by avoiding doctrinal issues and concentrating on 'practical' Christianity', Johnston was for a time able to please almost everyone.[25]

If any of Johnston's hearers were alienated by his doctrine (or lack of it) there was, throughout most of his ministry, nowhere else for them to go. If they had gone down hill to the Lower Meeting they would have found similar fare on offer. James Watkins, who had succeeded Force as minister there in 1742 shortly before Johnston's installation at Westgate, was probably unorthodox in his opinions. He had been educated at the Dissenting academy maintained by Samuel Jones, first at Gloucester and later at Tewkesbury, where the future Archbishop Secker had been a contemporary. Under the influence of Jones, who was one of the first tutors to put Locke on his lecture list, Watkins is likely to have become a critical questioner of Calvinism. He certainly seems to have enjoyed good relations with Johnston, participating in his ordination and later baptising some of his children. Had he been a conservative in theology he might have drawn away any Westgate hearers who were unhappy with Johnston's liberal views. But in the event the two congregations drew ever closer together and, when Watkins retired in 1759, his people decided to shut up their meeting-house and move up to Westgate. They brought with them some of the Lower Meeting's woodwork, which was used to extend the building by the addition of a fine new vestry, erected on stilts at the rear of the meeting-house.[26]

This was a very satisfactory situation for Johnston. He had succeeded in keeping his people together at a time when other Dissenting congregations were falling apart. Contrary to Jennings's prediction, here 'Jeremy's two figs' had been 'squeezed together' and had fully 'incorporated'. Not only that, but another congregation in the town, which in other circumstances might have been a resort for disaffected hearers, had now merged with his own, bringing welcome new subscribers to Westgate Meeting's funds. But Johnston was also unusually fortunate in that he was not solely dependent on his stipend. Following his marriage into one of the wealthiest Westgate families he evidently acquired considerable private means. His financial accounts, kept with meticulous accuracy, show that he came to enjoy a useful income from investments in various enterprises, including 'the building of a ship at Newhaven' for carrying on 'a trade from Lewes to Barbados'. For a time importing sugar from the West Indies was a highly profitable activity and his decision to participate in it suggests that Johnston, the founder of a long line of Lewes grocers, had the kind of business acumen for which his countrymen were famed.[27]

Anglicans in Adversity

The strength of Dissent in Lewes, as indicated by the prosperity of Westgate Meeting and its minister, continued to be a cause of concern to the ecclesiastical establishment. In 1718 the bishop of Chichester, Thomas Manningham, had complained that Lewes was 'miserably overrun' with Dissenters – so much so that he feared that the Church of England had 'little reputation' there. His successor, Thomas Bower, was to find ample confirmation of this sorry state of affairs when he came to study the returns of the diocesan survey that he ordered to be made in 1724. These show that out of a total of 324 families living in Lewes (including Southover but excluding Cliffe) 75 were Dissenters. Allowing for an average of three to a family the indications are that the Dissenting 'hearers', excluding those from surrounding villages who came into Lewes to worship on Sundays, were about as numerous as the communicants in the five parish churches, who totalled approximately 220. But how many of the Anglicans were regular worshippers? If some were accustomed only to attend church on 'sacrament Sundays', then the number present on an average Sunday may have been much smaller than the quoted figures suggest. At this period, as the surveys show, 'sacrament Sundays' were few and far between. At All Saints', St John sub Castro, Southover and Cliffe communion was administered only four times a year –- at Christmas, Easter, Whitsun and around Michaelmas. At St Anne's and St Michael's it was normally nine times a year: at 'the three solemn festivals' and on the first Sunday of every other month. It was reported that, with the exception of St Michael's (where there was a morning service on Wednesdays, Fridays and holy days) each church usually had only one service (with sermon) each week, on Sunday morning or afternoon. These arrangements, however, could sometimes be upset by the elements. Thomas Peirce, rector of St Michael's and St Anne's, recorded that he conducted worship in both of his churches every Sunday, except when stormy weather, 'to which the church is very much exposed', made it impossible to meet at St Anne's; in which case he held two services at St Michael's.[28]

The 1724 survey provides interesting information about the material condition of the parish churches. Although St John sub Castro was commended as a 'church in good repair within and without', it was reported that 'there has been no chancel in the memory of man' and, as a consequence, the communion table and rails were 'very small for want of room'. Southover church was also minus a chancel, 'a very large one having fallen down many years ago'. Moreover, a new steeple (intended to replace one that had collapsed in 1698) 'not being finished for want of a sufficient collection, the timber is in a few years so much decayed by being exposed to the weather that they have been obliged to take down three of the bells.' St Michael's was said to be 'in decent order within', but clearly in a bad state without, for the south-east wall of the chancel was in need of repair. Here is an indication of the dilapidation that 20 years later was to become so serious that 'parishioners could not attend divine service without great danger to their lives'. Things were apparently much better at St Anne's, where the 'very large' chancel had lately been repaired at the expense of Joseph Graves, rector there from 1683 until his death in 1720. A wealthy man, Graves is best remembered in Lewes for his generous bequest to the town of a library of 523 books and of an endowment with which to maintain and extend it. However, under later, less prosperous incumbents St Anne's fell into disrepair. Part of the problem was that, as the 1724 survey expressed it, 'almost half the great tithes are enjoyed by a layman, who pays nothing to the repairs of church or chancel'. Here was a reminder of the way in which the laity were perpetuating the process of ecclesiastical plunder that had begun with the Reformation. 25 years later, in 1749, the *Lewes Journal* reported that a 'great part of the roof' of St Anne's had fallen in and had seriously damaged the pews. However, the report continued, 'it was very providential it did not happen on a Sunday in time of divine service which, if it had, must inevitably have killed several people'. In 1750, after the chancel of St Anne's had become so 'very ruinous' that the church was virtually unusable, the parishioners agreed to collect voluntary contributions towards the cost of the repairs. But it is significant that they insisted that their shouldering of a responsibility that properly belonged to the rector should not constitute a precedent.[29]

The parish gaining the most favourable comments from the commissioners who carried out the 1724 survey was All Saints'. Here, surprisingly, the chancel as well as 'the church' had been repaired 'at the expense of the parish'. The steeple and its three small bells were said to be in 'good order' and the interior furniture and furnishings, comprising communion table, carpet, rails and 'cushion of crimson velvet' were 'all very decent'. Full marks were also awarded for the communion linen, a silver chalice with cover and a 'silver plate for the bread'. In fact All Saints' picked up only two black marks. One was for the absence of the statutory 'poor box', a deficiency reported in every Lewes parish except Southover. The other was for the state of the surplice, an essential item of clerical apparel that it was the parish's responsibility to provide. While those in the other churches in the town were graded 'good' or 'very good' the All Saints' surplice was condemned as 'very old and decayed' – which raises the question of whether it was ever worn.[30]

It is not always easy to discover who actually wore the surplices in Lewes churches at this date. At All Saints' there was no incumbent in 1724 and services were 'supplied by the sequestrator', who was named as Jonathan Leatherbarrow, A.B. of Brazen Nose College, Oxford. Had there been a resident rector at this date there would have been no parsonage for him to live in, 'but only a small garden let at 16s per annum'. The absence of a parsonage was also reported at Southover, another parish then in the hands of a sequestrator. He was Joseph Stedman, a graduate of Glasgow university, who had served as Presbyterian minister at Lindfield before conforming to the Church of England in 1717. He was now the resident curate at Hamsey, where he preached every Sunday (usually in the morning), in addition to being responsible for supplying the service held at Southover each Sunday (usually in. the afternoon). Every other Sunday he also conducted worship at St John sub Castro, where the incumbent Richard Davis (who was also patron of the living) was evidently wealthy enough to be able to pay someone else to do half his work for him. It is known that Stedman who, like other ex-Dissenters, may have joined the Church of England in search of better career prospects, later got into serious financial difficulties. His situation had not been helped by the Quaker Thomas Beard's refusal to pay tithes due to him at Southover.[31]

Another clergyman with financial problems – and the only other one in Lewes at this time known to have pursued Quakers for non-payment of tithes – was John Bristed, rector of St Anne's 1725-83 and of St Michael's 1731-52. The tithe income from these parishes, as the 1724 survey revealed, was much less than it ought to have been. Not only had half St Anne's tithes been impropriated by a layman but barely two-thirds of those at St Michael's could be collected 'by reason of the poverty of many of the parishioners'. In 1733 Bristed was obliged to lease St Anne's parsonage to a dancing master and later sought to supplement his meagre income by teaching at the grammar school. He also, like his predecessors Underdowne and Innians, earned extra fees by acting as surrogate in the Lewes archdeaconry court, whose activities were now largely confined to probate matters. One of the wills presented to him in 1750, the year in which the St Anne's churchwardens reported that their rector could not pay the £35 required for chancel repairs 'without reducing himself and family to great distress', must have been particularly painful to prove. This was the will of his wealthy kinsman Richard Bristed of Warbleton, a landowner who had died childless leaving most of his property to various cousins (one of whom was also named John Bristed) but nothing to the one who was probably the neediest of them all.[32]

Poverty also afflicted Edmund Lund, rector of All Saints' and St Thomas's from 1725 to 1776 and another who supplemented his income with surrogate's fees. In May 1744 a request was made to the duke of Newcastle that 'poor Mr Lund' and his 'large though poor family', who had been stricken with smallpox, might be allowed to live rent-free in an isolated house that the duke owned in Friars' Walk. In some respects, however, Lund may have been more fortunate than Bristed. It was reported in 1724 that, although 'the tithes demandable' in All Saints' parish were worth only £9 14s. 2d, the total collected amounted to three times this figure thanks to 'voluntary contributions' from parishioners. Subventions on such a scale were evidently not forthcoming at St Michael's, which had a higher proportion of Dissenters than any other parish in the town. Here it is likely that many of the parishioners' 'voluntary contributions' went to support the minister of Westgate Meeting rather than the rector of the church over the road.[33]

Beyond this bare record of their financial difficulties little information survives about the men who staffed the Lewes parish churches in these unpropitious times. That Bristed was a conscientious, practical preacher is suggested by the information that a sermon he once delivered at St Michael's on the subject of Repentance was so well received that it was subsequently published in pamphlet form. That Lund was regarded as a faithful 'guide and teacher' of his flock is clear from the contemporary testimony of one of his leading parishioners. The only indication of the tenor of his preaching comes from the diary of Thomas Turner of East Hoathly, who attended the morning service at All Saints' on 27 June 1762, when Lund took his text from Galatians 6. 2: 'Bear ye one another's burdens and so fulfil the law of Christ.' All the indications are that Lund fulfilled this law and practised what he preached. It would be good to know more about him and the other parish clergy who ministered in Lewes at this period. Knowledge of the good they did died with them and only the reports of their misfortunes have survived.[34]

By 1760, the year in which their church acquired a new Supreme Governor in the unlikely person of George III, the Anglicans of Lewes were evidently in the doldrums and the Dissenters were clearly prospering. Serving a wealthy congregation in a well-maintained meeting-house, Johnston may have been thankful that he was so much better off than the local parish clergy, but even so he is unlikely to have looked forward with great confidence to the future. England was beginning to experience the Evangelical Revival and this, by and large, was not good news for Presbyterians. Distrustful of the 'enthusiasm' of Wesley and Whitefield, which they deemed dangerously emotional, they stood for a rational form of piety in harmony with the world-view of Locke, Newton and other thinkers of the Enlightenment. Distancing themselves from the Independents, most of whom welcomed the Revival, the Presbyterians began to think of themselves as 'Rational Dissenters'. In holding firm to common sense and 'catholicity' in the face of fanaticism and sectarianism they hoped to promote the peace and unity of Protestant Dissent but, as it transpired, they merely helped to create a permanent rift between its 'liberalising' and its 'energising' forces. In Lewes, however, the rift was not at first as clear-cut as it was elsewhere because, since Westgate Meeting had succeeded in avoiding a schism, there was no orthodox Dissenting congregation in the town to host the new 'energising' forces. And so it came about, as the next chapter relates, that the Whitefieldians' first stronghold in Lewes was not, as was often the case, a reinvigorated Independent congregation but a 'chapel' newly-built without benefit of much assistance from conservative elements within Old Dissent.[35]

VI. Evangelical Revival and Sectarian Strife

On 15 September 1760 the *Lewes Journal* reported that George Whitefield, the celebrated Calvinistic Methodist divine, intended to preach that day in Lewes, but it is not known for certain if he did so. At the time he was staying in Brighton with his patroness and chief disciple, Selina, countess of Huntingdon, who had lately taken a house there and was in the process of establishing a base for the re-conversion of Sussex. A devout Anglican, she at first had no intention of setting up a separate denomination. Her hope was that the evangelical clergymen in her entourage, whom she (as a great lady was entitled to do) liked to call her 'chaplains', would be allowed to preach in parish churches throughout the county. In 1765 she 'began to concert measures for introducing the Gospel into the town of Lewes' and gained permission for William Romaine (the famous preacher at St George's, Hanover Square) to occupy the pulpit of one of the local churches. It may have been All Saints', where the rector Edmund Lund was a man likely to be sympathetic to evangelical piety. Nevertheless it was reported that Romaine's sermon had given 'great umbrage' to some of his hearers and he was subsequently obliged to preach in the open fields. According to Lady Huntingdon's account the common people heard him gladly: 'All gave earnest heed while he applied those solemn words, "Behold the Lamb of God that taketh away the sins of the world". I did not see one careless or inattentive person, and there is reason to think that many poor sinners were cut to the heart.' Later that year she obtained a pulpit for two other famous evangelical preachers, Martin Madan and John William Fletcher, but 'the clergy opposed them very violently and they betook themselves to a large room where they preached alternately to great numbers'. She was back in Lewes again in 1767 with Richard de Courcy, who preached twice to a large congregation in the open air.[1]

Opposition to the Calvinist evangelists came not only from the local clergy but also from riotous townsmen. On Bonfire Night 1769 an 'enraged mob' tried to set fire to a house on School Hill which, 'to the great annoyance of that neighbourhood and the principal part of the borough', had been let to a Calvinistic Methodist who planned to preach there twice a week. In January 1770 the *Lewes Journal*, which at this time was consistently hostile to the Huntingdonians, was glad to report that 'a journeyman carpenter, who has lately commenced Methodist preacher' had been 'hung in effigy on a signpost in Cliffe' and later 'taken down and committed to the flames'. The local press evidently regarded Methodism as a form of madness. When in August 1771 a man from Beeding ran stark naked through the streets of Lewes it was explained that he had been 'brought almost in a state of insanity by following the Methodists'. It was because Lewes was proving to be such infertile ground for evangelism that in due course Lady Huntingdon decided to open a permanent place of worship in the town. As with the one she had built for her 'chaplains' in Brighton, she avoided the term 'meeting-house' (which smacked too much of Dissent) and called the place a 'chapel' – a word hitherto almost unheard of in Lewes. Cliffe Chapel, a capacious building said to have had seating for 600, prominently situated on what was subsequently to be called Chapel Hill, was formally opened on 13 August 1775. The lease of the premises stated unequivocally that the cause had been established 'upon those principles and tenets which are commonly called Calvinistical'. This was a clear indication of the countess's determination to distinguish its doctrinal position from that of Wesleyan Methodists, General Baptists and Presbyterians, of whose Arminianism she strongly disapproved.[2]

The opening of the new chapel, which some Lewes people (doubtless to Lady Huntingdon's annoyance) insisted on calling a 'meeting-house', aroused considerable local hostility. In January 1776 it was reported that those frequenting it had been

> divers times disturbed in their religious worship by disorderly persons, who have made a practice during Divine Service of besetting the said meeting-house and, with indecent noise and clamour, and by flinging stones and bricks against and through the walls thereof and lighted combustibles into the house, interrupting the congregation in their devotions and putting them in fear of their lives.

Later that year, undeterred by such violent opposition, 'the serious people in and about Lewes', numbering 59, formed themselves into a single 'society'. Lacking a permanent pastor, the members at first had difficulty in keeping themselves together, but things began to look more promising in 1781 with the appointment of Joseph Middleton as full-time minister. Middleton, who had been trained at Lady Huntingdon's college at Trevecca in Wales, was an energetic young man of 27 who soon found favour both for his public preaching and 'private character'.[3]

Calvinists in Conflict

Soon after his arrival Middleton became convinced of the necessity of restricting baptism to believers, since 'the Holy Scriptures held out a believer as the only proper subject and immersion as the only proper mode of that ordinance'. His change of mind caused consternation in the Cliffe congregation but, after the young minister had undertaken not to try to impose his views from the pulpit, matters settled down for a time. However, in 1784, shortly after preaching a sermon on 'Brotherly Love' so pleasing to his hearers that they asked him to repeat it, fratricidal strife broke out and as a consequence Middleton and his supporters were expelled from the chapel. They then moved to the meeting-house lately vacated by the Quakers at Puddle Wharf, which in the following year they exchanged for a wooden chapel in what is now Foundry Lane. Not long afterwards they clarified their denominational identity, and at the same time distanced themselves from the old-established General Baptists in Eastport Lane, by joining the Kent and Sussex Association of Particular Baptist Churches. However, they were more liberal in outlook than some of the other churches in the Association whose refusal to admit non-Baptists to communion led them to classify themselves as not only 'particular' but 'strict'. The strictness of the Foundry Lane folk lay less in their doctrine than in the discipline they exercised through the officers appointed to seek out absentees to explain their failure to turn up on Sundays and to visit applicants for membership to 'enquire into their Christian experience'.[4]

For some years the new Baptist congregation grew and flourished but in 1794, as Middleton reported to the Association, they were beginning to experience the 'lukewarmness' and 'want of spirituality' that, he said, had been afflicting all the churches. In addition the Foundry Lane people had been upset by 'a censorious, ill-natured and condemning mode of preaching which has been introduced into our neighbourhood', which had caused many to be 'thrown from their steadfastness' and to be left 'stumbling upon the dark mountains of uncertainty, doubt and unbelief'. Middleton did not name the person responsible for this 'great decay of brotherly love', but it was almost certainly Jenkin Jenkins, his successor in the pastorate at Cliffe Chapel, who had recently adopted a most abrasive oratorical style. There were, however, other factors that had led to the Baptists' decline. Numbers attending worship had been reduced on account of deaths from smallpox, emigration to America and the 'exclusion' of 13 people – six for 'disorderly walking', one for 'considering the Pastor as a Priest of Baal' and another for 'holding Socinian opinions'. The holder of these opinions may have caught the infection from the General Baptists at Eastport Lane, whose theology was judged to be as reprehensible as Rome's. Middleton clearly

had Socinians in mind when, in his annual report to the Kent and Sussex
Association in May 1799, he wrote:

> We have observed that, instead of an ignorant and barbarous
> superstition that had enslaved mankind for more than a thousand
> years, a false philosophy is now endeavouring to take the lead,
> equally injurious to Christianity.

In the following year, however, the tone of his report was more
optimistic. The chapel was now full on Sundays and the members were
'agreed and comfortable' amongst themselves. They were apparently drawn
from a lower social stratum than the town's other Dissenters. Apart from
Thomas Dicker, a banker, and John Button, a school proprietor, the
congregation seems to have consisted almost entirely of artisans; but what
they lacked in material wealth they made up for in enthusiasm. By the end
of the century they were looking beyond themselves to the wider community
and had 'opened a house in a distant part of the town for preaching the
Gospel'. In fact all continued to go well until January 1805 when, 'by the
immediate hand of the Almighty', the church was 'suddenly deprived of
their affectionate pastor', who was seized with an apoplectic fit and died
soon afterwards. A great company of members and friends of the
congregation, 'solemnly impressed by this awful dispensation', attended
Middleton's funeral in All Saints' churchyard. It was an indication of his
abiding influence that ten years after his death the Foundry Lane meeting-
house was still known as 'Middleton's Chapel'.[5]

Meanwhile back at Cliffe Chapel many members of the congregation
had for some time been unhappy with the ministry of Jenkin Jenkins. In
1792 he had listened to William Huntington, the 'Redeemed Coalheaver',
preaching at Maresfield and had been deeply moved: he alone seemed to
offer the 'whole gospel' that sinners needed to hear. Thereafter Jenkins
became much more outspoken in his preaching, using language not often
heard in Lewes since the seventeenth century. His emphasis on the vileness
of human nature fitted ill with 'the polite and moderate Calvinism' of the
Countess of Huntingdon's Connexion and eventually the chapel trustees
terminated the minister's appointment. When he left many went with him,
regrouping in due course in Jireh Chapel, a fine timber-framed building
newly built with the assistance of Huntington and his London congregation.
The Coalheaver himself preached at the opening services on 7 July 1805,
saying in the course of his second sermon: 'If you will hear me attentively
I will tell you in so many particulars wherein you may know whether or not
you have a pure heart.'

Such spiritual precision was music to the ears of those in doubt or
despair. William Huntington, SS ('Sinner Saved') and Jenkin Jenkins, WA
('Welsh Ambassador') offered something that the DDs and MAs of the
established Church could not provide – absolute assurance of personal

salvation. With Huntington's help Jenkins soon succeeded in building up a flourishing congregation. At his death (aged 59) in 1810 it was reported that he was 'greatly respected by his numerous followers, by whom his chapel was so liberally endowed as to enable him to keep his chariot and pair and live in affluence'. Huntington himself died three years later and, at his express wish, his body was buried in a vault at the back of Jireh Chapel alongside that of Jenkins. His tomb still bears the proud epitaph that he had composed for himself:

HERE LIES THE COALHEAVER,
BELOVED OF HIS GOD BUT ABHORRED OF MEN.
THE OMNISCIENT JUDGE AT THE GRAND ASSIZE
SHALL RATIFY AND CONFIRM THIS TO THE CONFUSION
OF MANY THOUSANDS;
FOR ENGLAND AND ITS METROPOLIS SHALL KNOW
THAT THERE HATH BEEN A PROPHET AMONG THEM

In view of the mile-long procession of mourners that followed his hearse from Tunbridge Wells to Lewes on 8 July 1813, was it really true to say that Huntington was 'abhorred of men'?[6]

One of those who was for some years a regular hearer of Jenkins at Jireh was a Lewes shoemaker named John Gibbs. Born at Ditchling in 1769, he had {after a long and painful spiritual pilgrimage described in vivid detail in his autobiography) eventually found peace for his soul at Jireh. One day he had a vision of 'a glorious person' who came up to him and smiled at him, 'which smile I shall never forget, or the rapture of joy that it communicated'. But when told about the experience Jenkins, far from agreeing that this was a vision of Christ, dismissed it as the work of the Devil. To Gibbs the rebuke 'was like wrapping a cold wet cloth round a warm bosom' and he soon gave up going to Jireh. Instead he began preaching to a small gathering in his own house, but even then his difficulties were not over. Because he spoke with such passionate intensity some of his hearers became alarmed 'for fear that if I preached so close and so rousing a doctrine I should set the whole town on fire'. Others, however, heard him gladly and in 1811 he and a small band of followers leased premises in Lancaster Street which they named 'Bethesda' ('house of grace'). Their stay was short-lived, for Vigors McCulla, the Brighton preacher who had assumed a kind of archidiaconal authority over the local Calvinists, judged that Gibbs did not 'speak consistently with the Spirit's work' and barred him from the building. Eventually in 1815 Gibbs and his supporters acquired a disused schoolroom in St John Street, where they opened a new chapel: enlarged in 1824 and rebuilt three years later, in 1829 it was said to house a congregation of 250. Here, although plagued by ill-health, Gibbs continued to preach until his death in 1838.[7]

The conflicts among the Calvinists that had produced four separate congregations by 1811 continued to be a dominant feature of the religious life of Lewes. In 1816 Cliffe Chapel, which seems to have made a good recovery following the exodus of the Huntingtonians, experienced yet another secession. A substantial body of members withdrew to a handsome new building close to Lewes bridge which, after Whitefield's famous chapel in Moorfields, they called the Tabernacle. What prompted this third major exodus from Cliffe Chapel is not at all clear, but the disagreements may have been political rather than doctrinal. While the minister Joseph Kerby and his leading supporters were Tories, most of the principal seceders were Whigs, eager to work with the town's traditional Dissenters for constitutional reform. Social considerations may also have been significant, for the founders of the Tabernacle included some of the most prosperous tradesmen in Lewes: the coal-merchant Nehemiah Wimble, the timber-merchants George and Charles Wille, and the wine-merchant John Harvey. It is likely that such men would have been attracted by the idea of moving to a more prestigious building in a more central location. But whatever the political and social considerations the seceders doubtless believed that in setting up their Tabernacle they, like the Israelites of old, were guided by the hand of God. The same belief was held by another group of Independents, this time secessionists from Jireh, who in 1827 received a licence to worship in the Lancaster Street building that had housed the original Bethesda Chapel and was now, appropriately enough, to be re-named 'Providence'.[8]

Belief in Providence was strong among the Calvinists and it affected every department of their lives, as is seen in the case of Ebenezer Morris, a prosperous ironfounder and Jireh Chapel member. In November 1837, while awaiting a consignment of 60 tons of pig iron being shipped along the coast from the west, he was awoken in the night by a high wind. He said that 'in his alarmed imagination' he saw the ship, with its precious cargo, 'tossing and rolling on the boisterous main' and in danger of sinking. But although, having 'committed the matter to the care and disposal of the eternal and Almighty God', he experienced some calmness of mind, the failure of the shipment to arrive at the expected time gave him great anxiety. Aware of his plight, a group of friends assembled at his house to pray about the matter, whereupon Morris 'felt great enlargement before the Lord'. Everyone present was convinced that God would honour the trust that the ironfounder had shown 'in committing the cargo to His care and not falling down to worship the God of carnal contrivance, the Golden Calf of an insurance office'. There was much relief among those in the Morris counting-house when eventually the pig-iron arrived safely at Newhaven, ready to be brought by barge up river to Lewes.[9]

Competing Schemes of Salvation

Cliffe Chapel and the four congregations that had sprung from it represented an expansion of Dissent without parallel in Sussex at the time. In a period of rapid population growth and adverse economic conditions the evangelical Dissenters had responded energetically to the challenges that faced them, offering the poor both comfort in this life and the hope of better things hereafter. When it came to evangelical enthusiasm, however, the Calvinistic congregations did not have a monopoly. 1816, the year that saw prominent Lewes tradesmen setting up the Tabernacle, also witnessed the sudden conversion of Thomas Read Kemp, a young Cambridge theology graduate who had been the town's Whig MP since 1812. The experience led him to resign his seat and abandon politics in favour of preaching, his first sermon being delivered in the Foundry Lane chapel, 'every part of which was crowded to an excess at an early hour'. On 15 July the *Lewes Journal* reported that 'Mr Kemp's discourse was persuasive and argumentative, his language was mild but energetic, and his manner easy and unassuming'. His sermon, it was said, 'riveted the attention of all his hearers', including one man, 'not of the most sanctified exterior', who was moved to proclaim: 'Beyond anything I ever heard, it did my very heart and soul good.' Encouraged by this initial success Kemp obtained the use of a former fire-engine house close by the castle and turned it into a chapel, which was opened in December 1816. In reporting how crowded it had been for the opening service the local paper exclaimed: 'Would it were so at our established churches!' But the experiment was short-lived. Kemp's evangelical enthusiasm waned and by 1823 his congregation had disintegrated amid 'awful extremes of error'. The evangelist returned to the Church of England and to the House of Commons and is now best remembered neither for his politics nor for his preaching but as a property dealer on a grand scale and the founder of Kemp Town, Brighton.[10]

It seems that Kemp, although permitted to preach his first sermon in a Particular Baptist chapel, was not a Calvinist; theologically he was probably closer to the Wesleyan or 'Arminian' Methodists who had been preaching the gospel of universal salvation in Lewes since 1807. In April of that year the *Lewes Journal* gave the alarming news that 'a sect of Dissenters denominated ARMENIANS' had opened a 'commodious chapel' in St Mary's Lane in a former 'warehouse for wool and other purposes of trade'. Few of these Methodists were local people: there were no born-and-bred Lewesians among the chapel's trustees and much of the initial support came from immigrant paper-mill workers. The leading spirit among them was a former shepherd from Rottingdean, John Dudeney, about whose beliefs and actions much can be gleaned from a diary that he kept from June 1821 to March 1822. On Sundays he sometimes preached three times, either in

Lewes or further afield, and on some afternoons there were Love Feasts. On weekdays he attended house meetings at which prayers were said, hymns sung and anguished souls 'set at liberty'. Once there was a big missionary meeting at the Lewes chapel, attended by the eminent divines Jabez Bunting and Richard Watson. Sometimes the Wesleyans' activities aroused 'much talk' in the town and 'many false things' were said about them, almost certainly by militant Calvinists at the bottom of the town. Dudeney duly prayed for their forgiveness and derived much comfort from reading 'Mr Wesley's sermon on Bigotry'. With Dudeney's help the Lewes Wesleyan circuit prospered and in 1829 it was reported that there were 300 hearers at St Mary's Lane.[11]

By this time there were also 50 members of a break-away Arminian Methodist sect known as Bible Christians worshipping in the Eastport Lane meeting-house lately vacated by the General Baptists. Unlike the main body of Wesleyans the Bible Christians (later to become part of the United Methodist Church) admitted women to the ranks of their local preachers – something that caused astonishment when they first came to Lewes. In May 1824, when these 'Ranters' (as the *Lewes Journal* insisted on calling them) first arrived in the town, a young woman preached for nearly an hour and a half at an open-air service attended by between 500 and 600 people. The paper pointed out rather patronisingly that, although she spoke with 'a broad northern accent', her harangue was 'couched in good language and for the most part delivered with ease and grammatical accuracy'. But it was the sight rather than the sound of the preacher that most impressed the reporter, who commented on her 'interesting appearance' and 'fascinating features'. Knowing that, like the main-stream Wesleyans, these Methodists celebrated the *Agape* of the early church, he suggested that 'her attractions at their Love Feasts must be powerful'.[12]

Political and Theological Controversies

One effect of the proliferation of sects was to deprive Westgate Meeting of its historic role as the town's major bastion of Protestant Dissent. But even before the arrival of the Huntingdonians the cause had clearly been in decline. In a memorandum of 1773 Westgate's minister Ebenezer Johnston gave a gloomy report of the situation in Sussex:

> The Dissenting interest here is manifestly in a declining state. The congregations are generally small and it too often happens that when a minister dies or removes the people, either through want of ability or want of heart, suffer the interest to be lost among them.

Thanks largely to his continuing presence, Johnston's own congregation had not suffered extinction, but there is evidence that in the 1760s and 1770s new members were not coming forward in sufficient numbers to make up for those who had died, defected or left the neighbourhood. It is likely that some who were out of sympathy with Rational Dissent decided to leave and join the evangelicals. In 1775 William and John Ridge, who may all along have had reservations about Johnston's liberal theological stance, became trustees of the newly-built Calvinist chapel in Cliffe – while continuing to contribute, albeit at a lower level, to their brother-in-law's ministerial stipend. But one leading Westgate family did sever its connections completely.

After the death in 1792 of John Morris, the celebrated Lewes architect who had been appointed a trustee of the building three years earlier, there were no more Morrises at the meeting-house. Within weeks of his death John's nephew and heir, another John, whose first wife had belonged to the prominent Westgate family of Boys of Ashcombe House, married again – this time to the daughter of a Calvinistic Independent minister from Burwash. Since, as is usually the case, the religion of the mother determined that of the children, it was inevitable that the next generation should be brought up as evangelicals. The same thing evidently happened in the case of the younger John Morris's brother Joseph, a butcher by trade, who in 1782 had been the first member of his family to marry outside the old Dissenting establishment. Such switches of allegiance – from the Old Dissent to the New, from the ranks of the 'liberalising' to those to the 'energising' forces – were now becoming common. And the vigorous, combative Calvinism of men like Joseph Morris, one of the principal founders of Jireh Chapel, was to have a decisive influence upon the subsequent course of events in Lewes.[13]

To make up for those who departed the Westgate congregation seems to have attracted a few new supporters, the most celebrated of whom was Tom Paine. Paine, then an exciseman, moved to Lewes in 1768 and lodged with Samuel Ollive (son of the former Westgate minister) at Bull House, next door to the meeting-house. Baptised an Anglican, brought up a Quaker, he had for some years had close links with Rational Dissenters. It is therefore likely that, if he worshipped anywhere, it would have been at Westgate. When he married Ollive's daughter Elizabeth in 1771 the couple are said to have exchanged vows in the meeting-house, presumably in Johnston's presence, before going over the road for the legal ceremony in the parish church – a formality which, prior to 1837, was still binding on all Dissenters. But there is no evidence that Paine actually joined the Westgate congregation. The shilling a year that he paid to the meeting-house trustees was not a subscription but (to quote his own words) 'an acknowledgment of their suffering the droppings of rain' on to their courtyard from the eaves of the new extension he had made to Bull House. If he had attended services, would he have been comfortable with Johnston's preaching? Although much is known about his later position, it is not clear where Paine

Protestant Dissent in Lewes 1650-2000

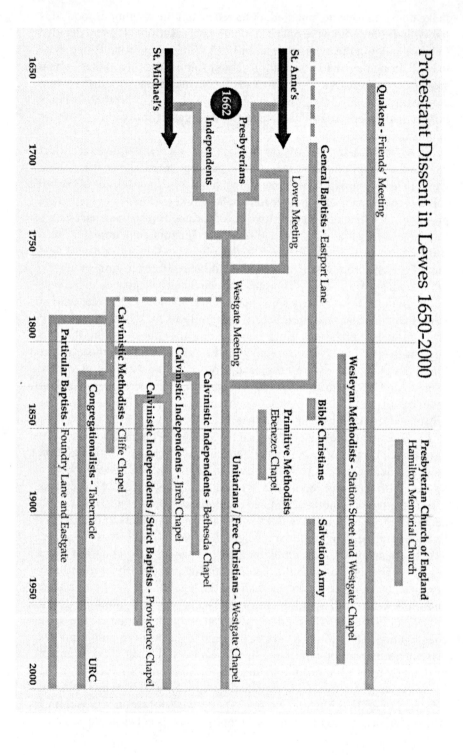

stood theologically at this time. As a militant anti-Calvinist, he would have
warmed to Johnston's Arminianism, but he would probably not have shared
his insistence upon the centrality of the Christian revelation: for all his
liberalism Johnston would have had no truck with the Deism for which
Paine was later to be famed. But the two would have been at one in
emphasising the goodness of God and the necessity for human beings, made
in his likeness, to imitate his benevolence. Had he lived long enough to be
able to read it, Johnston would certainly have approved of this passage
from *The Age of Reason*:

> The moral duty of man consists in imitating the moral goodness
> and beneficence of God manifested in the Creation towards all his
> creatures. Seeing, as we do daily, the goodness of God to all men,
> it is an example calling on all men to practise the same towards
> each other; and consequently everything of persecution and revenge
> between man and man, and everything of cruelty to animals is a
> violation of moral duty.

In including kindness to animals in his credo Paine was well 'ahead of his
time', but the rest of the passage might have been taken from one of
Johnston's sermons.[14]

After Johnston concluded his remarkable 40-year stint at Westgate in
1782 there was a succession of brief ministries, during which numbers
continued to decline. In fact by the end of the century the membership
seems to have been composed almost entirely of the Ridges and their
relations – Boyses, Johnstons, Snashalls and Wellers. However, things
looked up in 1803 with the appointment of Samuel Parker, a gifted scholar
and dedicated teacher. Some of his lectures, in which he defended revealed
religion against Deism, were published in 1805 under the title of *The Old
Testament Illustrated*, with the aid of numerous subscriptions from local
residents of varying religious persuasions. The subscribers included John
Button, Thomas Dicker, John Dudeney, John Wimble, John Godlee, four
Rickmans, 13 Ridges and the bookseller John Baxter, who put his name
down for 25 copies. Another of his books, *Primitive Christianity*, written
in Lewes and published soon after his departure in 1811, sought to recover
and proclaim the original New Testament message which, he believed, had
been overlaid by later accretions. Unlike Evangelical Dissenters, who
wished to change people's hearts, Parker and the Rational Dissenters were
mainly interested in enlightening their minds.[15]

If some people were put off by Westgate's rather arid intellectualism it
is possible that others, in this age of revolution, were frightened away by
its political radicalism. In 1785 a prominent Presbyterian, the surgeon
Joseph Ridge, had been instrumental in setting up the Lewes Library
Society, nearly half of whose original members worshipped at Westgate. It
bore a close resemblance to the Birmingham Library Society, which had

been established largely at the behest of members of the Presbyterian New Meeting in that town and which its new minister (Joseph Priestley) had just re-organised. Like the Birmingham Library the Lewes one was notable for the political and theological radicalism of the books that it purchased. After the outbreak of the French Revolution in 1789 the Society ordered, on Ridge's recommendation, Priestley's *Answer to Burke's Reflections* and a sermon by Richard Price that was also sympathetic to the Jacobin cause. But following the 1792 Reign of Terror these books, which had caused Priestley's New Meeting-house to be burned down by the Birmingham mob, could hardly be regarded as safe to read in Lewes. In fact by 1794 life had become so difficult for revolutionary thinkers that James Drowley, who was among the Library Society's most active recommenders of radical books, decided to follow Priestley into exile in America, where he and other Sussex emigrants established the 'English Jacobin colony' known as Sparta.[16]

Drowley, a draper by trade, was not a Westgate member but the lay pastor of the General Baptist congregation in Eastport Lane. By this date the congregation was abandoning the practice of baptising adults by total immersion and was ceasing to be Baptist in anything but name. In Lewes as elsewhere the General Baptists had for some years been drawing closer to the Presbyterians, with whom they now shared the appellation of Rational Dissenters. Those in Sussex, moreover, who had long been especially prone to Socinianism, were responding positively to the 'humanitarian' Unitarianism being propounded by Priestley. Like him they took the view that the doctrine of the Trinity had no biblical basis and that Jesus Christ was not God but rather the man whom God had sent to save the world. Under the terms of the 1698 Blasphemy Act the dissemination of such opinions was technically a criminal offence, but in reality the statute had become a dead letter long before its eventual repeal in 1813. Many people, however, still deemed the denial of the Trinity a most dangerous heresy and it was especially repugnant to the Particular Baptists in Foundry Lane, whose minister (as has already been noted) condemned Socinianism as a 'false philosophy'. Was it because Joseph Middleton, who at the time was the only Evangelical Dissenter in the Lewes Library Society, felt so uncomfortable in the company of a Socinian that in 1791 he resigned from the society shortly after Drowley had been admitted into membership? [17]

Although the Library Society, on the recommendation of its Presbyterian and General Baptist members, purchased many volumes of liberal theology, few of those attending Westgate Meeting at this time seem to have had much enthusiasm for Unitarianism. But the situation was to change after 1817 when a new minister, who had strong Priestleyan views, was appointed. Thomas Walker Horsfield, a 25 year-old Yorkshireman fresh from the heady atmosphere of the Unitarian Academy at Hackney, made it a condition of his coming that he should be permitted to introduce 'doctrinal and other subjects in preaching'. In spite of the reservations of some members his conditions were eventually agreed to and the young minister, taking advantage of 'the favourable opportunity that there appears to be in Lewes of extending widely the glad tidings of salvation', set about his task with great vigour. His heterodox doctrinal stance gave great offence to orthodox Dissenters such as John Hyatt, minister of Whitefield's Tabernacle who, in a sermon evidently preached in Lewes shortly after Horsfield's arrival, made a vigorous attack on Unitarianism. 'Those professing Christians who deny the Godhead of Jesus Christ', he said, were 'guilty of the grossest blasphemy' which, if persisted in, would bring them to the 'damnation of hell'. Undeterred by such opposition Horsfield persevered in his attempt to transform a motley collection of unsectarian Dissenters into a distinctively 'Unitarian' congregation. By 1825, when the General Baptists, always more sectarian in outlook than the Presbyterians, left Eastport Lane and moved up the hill to Westgate, he may have felt that his attempt had succeeded. In contrast to Chichester, where the Presbyterians and General Baptists remained separate throughout the nineteenth century, the merger of the two Rational Dissenting congregations in Lewes resulted in a significant strengthening of the Unitarian cause.[18]

Practical Christianity

Political and theological controversies, which occupied much of the energy of the Presbyterians and General Baptists, seem to have had little appeal for the only other long-established body of Dissenters in the town, the Quakers. In 1784, having sold their old meeting-house to the Particular Baptists, the Lewes Friends built themselves a new one in a more peaceful location adjoining All Saints' churchyard. Much of the cost of the new building was borne by members of the Rickman family, who at this time were prospering in business as brewers, millers and merchants in corn and coal. As the preponderance of their headstones in the Friends' burial-ground indicates, the Rickmans were as prominent among the Quakers as the Ridges were among the Presbyterians. At this time the numbers of Friends remained small because, unlike the newly-established sects, they did not actively seek converts. But newcomers were continually being attracted to their meetings, whose silence was in such sharp contrast to the noise and bustle of a busy commercial town.[19]

One such newcomer was the draper William Marten who, after sampling the services of the General Baptists in Eastport Lane (where his father was a member), the Calvinists at Cliffe Chapel and the Anglicans at All Saints' and St Thomas's, eventually found peace for his soul among the Friends. He particularly valued their totally silent meetings, when no one was moved to speak and he could feel that 'the great Master was near'. He also took pleasure in adopting the Quakers' distinctive life-style. In his journal he tells how in due course he 'became convinced of the propriety of wearing plain apparel, of using the singular pronoun in addressing one person, and of forbearing to take off my hat by way of compliment'. With some trepidation he joined with other Friends in bearing 'public testimony against stage entertainments', by distributing leaflets outside the local theatre. On another occasion he 'expostulated' with a young clergyman who had come to Lewes to attend a ball and did so with such persuasion that the cleric decided not to go dancing after all. But what most set the Friends apart from their neighbours was their refusal to place lights in their windows at times of national celebration: for failing to do so in March 1789, when the townspeople were dutifully celebrating George III's recovery from illness, Marten had three panes of glass broken. It took even more courage to make such a stand after war had broken out with France and patriotic feelings were running high, but Marten steadfastly maintained the Quaker peace witness. In November 1805, when 'the town was illuminated as a testimony of rejoicing' after the great naval victory at Trafalgar, he commented: 'Oh that men would learn the religion of Jesus Christ, the Prince of Peace; then would they cease to rejoice at the destruction of their fellow-creatures.' At a later date his humanitarian zeal led him to collect 693 signatures in Lewes to a petition calling for the abolition of the slave trade. Since the demise of the 'Association of Merchants trading from Lewes to Barbadoes' it is likely that no-one in the town was now benefiting directly from this cruel triangular trade, but it would still have taken courage to campaign openly against it. In Marten the light of the Spirit shone forth brightly like a good deed in a naughty world.[20]

Marten's missionary zeal was also demonstrated in his work on behalf of the Lewes Bible Association, which he helped to found in 1812. The main purpose of this body, which was supported by both Anglicans and Dissenters, was to sell the Scriptures cheaply to the local poor, and in the first four years of its existence it disposed of no fewer than 1,233 copies. In December 1816, at its fourth annual meeting, there was a lengthy discussion about the association's aims and objectives. One member said that it existed not only to 'promote individual happiness by the introduction of religious hopes and principles' to the poor but also to advance 'the peace and prosperity of society in general'. He went on to say that the importance of the second objective had been demonstrated in other towns that had Bible Associations and had, as a consequence, experienced 'a considerable improvement in the morals and general behaviour of the lower classes' and a marked reduction in the crime rate. At this time of severe social unrest many men of property in Lewes would probably have been gratified to think that their philanthropy was helping to keep the poor in their appointed place.

However, for Marten, with his compassionate concern for the well-being of the weak and downtrodden, the first objective was always more important than the second.[21]

The Bible Association enabled Marten to keep in touch with others who shared his evangelical enthusiasm. At a time when sectarian differences were causing serious conflict in Lewes he took a remarkably benign attitude towards those of a different religious persuasion. After entertaining a Methodist preacher and his wife to tea he confessed himself 'pleased with their company and religious conversation' and prayed that 'the Lord bless his labours in the ministry to the conversion of sinners'. On another occasion he was moved 'to go to a minister of the Church of England and advise him against being lifted up with having a large congregation, but to continue humble'; to his delight the clergyman 'received the message in love'. Some years later he recorded an evening stroll with another Anglican clergyman, with whom he had an 'edifying' conversation. 'I am persuaded', he wrote, 'that there are many in this establishment, both ministers and others, who are members of the church of Christ, to whom my soul must be expanded in charity.'[22]

Revival in the Church of England

The first clergyman, whom Marten warned against pride, may have been Richard Cecil, who had succeeded Lund as rector of All Saints' with St Thomas's in 1777. The wealthy son of an Anglican father and a pious Dissenting mother, Cecil had embraced evangelical Christianity after an ill-spent youth and he possessed all the fervour of the 'twice-born'; but his reforming zeal was evidently not at first appreciated by some of his parishioners. At a Sunday evening service at St Thomas's soon after his arrival he 'openly accused the clerk of being drunk and unable to perform his duty' and ordered him to resign his desk. The rector's action, it was said, 'threw the whole congregation into uproar and confusion' so that 'the house of God became a house of bickering'. So incensed were some of the parishioners that it was Cecil, not the clerk, who had to vacate his place. In the end, states the *Lewes Journal*, 'they beheld a *holy* minister of the gospel retiring from his duty and the church amidst the hissings of a crowded congregation' – whereupon another, more acceptable, clergyman had to be called in to take over. Meanwhile the clerk who, according to one witness, was 'neither intoxicated with liquor nor besotted with enthusiasm', was able to continue with the service.

The editor of the *Journal* seems to have carried on something of a vendetta against Cecil, whose 'enthusiasm' he evidently found distasteful. Some months later, in June 1778, he went out of his way to report a 'most excellent sermon' by a visiting clergyman at Cliffe, who had taken as his text I Timothy, 4. 16: 'Take heed unto thyself and unto thy doctrine; continue in them: for in doing this thou shalt both save thyself and them that hear thee.' The report was followed by an editorial comment that was clearly directed at Cecil: 'It is much to be wished that the doctrine then enjoined may in future be adopted by a certain pastor, which will neither bewilder the imagination nor lead the unthinking vulgar into a state of despondency.'[23]

In due course, however, Cecil triumphed over his adversaries. Far from causing bewilderment or despondency his preaching had a strong appeal to his audience, as a contemporary account makes plain:

> He was capable of riveting the attention of a congregation by the originality of his conceptions, the plain straightforward force of his language, the firm grasp of his subject, and by the happy power of illustration which gave freshness and novelty to the most familiar subjects.

By 1780 Cecil had attracted hearers from other congregations in the town including that of Cliffe Chapel, one of whom was the future Quaker William Marten. 'Under his ministry', Marten recorded in his journal, 'I was made sensible of my sinful nature and undone state, and that without a Saviour I must perish for ever.' Although he retained his two Lewes livings for 20 years Cecil seems to have left the town in about 1787, when he was appointed evening lecturer at Christ Church, Spitalfields. The dampness of his Lewes rectory had apparently produced a 'severe rheumatic affection in his head' and he was evidently relieved to return to London.[24]

Cecil was succeeded as rector of St Thomas's in 1797 and of All Saints' in 1798 by Thomas Aquila Dale. He too was to become famed for his sermons. John Dudeney, before he became a Methodist, heard them gladly. And many years after his death Gideon Mantell, the distinguished Lewes geologist, wrote that Dale's 'earnest and impressive style of preaching and the eloquent and fervent piety which characterised his discourses are still vividly present in my mind'. When he died prematurely after a short illness in 1807 a correspondent in the *Lewes Journal* described him as 'a truly pious man, an evangelical minister, a kind husband, a tender parent and a man who laboured much to do good'. He was widely respected in the town. Among the most generous contributors to the fund raised to support his widow and nine children were several leading Dissenters: John Boys of Westgate, George Wille of Cliffe Chapel and the Quaker John Rickman. Ten weeks after Dale's death All Saints' church, which had been rebuilt on a grand scale to accommodate its growing congregation, was formally consecrated. At the service John Buckner, bishop of Chichester, presided and the preacher was Edwin Merriman, Dale's successor at All Saints', who likened the new building to 'the magnificent temple at Jerusalem which the Great Jehovah filled with his glory at its consecration'. It was in fact a 'galleried preaching box' which, but for the retention of its medieval bell-tower, might have been mistaken for a Dissenting meeting-house. With seats for 800 people its congregation could now take pride in possessing a church more than twice as capacious as the former warehouse in their parish that had recently been converted into a place of worship for Wesleyans. But, according to the newspaper report of the consecration, there was disappointment that the occasion had not attracted 'so large an attendance as was expected'.[25]

There is a possible explanation for the low turnout: the rebuilding of All Saints' had caused conflict in the parish. The whole operation was strongly opposed by many influential parishioners, including the two churchwardens, Sir Henry Blackman and Captain William Hick, and the astute ecclesiastical lawyer John Hoper. When, at the behest of the bishop, a Bill for the rebuilding was introduced into the House of Commons in the summer of 1805, these parishioners petitioned against it, urging instead that the existing church should be repaired and extended. Their action drew an angry response from Buckner, who suggested that the main opposition came from 'Dissenters and Methodists' who were bound to object to having to pay for 'the improvement of a place of divine worship in which their difference of opinion forbids them to assemble'. Loyal Anglican parishioners, on the other hand, ought to know better than to oppose the scheme, and in his letter to Hoper he underlined the word 'know':

> You *know* the ruinous state of the church in question and that divine service has been intermitted there for at least four years, in consequence of the supposed danger of assembling therein. . . . You *know* that the population of the parish is greatly of late increased [so] that, if a church were re-erected on its present site it would not contain one third of the inhabitants.

Hoper immediately wrote back to say that opposition to the rebuilding came primarily from parishioners who were 'firmly attached to the established church'. Those most in favour of it, on the other hand, were 'some individuals who possess new built houses' who were hoping to obtain the 'beneficial appropriation to their houses of pews in a new church without paying for them'. Nevertheless in due course the Bill was passed. The bishop had won, but it turned out to be a Pyrrhic victory; to the gratification of Hoper and his friends the Act contained an additional clause to which Buckner had objected strongly. This stated that, after pews in the new church had been allotted to those who had had them in the old one and ample space had been set aside for the poor, the rest of the pews should be let or sold by auction to other parishioners – and the proceeds used to pay for the rebuilding of the church.[26]

In some respects the new red-brick church turned out to be something of a white elephant. After Dale's death there was never again to be an

Anglican incumbent, either at All Saints' or anywhere else in Lewes, capable of attracting great crowds. At this time good preachers, like dedicated pastors, appear to have been something of a rarity in the Church of England. Writing about Lewes as he remembered it in his boyhood in the 1820s Edward Boys Ellman, who himself was to become a parson, described it as 'a time of dreadful deadness among the clergy'. Many of them, he suggested, had been neglectful of their duties:

> No parish even in Lewes had more than one service on a Sunday,
> and the time of those services was frequently changed without
> notice, the ringing of the church bell summoning the people when
> a clergyman came in sight.

He recalled that there were so many non-resident clergy then living in Lewes that the town was known as 'The Rookery', from 'the number that rode out of Lewes in black coats to their various duties each Sunday'. The absentee clerics included Charles Harrison, vicar of South Malling and Alfriston, Harry West, incumbent of Berwick and Laughton, and Edward Raynes, archdeacon of Lewes and rector of Beddingham, Firle and Ripe, who lived in grand style at Antioch House, Lewes and was best remembered as the 'head of a whist club' in the town.[27]

Ellman in fact had few good words to say about any of the Lewes incumbents. He remembered George Proctor, the headmaster of the grammar school (1821-29) and rector of St Michael's (1826-41), chiefly for his fondness for the cane, which used to be 'in constant use'. Another clergyman for whom he had little respect was Peter Guerin Crofts, rector of St John sub Castro (1799-1847), who shared Harrison's passion for fox-hunting. Like George Shiffner, rector of St Anne's and Hamsey (1818-48), Crofts had been in post since his ordination and owed his premature preferment primarily to family patronage. The presence of such men was a sign that the 'gentrification of the clergy', that familiar phenomenon of Jane Austen's England, was now a feature of the Lewes scene. Crofts did not live in his parish but at Malling House, a fine Queen Anne mansion (with nine bays and two storeys) situated in spacious grounds on the other side of the Ouse. According to one (admittedly not unbiassed) witness he was about as far removed as anyone could be from Chaucer's ideal 'poor parson of a town'. Gideon Mantell, who fell out with him in 1829 over a tree he had planted in St John's churchyard without his permission, called him a 'proud priest', displaying 'arrogance and utter want of taste and every finer feeling'. 'Talk of *catholic* intolerance!', he exclaimed, 'What can exceed this protestant overbearing spirit – and in *1829* too!' Two years later the rector's name crops up again in Mantell's journal when, having attended the funeral of an old friend at St John's, he referred contemptuously to 'that pompous priest, the Rev. P. Crofts', who had officiated at the service.[28]

Anglicans and Dissenters at odds

In other towns the presence of rich and powerful parsons like Crofts might have meant that the social and cultural life of the place was firmly under Anglican control, but this was not so in a hotbed of Dissent like Lewes. Although it controlled the grammar school, where the headmaster was always in holy orders, the established church had no monopoly of education. In addition to the 'subscription school' opened in 1809, with about 200 boys and girls on the roll, under the auspices of the inter-denominational Lancasterian Society (with premises in what was subsequently called Lancaster Street) there were several flourishing private schools owned and managed by Dissenters. In 1791 the Particular Baptist John Button opened an English Grammar School which a knowledgeable contemporary described as among 'the best infant seminaries in Great Britain': it offered instruction in English, Arithmetic, Geography, History and Elocution to the sons of local tradesmen. An even broader education, including foreign languages, was provided by Victor Amadeus Raymond, a Swiss Protestant attender at Westgate Meeting, who ran a boys' school on School Hill from 1789 to 1820. Other less ambitious establishments included the commercial school founded in 1804 by the Methodist John Dudeney and the miniature Dissenting academy on St Anne's Hill over which Horsfield presided during his ministry at Westgate. Horsfield, moreover, was a principal founder of the Lewes Mechanics' Institution, established in 1825 to disseminate 'Useful Knowledge' to young men of slender means. He himself lectured on Pneumatics, while Dudeney taught Astronomy and Burwood Godlee, the Quaker coal merchant who ran the local gasworks, gave talks on Electricity and Steam Power.[29]

The Anglican-Dissenting divide, apparent in the sphere of education, was a much more serious matter when it came to party politics. In Lewes, as elsewhere in England at this time, the Church of England could properly be described as 'the Tory party at prayer'. This was evident in the parliamentary by-election of 1816, caused by the sudden conversion of Thomas Read Kemp. On this occasion, as on others, the Lewes electorate was divided more or less on confessional lines. The successful Tory candidate, Sir John Shelley, was nominated by Archdeacon Raynes and supported by Crofts, Merriman and William Gwynne, rector of St Michael's. The narrowly defeated Whig candidate, James Scarlett, a favourer of reform in Church and State, was supported by the great majority of the town's Dissenters, with only the minister of Cliffe Chapel providing any significant backing for the Tories. Religious affiliations appear to have been particularly important in this election, in which the repeal of the Test and Corporation Acts, debarring Dissenters from civic office and degrees at English universities, was a major issue.[30]

Ten years later, in the general election of 1826, Church control of education became a major issue when George Shiffner of St Anne's (whose father was the outgoing Tory MP) and John Scobell (who had been recently installed as rector of All Saints' and Southover) tried to strangle the infant school in Lewes run by the non-Anglican British and Foreign Schools Society. This time, however, the politico-religious situation was complicated because, in addition to the Tory Shelley and the Whig Kemp, there was an outside candidate, a radical Whig of Irish descent named Alexander Donovan, who had been proposed by Benjamin Ridge, a leading Westgate member, and seconded by Horsfield. In the event Donovan failed to get elected, partly perhaps on account of his advocacy of Catholic Emancipation, a cause close to Horsfield's heart but not one to win the support of many people in Lewes. Horsfield's political activities, in fact, were making him very unpopular in some quarters. According to Henry Acton (the former Eastport Lane pastor who wrote his obituary in 1837) his school was 'much injured through the influence of political enmity on account of the active part he had taken on the liberal side in public affairs'. By causing pupils to be withdrawn from his school Horsfield's opponents deprived him of a large part of his livelihood and forced him to leave Lewes in 1827 and move to distant Somerset with his monumental *History of Sussex* uncompleted.[31]

It is important, however, not to exaggerate the seriousness of the Anglican-Dissenting divide. Most of the time churchgoers and chapelgoers worked together quite harmoniously for the well-being of the community. Their unity was publicly demonstrated in 1830 when, to the delight of the townsmen, the newly enthroned William IV agreed to visit Lewes – reportedly the first monarch to do so since Henry III in 1264. Appropriately it was a prominent Dissenter George Adams, currently serving as senior constable, who formally welcomed the royal visitor to a town whose inhabitants were (as he put it in his speech) 'for the greater part a plain trading people'. In response the king praised the 'plainness of manners and industrious habits' of such people, who 'render this nation supreme to any other'. But did he know that so many in this highly commendable category, in Lewes as elsewhere, refused on principle to acknowledge his supremacy in matters ecclesiastical? Was he aware that not only Adams but also Nehemiah Wimble, who later entertained him and the queen at his fine house called The Friars, worshipped regularly at the Tabernacle next door? If previously not aware of the strength of Dissent in his kingdom he probably was so after his visit to Lewes, where among those formally presented to him along with the Anglican clergy were those officially designated 'the Dissenting ministers of the different parishes and congregations' in the town.[32]

By 1830 the population of Lewes, which in 1760 had stood at some 2,500, had risen to about 8,500. Some of this expansion had taken place in All Saints' parish, where the doubling of the number of houses in the previous 30 years had been put forward in 1805 as a reason for enlarging the church. The greatest growth, however, had occurred in the parish of St John sub Castro, where the early years of the nineteenth century saw the building of the 'New Town'. The consequence was that by 1830 over 2,500 people were living in a parish whose church had a mere 270 sittings, of which only 56 were described as 'free and unappropriated'. Accordingly in 1839, in order 'to remedy so great a want of church accommodation', Crofts (who was patron as well as rector of the parish) obtained permission to pull down the old church and build a much bigger one on the same site. Money was quickly raised and on 3 June 1840 Bishop Otter came to Lewes to consecrate the 1000-seater church. The new building represented a departure from tradition in that its axis was north-south instead of east-west, but in another respect it represented a return to a remoter past. Unlike All Saints', with its plain 'meeting-house' windows, St John's was solidly gothic. Here was a sign that the Georgian era, inspired by the 'enlightenment' associated with classical antiquity, had ended and that the Victorian, seeking inspiration in the Middle Ages, had begun.[33]

The Religious Census of 1851

Church/Chapel	Seats		Adults	Children
Anglican				
All Saints'	783	*(160)*	365	107
St Anne's	444	*(164)*	242	67
St John sub Castro	[850]	800	-	
St Michael's	[500]	50	-	
St Thomas's	500	*(40)*	297	99
Southover	423	*(167)*	302	-
Sub-total	3500	*(531)*	2056	273
Nonconformist				
Bethesda	300	*(300)*	95	-
Bridge	180	*(180)*	180	-
Cliffe	450	*(145)*	388	150
Eastgate	400	*(150)*	231	99
Ebenezer	150	*(50)*	230	50
Friends	105	-	82	-
Jireh	950	*(450)*	775	-
Licensed Room	20	*(20)*	66 [sic]	-
Providence	280	*(190)*	370	-
Tabernacle	1031	*(517)*	800	225
Wesleyan	315	*(125)*	261	89
Westgate	400	*(50)*	126	63
Sub-total	4581	*(2282)*	3604	676
TOTAL	8081	*(2813)*	5660	949

Notes

1. Seating. Where the actual number of seats is unknown the estimated number has been placed in square brackets. Numbers of free seats have been set in *italic* and placed in round brackets.
2. Attendance. The numbers given are of those reported to have attended service on Census Sunday, 30 March 1851. Where there were two services half the smaller attendance figure has been added to the larger one; where there were three, one third of the smallest figure has also been added. *Average* attendance figures, provided by some churches and chapels, have not been included in the table.

VII. Protestants, Papists and Puseyites

In Queen Victoria's day everyone went to church – or so it is sometimes said. But the returns of the religious census of 1851 clearly show that, if they had all wanted to do so, there would not have been room for them. When all the available seating in all the churches and chapels in England and Wales is totalled up it transpires that only 57% of the population could have been accommodated. Sussex, where there were enough seats for 56.5% of the people, conformed to the national average. In the larger towns, however, the percentages were always lower: for Hastings it was 43.3% and for Brighton only 38.9%. But in Lewes, it may come as no surprise to discover, the situation was very different: nearly 90% of its inhabitants could have been seated. For a population of just over 9000, it had a total of just over 8000 seats; and since the 9000 included babes in arms, it is possible that on Census Sunday, 30 March 1851, all the inhabitants of the town could have been squeezed in somehow, provided only they were not too particular about where they went to worship.[1]

It is certain, however, that worshippers would not normally have been allowed to sit where they liked; as was customary in England at the time, most places of worship in Lewes imposed restrictions on their seating and often charged 'pew rents'. Only at Bethesda and at two 'licensed rooms' in Cliffe were all seats recorded as being 'free' and, among those imposing restrictions, only at Providence did the free seats outnumber the rest. At the Tabernacle half the seats were free, but they included 324 in the children's gallery and '27 sittings under and about the pulpit which are seldom occupied'. Elsewhere the free seats were very much in the minority. In St Thomas's there were only 40 free sittings 'on benches attached to the walls and pews'. Of the 160 unallocated seats at All Saints' 100 were reserved for 'charity children'. At Cliffe chapel, where two-thirds of the pews were reserved, latecomers unable to find a seat had the consolation of knowing that there was standing room for 100. Even the Primitive Methodists at Ebenezer, who might have been expected (in line with the practice of the primitive church) to have a more open policy with regard to seating, only kept a third of their seats free. While pew rents remained and the better-off continued to occupy the better seats, institutional Christianity would continue to make a mockery of the egalitarian teachings of its founder.

The main purpose of the census, of course, was not to count the seats but the people who sat on them. In some instances, as at St John sub Castro, where the figures recorded are suspiciously round, it looks as if the counting was not done very carefully. The returns give the numbers present at each service: at most places there were two services, with the Anglicans normally holding a second one in the afternoon and the Nonconformists holding theirs in the evening. It is, however, not easy to count the actual number of worshippers, for no-one knows how many attended more than once. Only for St Michael's and one of the licensed rooms in Cliffe (otherwise known as the Bridge Room or Chapel), where there was only a morning service, and for St John sub Castro, where there was only an evening one, is it possible to discover how many individuals were present. But by using a formula adopted by many demographers it can be estimated that for the Anglicans the total number of worshippers was 2340 and for the Nonconformists 4280. The Nonconformists thus outnumbered the Anglicans by 65:35 – a preponderance without parallel in Sussex, and perhaps anywhere in south-eastern England. Given that only 18.62% of the total population of England and Wales are estimated to have attended a Nonconformist place of worship on Census Sunday, the report that nearly half the inhabitants of Lewes did so is remarkable.[2]

The total number estimated to have attended worship in Lewes includes Sunday school children, who are found in nine out of the 18 congregations. There were none at St Michael's, St John sub Castro or Southover, but the three other parish churches had children attending both morning and afternoon. Using the formula adopted for adult attendances it is estimated that the total number of children present at Anglican services was 273, compared with 676 at the Nonconformist ones. The biggest attendances were at the Tabernacle and Cliffe Chapel, where the children present were said to number 225 and 150 respectively. Cliffe Chapel had the oldest Sunday school in Lewes. Horsfield, in his *History of Lewes* (1824) says that it had been established 16 years previously and that 'upwards of two hundred children at a time enjoy the advantage of instruction'. He also mentioned the Wesleyan Sunday school, where there were 140 children, and the one at the Tabernacle, where 250 children were taught by 'about forty of the most respectable young persons belonging to that congregation'. At Eastgate the first mention of a Sunday school occurs in 1830, but there may have been one earlier: by 1836 there were 140 children on the roll and 24 teachers. Rather surprisingly Jireh had no school until

1858 but, once established, it grew very quickly and by 1877 there was an
average afternoon attendance of 278. The expansion led Isaac Vinall, the son
of a former minister at the chapel and a leading local solicitor, to establish a
separate evening 'Ragged School' in St John Street, which by 1884 had 250
children on its roll.[3]

If the figures given in the census are accurate it seems that in 1851
about 72% of the population of Lewes attended public worship on a Sunday
– which compared very favourably with a county average of 56.5% and a
national one of 58.1%. The other interesting statistic that emerges is that,
with a total seating capacity of about 8000 and a total attendance (including
children) of over 6500, the town's churches and chapels were, on average,
more than three-quarters full. It is a pity, however, that no such statistics
are available for any year after 1851. Only by a laborious process of piecing
together the membership and attendance figures of individual congregations
(where such evidence survives) would it be possible to plot the peaks and
troughs of public religious observance in Lewes throughout the Victorian
period.[4]

The Ups and Downs of Nonconformity

It is clear from the limited range of surviving records that the fortunes of
the various congregations, and especially the Nonconformist ones, were
affected to a very high degree by the performance of their ministers. The
history of the Particular Baptists, who in 1819 had moved from Foundry
Lane to a new meeting-house in Eastgate Street, illustrates this well. When
Ebenezer Davis, a dynamic and dedicated Welshman, became minister in
1840 the people prayed that 'a new era might be opened in the history of
the cause, which had long been in a languid and declining state'. The prayer,
it seems, was soon answered; within a year the congregation had become
so much stronger that they were planning a bigger chapel, which was duly
opened in October 1843. By 1845 its membership had, probably for the
first time in its history, topped the 200 mark and the future looked brighter
than it had ever done. But the gifted Welshman was succeeded by a less
charismatic Englishman and by 1853 the membership had fallen to below
100. 'Compared with what we wish to see', ran a congregational report that
year, 'there is little spiritual life and vigour amongst us, and the word of
truth seems to have small effect in awakening sinners.' But in 1854 another
minister came: soon things began to look up and by 1860 numbers were up
to 145. Thereafter the church's fortunes waxed and waned, as ministers
rapidly came and went. The last of the short-stay pastors was William Scott,
a spirited young man who did much for the youth of the town and helped to
found the local YMCA. He came in 1874 but left in 1878, announcing that
he now believed the 'one-man ministry' to be unscriptural, unnecessary

and even positively harmful to the church. After such an unsettling experience it is not surprising that the congregation decided to look for a minister of more advanced years and less radical opinions. In 1879 they called William Kingo Armstrong, a former Scottish Presbyterian who had become a Baptist by conviction. Here at last was a safe pair of hands and in due course the congregation once again began to grow: in 1893 it was stated that 'the cause had gone through many vicissitudes but has never been in a more flourishing condition than at the present time'. Armstrong was a great admirer of Charles Haddon Spurgeon, supporting him in his endeavours to uphold Calvinist orthodoxy within the Baptist denomination. After his death in France in 1892 the great preacher's coffin (straight off the boat from Newhaven and awaiting the next train to London) rested for a while at Lewes station, where Armstrong and some of his friends sang 'For ever with the Lord' on the platform. They may have sensed that this death marked the end of an era; 'No Calvinist after Spurgeon', writes Owen Chadwick, 'became a leader of English religion.' Armstrong himself died four years later at 74, deeply mourned by his people, and was succeeded by John Penfold Morris, who was to minister to the congregation with conspicuous success for 25 years.[5]

At Jireh Chapel the people enjoyed greater continuity of leadership than their fellow-Calvinists at Eastgate. The celebrated John Vinall, who had come to Lewes from Henfield as a young man in 1802 and had first preached at Jireh in 1810, was appointed minister in 1822 and continued to have oversight of the congregation (and that of Providence chapel, Brighton) until 1856. Although constantly afflicted with illness, which he saw as a sign of the chastening hand of God, this 'poor trembling faint-hearted sinner', as he described himself, exercised a highly successful ministry. His main difficulties seem to have stemmed from a bitter and prolonged conflict between his two sons. When he retired in 1856 he hoped to be succeeded by his favourite younger son Ebenezer, then ministering at Providence Chapel in Lancaster Street. But the Jireh trustees, who had the power of appointment, decided instead to choose the elder son John, then in charge of the congregation meeting in the 'licensed room' by Lewes Bridge. This greatly displeased a section of the Jireh people, who sent a strongly worded protest to the trustees. 'Believing the dear Lord . . . has been pleased to anoint our brother in the faith Ebenezer Vinall for the work of the ministry', they implored them not to 'hinder the work and grieve the Holy Spirit' by refusing to accept him. However, the trustees stood by their decision and John II, whom Ebenezer likened to the jealous elder brother in the parable of the Prodigal Son, moved into Jireh, taking the Bridge folk with him. Thereupon the malcontents withdrew to Providence Chapel (soon to be rebuilt), where Ebenezer continued to minister until his removal to London in 1865, and where John I, who had left Jireh with the secessionists, worshipped until his death in 1860. But John II did not long enjoy his elevation, for in 1859 he died suddenly and was succeeded by Matthew Welland, who was to remain as minister for over 40 years.[6]

There was a similar continuity of ministerial leadership at the Tabernacle. After thirteen years without a settled minister Evan Jones, a Welsh farmer's son, was appointed to the pastorate in November 1829. After three years numbers attending had increased so greatly that the building had to be enlarged, but in 1839 progress was temporarily halted by a serious conflict in the congregation. A group of members, reportedly appalled by the 'irregularities' of the minister's children, resigned and migrated to Cliffe chapel. But misfortune swiftly befell the seceders: many lost children by death; Nehemiah Wimble, formerly a very rich man, died insolvent in 1843; and in the same year John Adams 'bled to death from his mouth' in London. After the last event, so it was reported, 'the people of Lewes were ready to think, and some said, "The judgment of God is upon this family".' After 1839 there were no more secessions, and Jones continued to minister with great acceptance until his retirement, shortly before his 72nd birthday, in 1862. It was recorded that during his time there he had received into the congregation about 500 people, 'most of whom were converted under his ministry'. Thereafter there was a succession of fairly brief pastorates until 1887, when the congregation called Burgess Wilkinson, whose 23 year ministry was to prove to be the most distinguished in the history of the Tabernacle.[7]

Much of the information about events at the Tabernacle in the middle years of the nineteenth century comes from the diary of Charles Wille, a wealthy timber merchant who was a trustee of the building from 1829 until his death in 1878. A close friend of Evan Jones, he stood by him loyally during the 1839 crisis and had some harsh words to say about his critics. At this time, however, he was even more angered by the 'awful and wicked' behaviour of a group of men who met regularly at a tavern close by the Tabernacle. Here they amused themselves by 'ridiculing the preaching of the gospel (imitating the minister, 'tis said) and also mocking the prayer and singing'. In 1840, when one of the miscreants drowned himself, he saw it as a clear sign of divine displeasure. A man of singular piety, Wille was a regular attender at the Tabernacle's Sunday services and weekday evening prayer meetings. Early in January 1860 he took a prominent part in a series of five 'special meetings for prayer for the outpouring of the Spirit', in the course of which there was 'much feeling manifested and some evidence of good'. He was actively involved in the affairs of the Sussex Congregational Union, over whose meetings he sometimes presided, but he was no narrow denominationalist. Although he never apparently went to Jireh or Westgate he was happy to attend the services, lectures or missionary meetings hosted by the mainstream Nonconformists – Baptists, Wesleyans and Presbyterians. Sometimes he also went to weekday services at Southover church, where the preaching was suitably evangelical: in October 1859 he reported 'an overflowing congregation' and 'an excellent sermon' from the celebrated Samuel Waldegrave, who in the following year was to be appointed bishop of Carlisle. But the most famous visiting preacher that he heard was Spurgeon, who on 23 May 1860 gave two sermons at the Corn Exchange to congregations totalling 2100. Thereafter Wille continued to be an avid sampler of sermons until, in his seventies, increasing deafness led him to listen only to preachers whose voices were loud and clear enough for him to be able to hear them.[8]

Wille's journal is also a source of information about what was happening at Cliffe Chapel. Evidently the accession of the dissidents from the Tabernacle, far from strengthening the cause, hastened its decline. The new arrivals promptly pushed the settled minister, Samuel Franklin, aside arranging for the pulpit to be supplied by preachers more to their liking. A new minister was appointed in 1843 but, according to Wille, there were 'continued contentions' between the newcomers and the established chapel deacons, some of whom were unceremoniously turned out of office. Although the 1851 census records that 232 adults and 150 children attended in the morning and 272 adults in the evening, the congregation was not really flourishing. In March 1852 Wille recorded that the 'Cliffe chapel people [had] divided into two congregations', with one withdrawing to worship in Mrs Adams's warehouse. Later that year a new minister, a Scotsman named John Irvine Dunlop, arrived to lead the much reduced Cliffe congregation and remained in post until 1860; but soon after his departure the cause finally folded. The surviving members probably joined other congregations in the town. Some, who continued to like their Calvinism plain and undiluted, may have joined Jireh, Providence or perhaps Bethesda, where Thomas Geering, who worked in the week as a gardener-cum-greengrocer, was the part-time pastor. Others less strict in their beliefs may have gone to the Tabernacle, where the theology was becoming more liberal, or to the Wesleyans, where the hymn-singing was probably the best in town.[9]

Divisions within Wesleyan Methodism

The Wesleyan Methodists, who disliked the term 'Dissenter' and preferred to be called 'Nonconformists', were now firmly established in Lewes, but in the early Victorian period their cause was experiencing difficulties and disturbances. In 1837 John Stevens, the superintendent of the Lewes circuit, informed Jabez Bunting, the chief administrator of the Wesleyan Connexion, that since coming to the town three years earlier he had met with 'a succession of discouragements and disappointments'. 'I have laboured harder and done more to advance the interests of Methodism in this circuit than any of my predecessors and yet', he complained, 'it is a melancholy fact that the circuit is in a declining state.' He said that 'some of the leaders and many of the people' were arrayed against him. For this he attached much of the blame to the local Dissenters, 'who are exceedingly bitter against me and have taken every opportunity to inflame the minds of our own and other people, and to injure us and our cause'. In this they had been supported by '20 of Paine's disciples', who were possibly continuing members of great Tom's beloved Headstrong Club. Defamatory papers had been distributed and 'the most infamous reports against the preachers' had been circulated. The odium was clearly not so much theological as political. The Unitarians and many of the Independents and Baptists had 'formed themselves into a political society for the accomplishment of certain objects', foremost among which was the abolition of church rates. To Stevens's horror and dismay some Wesleyan leaders and preachers had joined this society and many of the rank and file members, being 'exceedingly ill-informed on public questions' and 'easily made the dupes of designing men', had taken 'the radical side in politics'. In the recent parliamentary election they had supported the Liberal candidate and, because he himself had voted Conservative, he was now 'hated by many Methodists'. As a consequence Stevens had decided that he would not seek an extension of his superintendency, and in fact left Lewes soon afterwards.[10]

It is likely that in due course many local Wesleyans split off and joined the Primitive Methodists, who (following the demise of the Bible Christian congregation some years earlier) may have offered the only alternative haven. The Primitives, who had broken with the main Wesleyan body in 1811, apparently arrived in Lewes some 30 years later. At the time of the 1851 census the society (as the congregation was called) was renting a dual-purpose building in Fisher Street called 'Ebenezer' and was reportedly attracting as many people to its evening services as the Wesleyans. Drawing their support from a lower social stratum, the Primitives were noted for their more radical political stance and greater religious zeal but, although numerous 'hearers' attended their services, their committed membership remained small: there were only 34 on the roll in 1852 and even fewer thereafter. By 1862 the quarterly meeting of the Brighton Primitive Methodist circuit noted that 'the decrease of members in Lewes is occasioned by young persons falling away and none as yet converted to fill their places'. The congregation was described as 'a dead weight'. It was thought that only a resident preacher 'of considerable nerve, tack [sic], power and experience' would be able to 'keep the society in gear and grapple properly with that town of 10,000 inhabitants in which as yet we, as a Connexion, have done so little for ourselves'. They were especially critical of some obstreperous women members who had been threatening to withhold their seat rents unless a resident 'single man preacher' was appointed to Lewes. Eventually, in September 1863, four of the troublemakers were expelled from the society on account of their 'long continued agitation' and 'rebellion against our rules and official authority'. Although in the following year it was eventually agreed to appoint a resident preacher, the situation did not improve. In March 1877 the Fisher Street meeting-room was abandoned and it was decided that the eight surviving members should meet for worship in the Mechanics' Institute; that September it was agreed that 'Lewes come off the Plan' and so ended the Primitive Methodist presence in the town. But as their fortunes had been declining those of the main-stream Wesleyan Methodists had been in the ascendant. In 1867, having grown out of their old premises in St Mary's Lane, they erected a new red-brick gothic building (henceforth upgraded from 'chapel' to 'church') on the same site, with seating for over 500 people. And there, having consolidated their position, they were to remain for another 100 years.[11]

In the year after the erection of the Wesleyan church another brand new red-brick building, this time in Lombardic style, was opened for worship not far away in Market Street to house yet another Nonconformist congregation. They belonged to the moderately Calvinistic, newly formed 'Presbyterian Church in England' which, rooted in Scotland and the far north of England, had lately established a southern outpost in Brighton. Once again, as in the time of Lady Huntingdon, this rapidly expanding coastal resort had become the base for evangelical activity throughout Sussex. It was through the endeavours of missionaries from Brighton that in 1864 a new Presbyterian cause was established in the Old Chapel (now lying unused) in Cliffe. The first minister in Lewes was a young man named John Prentice, who hailed from North Shields. 'An able and earnest preacher, most assiduous in his attention to the sick and the poor', he soon built up a strong following. In 1868 the congregation was able to move to a new place of worship in the heart of Lewes, which was named 'Hamilton Memorial Church' after his old mentor, the eminent Scottish divine James Hamilton. The congregation was also prosperous enough to provide Prentice with a fine house in Grange Road that, after the Scottish fashion, was called 'The Manse'. But the southern air does not seem to have suited him, for he soon became afflicted with consumption and died in 1877 at the early age of 40. His place was taken by a succession of Scotsmen, none of whom appears to have made much impact on the life of the town.[12]

Christianity without Creeds

The establishment of the Hamilton Memorial Church may have caused some confusion locally, since 'English Presbyterian' was still the official designation of the old-established congregation of Westgate Meeting –

or, as it was now coming to be known, Westgate Chapel. Although by this time largely Unitarian in their theology many Westgate people did not like their building to be referred to as the 'Unitarian chapel'. Their position remained similar to that of Samuel Ridge, who died in 1838 and was described in his obituary as 'a Protestant Dissenter in the sense in which that character was and is understood by the English Presbyterians, whose distinction is not a creed but the freedom of individuals to choose and profess their opinions without any external interference'. Members of the Ridge family continued to be trustees of Westgate until the 1870s and their unsectarian outlook long seems to have prevailed there. Their influence and that of other lay people who thought like them was possibly more decisive than that of the ministers who, throughout the Victorian period, came and went with great rapidity.[13]

Between 1840 and 1901 the congregation was in fact served by no fewer than eleven ministers. At Westgate, as at Eastgate, the smallness of the ministerial stipend meant that some men, particularly if they had a family to support, were disinclined to remain for long. For a man like William Smith, the distinguished Irish botanist who came in 1850 and left in 1854 to become Professor of Natural History at Queen's College, Cork, the Westgate pulpit was clearly a staging post on the way to better things. Others, however, were men of independent means who were free from financial constraints and could even afford to subsidise the congregation. One such was Samuel Wood, minister from 1843 until his retirement at the early age of 51 in 1848. The son of a wealthy Liverpool merchant, he was able to contribute substantially to the cost of the major alterations carried out at Westgate (including the building of a back addition to house the Sunday school) soon after his arrival. Another was Thomas Carter, minister from 1856 to 1867, who augmented his inherited fortune by marrying the daughter of the congregation's wealthiest member, John Every, and was responsible for installing new seating in the chapel, largely at his own expense, in 1863. Carter's ministry was memorable for a long and acrimonious correspondence, published in the *East Sussex News*, with a local Anglican curate who had attacked his views on the Trinity as being those of an 'ignoramus'. A more peaceful (and fruitful) ministry was that of Archibald Forbes Macdonald, an Aberdeen graduate who came in 1877, retired in 1882 and lived on in the town until his death in 1886. Spiritually he was very close to James Martineau, the most distinguished of the nineteenth century Unitarian divines. Like his mentor Macdonald had no interest in converting others to his views but, as he put it, only in 'pointing to the germs of truth already in themselves and helping to develop *that*'. It may be taken as a sign of his personal approval of his work at Westgate that, shortly after Macdonald's death, Martineau contributed towards the cost of renovating the chapel.[14]

Macdonald's stance was in some respects similar to that of those attending the town's other congregation without a creed. The Quakers continued to believe strongly in 'the true light which lighteth every man that cometh into the world' and simply sought to bring people into contact with 'that of God' within them. They put into practice the Lutheran doctrine that 'every man is his own priest', always insisting that 'every man' meant 'every man and woman'. In their quiet meetings for worship anyone who was 'moved by the Spirit' was free to speak, but in fact most of the speaking seems to have been done by those Friends who had been appointed 'ministers' and who sat in a special gallery. In Lewes meeting-house in the mid-Victorian period many of the men and women in the gallery were related to the Rickmans, who continued to play a prominent part in Quaker affairs. In the late 1850s the ministers included the prosperous merchant John Rickman, now in his 80s and living in retirement at Wellingham House near Lewes, and his unmarried daughters Rachel and Matilda, both of whom had become almost blind. Some years after John Rickman's death in 1859 other relatives of his are found occupying the ministers' gallery. They included his nephew and business partner Burwood Godlee, who with his wife Priscilla (also a minister) lived in a fine house formerly standing over the road from the meeting-house called Leighside; Sarah Rickman (nee Godlee) and Mary Ann Godlee, Burwood's sisters, who had earlier run a successful girls' school at Dial House near Lewes Bridge; and Richard Peters Rickman, who was married to Priscilla Godlee's sister and had later moved into Dial House, which he had renamed 'The Friars'.[15]

In the later years of the nineteenth century the best known and most widely respected Quaker in Lewes was undoubtedly Caleb Rickman Kemp, a man of strong evangelical convictions who had been recorded a minister in 1857 at the unusually early age of 21. A partner in Rickman & Company, his cousins' old-established lime-burning, corn and coal business, he was wealthy enough to be able to devote a great deal of his time to religious and philanthropic work. An early visit to the West Indies with his father had inspired a life-long interest in overseas missions and in the work of the Anti-Slavery Society, on whose committee he served for 27 years. He took an active part in the work of the British and Foreign Bible Society and the YMCA, and he helped to set up the Lewes Evangelical Free Church Council in 1897. He was for some years both chairman and treasurer of the Lewes Town Mission, which had been founded in 1861 for 'the promotion of the moral and religious interests of the poorer classes, irrespective of denominational aims'.[16]

The Church Militant

It was out of concern for the moral and religious condition of the poorer classes, many of whom never went near a church or chapel, that in 1865

William Booth founded the missionary organisation that from 1878 was known as the Salvation Army. The Army, which had staged a spectacular invasion of Worthing in 1883 and not long afterwards had acquired a base in Brighton, was late in coming to Lewes. On 15 May 1891 the *East Sussex News* announced that 'the long talked-of attack by the forces of General Booth on the county town of Sussex has been commenced'. It told how on the previous Saturday a large van, bearing on its side the word 'Rescue' had passed through Lewes on its way to Brighton and had returned on the following Monday. One of six 'moving forts' that had set out from London to evangelise southern England, the van was parked on the green at the end of South Street, where a huge meeting-tent was promptly pitched. Thereupon the contingent of ten who constituted the advance guard proceeded to the railway station to meet the 'pioneers' who arrived by train from other parts of Sussex. Escorted by the police and headed by a brass band they then marched through the streets of Lewes, only silencing their instruments as they passed All Saints' out of respect for those then holding a service there. But there was no respite in the 'hooting and yelling of the mob' who followed the procession, throwing stones and in the process breaking some of the church's windows. When the Salvationists got back to the station there was 'a scene of wild confusion' when the mob tried to bar the way to the entrance and had to be driven back by a small army of porters. The parades continued throughout the week but without a band and 'largely attended' services were held each evening in the tent on South Street Green, where Lewes people experienced (in many cases for the first time) the sight and sound of a woman preaching. The singing was good, five converts were made and only 'a few hobble-de-hoys' were said to have given any trouble.[17]

The Army detachment, commanded by a 'very courteous' young man named Captain Whinnerah, remained in Lewes throughout the summer. In August it was reported that there had been 'rough conduct' and 'horse play' at some of the open-air meetings and on one occasion the Salvationists had been 'saturated' by a man throwing water at them in Malling Street. But for the most part local people seem to have been friendly and no fewer than 350 local children accepted the Army's invitation to a grand tea on the green, at the end of which each received a bag of sweets. That month saw the release of the Salvationists who had recently been imprisoned in Lewes for breaches of the peace in Eastbourne. On 1 August, when the first two were released, many comrades assembled at the prison gates to welcome them, but the authorities, fearing a disturbance, arranged for the freed men to be taken to the station in a cab with drawn blinds. However, although offered free tickets, they refused to board the train and were escorted to a house on School Hill, where they and the other Salvationists enjoyed a celebratory breakfast. It is evident that attitudes towards the Army in Lewes were on the whole rather different from those then prevailing in Eastbourne, where the authorities seem to have sided with the mobs of protesters. For one thing the *East Sussex News*, always a strong supporter of Nonconformity, was sympathetic to the missionaries. 'It may be hoped,' it said on the Army's first arrival in the town, 'that the Salvationists will receive similar treatment to that accorded to other religious bodies'. On the other hand the establishmentarian *Sussex Express* was less welcoming. Its report of the Army's 'attack' was shorter and less detailed than an accompanying item about the dedication of a new reredos at All Saints'. It concluded with the comment that several things militated against the Salvationists' chances of success: 'The town has no large slum population, it is well provided with places of worship, and lastly, the people of Lewes do not take kindly to strange and fantastic methods of religion.' The paper may have been right about the provision of places of worship and local attitudes to strange practices, but it was almost certainly wrong about the slums. That there were many living in dire poverty in Lewes at this period is clear from the annual reports of the St Michael's Provident Clubs. Each winter the clubs provided blankets, boots, clothing, coal and 'Christmas cheer' for some 250 people, some of whom doubtless lived under the town wall in Westgate Street in what until the 1930s was regarded as a little better than a slum.[18]

The year 1891, which saw the Salvation Army's invasion of Lewes and moves towards the setting up of a permanent 'citadel' in South Street, also witnessed other military-style missionary activities in the town. In September the Church Army, which the Anglicans had mobilised ten years earlier in imitation of General Booth's brigade, made a brief appearance in the town. But this time there were no moving forts or brass bands or processions through the streets: there was simply a sedate gathering in the grounds of Southover Rectory where a Captain Hotchkiss spoke to an audience numbering no more than 60. The same month also saw the arrival of a real-life Army officer, Captain Baring, who had served with the 17th Lancers in the Crimean War and who proceeded to mount a two-week 'evangelistic mission' in the Pelham Rooms, 183 High Street. Although his mission was conducted under the auspices of the local branch of the YMCA, which had been founded by local Nonconformists in 1877, it goes without saying that the captain was a member of the Church of England.[19]

Opposition to the Oxford Movement

The Victorian period, which saw Nonconformists playing an increasingly important part in the social and religious life of Lewes, also witnessed a remarkable revival in the fortunes of the Church of England. This had something to do with an improvement in the quality of the parish clergy.

After the retirement of Crofts from St John sub Castro in 1847 and of Shiffner from St Anne's a year later, there were no more sporting squarsons among the local incumbents. By the 1870s pluralism and absenteeism were things of the past and, for the first time for centuries, every parish in Lewes had its own resident rector. They were for the most part dedicated men, content to stay in one place and serve their cures conscientiously all their days. The later years of Victoria's reign saw some remarkably long incumbencies. Augustus Parsons was at St Anne's from 1863 to 1898, William Richardson at Southover from 1869 to 1900, and Arthur Perfect at St John sub Castro from 1868 to 1910. Perfect, who died in harness at the age of 71, was evidently a model parish priest. For most of his time at St John's he had no curate to assist him in what was then described as 'the largest and also the poorest parish in Lewes'. During his 42-year incumbency there were 2530 baptisms, 2070 burials and 532 marriages, at most of which he himself officiated. 'He did his duty simply and faithfully, unostentatiously and quietly.' 'Zeal' and 'earnestness' were his characteristic qualities and his sermons were remarkable for their 'breadth of view and intense human sympathy'. 'He was ever a man among men and behind a courtly bearing were a warm heart and not a little humour.' From the things said about him at his funeral it sounds as though Parson Perfect lived up to his name.[20]

The improvement in the quality of the parish clergy was accompanied by an improvement in the material condition of their churches. In 1866 a letter to the *Sussex Express* had condemned the Lewes churches, 'whose shabby exterior and pewed-up and pew-rented interior are a positive disgrace'. Soon after this, however, much attention began to be given to the renewing or refurbishing of fabric and to the enlargement of inadequate premises. In the 1880s chancels were added at All Saints' and Southover and coloured glass inserted into windows at two other churches – one at St Michael's later being described by Nikolaus Pevsner as 'good for its date' and one at St Anne's as 'very terrible'. Good or bad, the insertion of the glass helped to restore the 'dim religious light' lost at the Reformation, enabling the worshippers to feel that they were back in the Middle Ages. For High Churchmen the great aim became the restoration of the sacraments to the central place they had once occupied in the Church's life and liturgy. Paradoxically, however, the man who introduced the 'Oxford Movement' into Lewes came not from the university of Pusey, Keble and Newman but from Cambridge, for so long the power-house of puritanism. And its influence was first felt not at St John sub Castro, where the High Church movement had made headway in Laud's day, but at that historic bastion of militant Protestantism, St Michael's.[21]

The decisive event was the rejection in 1841 by the Lord Chancellor, who was the patron, of a petition from the parishioners of St Michael's

asking him to present their popular curate John Roper to the living. Instead
he appointed a newly ordained Cambridge graduate named Frederick Teed
– a rich young Old Etonian who apparently got the job because he had the
right social and political connections. He immediately introduced a daily
service and increased the number of celebrations of communion from four
to 16 a year. Because of his influence in high places he was able to obtain
a gift from Queen Adelaide of new furnishings that would help to make St
Michael's church once again fit for Catholic worship. This, as Roger Davey
has pointed out, was an astute move, since the parishioners, even if they
disliked the gift, could hardly say no to the giver. Nor could they easily
reject the new rector's generous donation of chairs and cushions for the
'altar', the new name given to the old wooden communion table that for
two centuries had been hidden away behind the high central pulpit.[22]

At St Michael's, as in every Lewes parish, the Word had long ago taken
precedence over the Sacrament: the town's Anglican churches were simply
'preaching-boxes', in which the seating was so arranged that it was easy to
sit and listen but almost impossible to kneel. Teed's task was therefore
even more difficult than that of the High Church revivalists in Laud's day,
and it was not until 1849 that he felt sufficiently confident to ask for the
offending central pulpit to be removed. The churchwardens reluctantly
agreed to his request, but only on condition that he paid for the pulpit's
removal and undertook to reinstate it at his own charge if he was ever asked
to do so. Then, early in 1851, came the backlash. Teed had introduced certain
liturgical innovations, involving 'the frequent repetition of chanting and
music', that were unacceptable to many of the parishioners and, after a
special meeting of the vestry at which objections were voiced 'in very
strong terms', he was obliged to withdraw them. His plans to replace all
the box-pews and to build on an apse at the east end of the church remained
unfulfilled at the time of his sudden death in 1863.

Teed was succeeded by another High Churchman named Frederick
Woolley, hitherto headmaster of the grammar school. In 1867 he was
strongly criticised in an article in the *East Sussex News*, headed 'High
Church Doings in St Michael's', for introducing a surpliced choir, intoned
prayers and chanted psalms, and for 'festooning' the church with flowers.
The paper piously advised him that if he were to 'preach the simple gospel
of Christ ably and earnestly' he would not need 'to get up an "exhibition"
to secure an attentive audience'. But Woolley was not deterred. In 1871 he
caused lighted candles to be placed on the altar, the first that had burned
there for more than three centuries. This innovation led to strong objections
from some parishioners, one of whom turned up to evensong arrayed in a
long white shirt and chanted the responses in a 'loud unnatural voice',
thereby creating such a disturbance that the police had to be called. The
rector also introduced a weekly communion service, at which he wore the

full sacerdotal regalia of chasuble and maniple but, as with Teed, illness prevented him from carrying out the projected structural alterations that would have made the church fully fit for 'Catholic' worship.

After Woolley's premature death in 1877 a parishioner named William Banks, who had a newsagent's shop close to the church and had been one of the rector's most vociferous opponents, wrote to the Lord Chancellor requesting him to appoint a 'sound evangelical clergyman' to St Michael's. But the Chancellor took no notice and instead presented Edgar Cross, an Oxford graduate with impeccable High Church credentials, to the living. The new rector, who evidently had ample private means, lost no time in applying for a faculty to build an apse to house an extended sanctuary, but the proposal aroused great opposition. A major objection was that the building would disturb several graves, including that of the ancestors of Richard Hobden, a former Keere Street cooper, who said that the rector's designs were 'Ritualistic' and even 'Romanistic'. In the end, however, a public poll approved of the scheme by 87 votes to 17, and the alterations went ahead, with Banks continuing to protest that the congregation at St Michael's was no longer composed of parishioners but mainly of people from other Lewes parishes 'who attended merely out of curiosity to witness the Ritualistic practices which were there carried on'. The alterations, which caused the church to be closed in 1878 from May to November, involved removing the galleries, repewing the nave, adding 12 feet to the chancel, raising up the altar on nine steps, erecting a barrier between the choir and the congregation and inserting a piscina in the wall of the apse. There was now also 'a super-altar with a pedestal bearing the Agnus Dei, with a massive gilt cross, two vases and two tall candlesticks'. When the bishop of Chichester, Richard Durnford, preached at the special service to mark the re-opening of the church he deplored the excesses of both 'Romanism' and 'Calvinism', but he did not say which of the two he believed to be the greater threat to the peace of the Church of England.

Rather more cautious in his approach than some other High Church clergy at this time, Cross was never prosecuted for his innovations. In 1878 he protested that he would always be 'careful to preach the Catholic doctrine of the Church of England and follow her ritual as ordered by her, and so avoid Romanism, Rationalism and Puritanism'. In the 1880s his main achievement was to make the Georgian south windows 'correctly gothic', insert the stained glass later commended by Pevsner and erect a fine stone reredos behind the altar. When he retired in 1891 Cross, who had personally borne part of the cost of the alterations, could comfort himself with the knowledge that Anglo-Catholicism had been firmly established at St Michael's. Furthermore, since he had purchased the advowson (subsequently to be transferred into the safe hands of the Society for the Maintenance of the Faith), he had ensured that his successors would be men of similar outlook to himself. Henry Belcher, who came in 1896 and stayed 20 years, introduced incense, called communion 'mass' and used wafers in place of the 'best and purest wheat bread' prescribed by the Prayer Book. When John Kensit, spying out the scene on behalf of the Protestant Truth Society, attended the service at St Michael's one Sunday in 1898 and asked the rector to give him 'bread as ordered by the rubric', Belcher refused and Kensit marched out of the church in protest. But by this time everyone in the regular congregation was apparently prepared to accept the changes. By the time of his death, aged 87, in 1906 even William Watts, a former churchwarden who had initially been opposed to the innovations, had apparently become 'an enthusiastic supporter of the new order'. This provides a corrective to the suggestion that the changes had been imposed upon an unwilling congregation by rich and powerful people whom they were too poor and weak to resist.

It is important; however, to put the Victorian developments at St Michael's into their proper perspective. Those directly affected by the High Church revival constituted only a minute proportion of the total population of Lewes. As the religious census of 1851 indicates, St Michael's (with only 50 people attending the sole Sunday service) had a much smaller congregation than any of the other parish churches. And although it expanded after 1851 it never grew as large as those of the other parish churches in the town: at the first service to be held after the re-opening of the church in 1878 there were only 50 communicants. In any event, after its box-pews and galleries had been removed, the church could never seat more than about 250, far fewer than the numbers that could be accommodated at All Saints' or St John sub Castro.

Anti-Catholic Agitation

It is clear that people in the other Lewes parish churches often looked askance at what was happening at St Michael's. One who was particularly hostile to the Oxford Movement was John Scobell, a strong evangelical who served as rector of All Saints' and Southover from 1821 to 1868. His hostility boiled over in 1855 when his daughter Emily joined the Sisterhood of St Margaret established at East Grinstead by the celebrated hymn-writer John Mason Neale. After her death two years later her body, accompanied by Neale in cap and gown and by eight sisters in grey cloaks and black bonnets, was brought back to Lewes by train for burial in All Saints' churchyard. It is reported that several hundred people, some of them shouting 'No Popery', watched the coffin, over which was draped a pall covered most offensively with crosses, being carried from the station to the churchyard. After the service Neale was physically assaulted, stripped of his gown and thrown to the ground. Rescued by the police he and the terrified sisters sought refuge in the King's Head tavern, where the mob besieged them for nearly an hour until eventually Neale was able to escape by climbing over a garden wall. Nothing daunted, he returned to Lewes the following night to pray at Emily's tomb, but a hostile crowd, forewarned of his coming, pelted him with stones, one of which hit him on the head. The incident led to an acrimonious correspondence between him and Scobell, who complained bitterly about how his daughter had been 'inoculated with Puseyism' and carried off by members of 'a deadly church faction' bent on the destruction of Protestant England.[23]

At this period Protestant fervour was growing because of newly kindled fears of 'Popery'. The first mention of a Roman Catholic presence in the town occurs in 1815, when a Lewes grocer Thomas Johnston (grandson of Ebenezer and a prominent Westgate member) made himself unpopular by letting them a room to worship in. Strong feelings were aroused against Catholics in the later1820s when a movement was afoot to emancipate them. At this time few people in Lewes had a good word to say about them apart from Horsfield, an active member of the Unitarian Association that in 1825 had publicly protested against the 'intolerant laws' denying civil rights to their 'fellow-Christians of the Roman Catholic persuasion'. The actual number of Roman Catholics in the town was then very small, but the appearance of natives of Dublin, Cork and Galway in the 1851 census returns suggests that, following the arrival of Irish immigrants in the Hungry Forties, their number increased considerably. Nevertheless it is unlikely that the presence of people like James Murphy, a 'hawker of linen', then lodging in South Street, or James Genetty, a fiddler, residing (along with three other Irishmen) in a Keere Street beer-house, would have aroused fears that the place was becoming swamped with dangerous papists. There is no doubt that what most provoked anti-papal paranoia was the restoration in 1850 of the Roman Catholic hierarchy in England and the appointment of Cardinal Wiseman as Archbishop of Westminster. In November of that year a public meeting was held in the Town Hall, with the senior constable in the chair, at which a motion was carried unanimously

> That the love of religious truth and liberty which has so often roused
> our Protestant Forefathers to resist and drive away any Popish Error
> and domination is as strong as ever in us their Children and that we
> are determined . . . to use every Loyal and Constitutional Method
> to resist and repel these dangerous Encroachments.

Not all the methods used to resist the papal threat were strictly constitutional. On Guy Fawkes Night that year the 'Bonfire Boys', who had long been in the habit of celebrating the Fifth of November in riotous fashion, dressed a man up as Wiseman 'in red from top to toe' to harangue the crowd about papal aggression. It is clear from the comments in the *Sussex Express* that nothing quite like this had ever happened in Lewes before. 'We may here remark', wrote its reporter in November 1851, 'that since Dr Wiseman's insolent usurpation the celebration of this anniversary has partaken to a much greater extent than formerly of an anti-Romanist character.' In 1853 the proceedings were extended and formalised, with a Grand Procession marching through the town, carrying a large banner proclaiming 'No Popery' and an effigy of the Pope, which was subsequently burnt in a huge fire in front of County Hall.[24]

1850 thus saw the introduction of a distinctive religious dimension into what the local press in the previous year had described as essentially a 'political anniversary'. People now began to look back not only to the Gunpowder Plot of 1605 but also to an earlier event of greater significance for Lewes. In this town, which had experienced the bitter consequences of the restoration of the Catholic hierarchy in Queen Mary's reign, 'Remember, Remember the Fifth of November' now acquired an additional refrain: 'Remember the Protestant martyrs'. On 5 November 1850, according to the report in the *Sussex Express*, 'at midnight a tar barrel was ignited in sight of the spot where the Papists were wont to light the faggot and burn to death their unyielding Protestant brethren'. Never before had the paper's annual Bonfire Night report made any mention of the Marian martyrs. But this time the reporter, who had evidently done his history homework, took the opportunity to indulge himself in a lengthy (if not entirely accurate) antiquarian digression:

> Although three centuries have passed away since these dreadful occurrences took place, their horrors have been handed down from generation to generation. . . . The names of their victims, Carver, Harland, Oswald, Ovington, Read, Wood, Miles, Woodman, Stephens, Maynard, Hoffman, Morris and his mother, Burgess, Ashdon and Grover's wives, who were burned to death in the month of June 1555, the last named ten in one fire before the Star Hotel . . . are still held in reverence, not only by their successors, many of whom yet live in the neighbourhood, but by the town generally.

The names of the martyrs were taken, as the writer acknowledged, from Horsfield's *History of Lewes*; it even included the man whom that book, compounding the original error in Foxe's *Acts and Monuments*, confusingly called 'Hoffman'. But the comment that the story of the martyrs had been 'handed down from generation to generation' and that the 'successors' of these (almost exclusively Wealden) men and women 'yet live in the neighbourhood' of Lewes was pure journalistic speculation. Until Horsfield published his account of the Marian persecutions in 1824 it is likely that few people in Lewes had ever heard of Carver or Woodman, let alone 'Hoffman' (*recte* Hosmer). And it was not until 1851, when the Lewes antiquarian Mark Antony Lower published the *Sussex Martyrs*, that they would have had an opportunity of reading Foxe's own graphic account of these tragic proceedings. As Lower indicated in his preface, the story of the martyrs, once so well known throughout England, had now become – in Lewes as elsewhere – largely forgotten.[25]

Contrary to what the *Sussex Express* reporter maintained, the strength of anti-Romanist feeling in Lewes probably had less to do with the past cruelties of Catholics than with the present activities of Anglicans. Lower made it clear that what moved him to publish the *Sussex Martyrs* was his anger against High Churchmen who had the temerity to contend that the Reformation, for which cause men like Carver and Woodman had gone to their deaths, was simply a 'mistake'. It is significant that the protests against the restoration of the Catholic hierarchy, culminating in a great bonfire in Lewes High Street, first took place at the very time when Frederick Teed, rector of nearby St Michael's, was introducing what many regarded as reprehensibly 'popish' practices. In this respect it is noteworthy that within a few years the burning of the effigies of dead popes was to be extended to include those of contemporary High Churchmen such as J. M. Neale and H. M. Wagner. And in 1868, following the disestablishment of the Church of Ireland, which was regarded by some in Lewes as 'an initiative hatched in Rome between Gladstone and the Cardinals', anti-Catholic feelings reached fever-pitch. On Bonfire Night that year a man dressed up as 'the Lord Bishop of Lewes' warned the crowd about the Catholic threat to the Church of England. 'Protestants of England', he urged, 'arouse yourselves; never since the Reformation has the Church been in such a state as she is at the present time.'[26]

By the late 1860s, however, the steady increase in the number of Roman Catholics residing in the town led the Lewes Bonfire Boys to turn their attention to what was happening nearer home. On 5 November 1869 they tried to explode an effigy of the Pope filled with gunpowder outside the house in Priory Crescent where a priest had recently established a Mission of the Sacred Heart. However, as a Roman Catholic observer gleefully recorded, 'the Fates decreed otherwise' and 'in spite of several torches being applied, the effigy would *not* go off'. At this time in fact the Roman Catholics were in the process of building a permanent place of worship next to the Pelham Arms on the corner of the road named (appropriately enough in view of the congregation's strong Irish associations) Irelands Lane. Since the inn was the headquarters of the Borough Bonfire Society the situation was potentially explosive. When in January 1870 the time came to consecrate the new church, the Roman Catholics were so fearful of disruptions that admission was by ticket only; and a Mrs Kelly, 'a very strong and powerful woman', was positioned at the door. They were wise to take such precautions, for soon a crowd estimated at between 2000 and 3000 assembled outside the church, 'singing bonfire songs, howling and jeering'. In due course a group of Bonfire Boys, who had climbed through

a window at the Pelham Arms and positioned themselves in the passage
between the inn and the church, made so much noise that the service had to
be brought to an abrupt conclusion. At this point the congregation, which
included the poet Coventry Patmore and others who had come over from
Brighton for the occasion, eventually managed to make their escape under
police protection. However, as a contemporary account put it, 'the ways of
God are truly wonderful', for the wife of the landlord at the Pelham Arms
had a change of heart and within two years of the disturbance she and her
two daughters were received into the Roman Catholic Church. The parish
priest, Hubert Wood, described as 'a fine looking man, strong and well
proportioned, about 6ft 2in in height', made other converts among people
in the town and the congregation appears to have flourished. When he died
suddenly of a brain haemorrhage in 1882 at the early age of 43 many
mourned the loss of this 'most loveable gentleman'.[27]

The main support for the Bonfire Boys and their anti-Catholic antics
seems to have come from evangelical Anglicans such as the Southover
brewer Francis Verrall, who was a patron of the Borough Bonfire Society.
William Richardson, rector of Southover, was also an enthusiastic backer
of bonfires. In 1893 he inaugurated an annual Thanksgiving Service in his
church on the Sunday before 5 November, which gave him a good
opportunity of warning people about the perils of Popery. The services,
which were initially for men only, were attended by 'crowded and reverent
congregations' drawn from all the town's bonfire societies, many of whom
also belonged to the newly formed Lewes branch of the Loyal Orange Lodge.
Seeing such people parading round the town in their bright orange sashes,
visitors might well have thought they were not in Lewes but in Lisburn.[28]

Church *versus* Chapel

Many Nonconformists in fact opposed the Guy Fawkes night celebrations
(as they also opposed the Lewes race meetings) because they caused
drunkenness and disorder. This was clearly the case with the Methodists,
who pioneered the Temperance movement in the town. As early as 1838
Lewes Wesleyans had helped to organise a great open-air anti-drink
gathering at Uckfield, which was eventually broken up by a mob rented by
the Lewes brewers. To make a stand for Temperance – which normally meant
teetotalism – in a town like Lewes, whose eight breweries provided
employment and enjoyment for so many people, was not easy but by the
1860s the cause was well established here. In 1868 Methodists and other
Nonconformists organised a Grand Temperance Festival, which was attended
by 300 people and resulted in the setting up of a Drinking Fountain Fund.
One of the principal supporters was Eliza Payne, a prominent Lewes Quaker,
who three years later paid for the building of the British Workmen's Institute

in Little East Street. Described as 'a public house without intoxicants open daily from six to ten', it served coffee and other refreshments and provided a meeting place for the Good Templar's Lodge. Particular attention was given to the welfare of young people and in 1878 the Wesleyans formed a branch of the Band of Hope, which soon had a membership of 150. Not long afterwards Bands of Hope were also established by Baptists, Congregationalists and Presbyterians. By this time, however, Temperance had ceased to be an exclusively Nonconformist cause. In July 1879, at a grand meeting in the County Hall chaired by Caleb Kemp, called to support a Bill for Closing Public Houses on Sundays, the incumbents of All Saints', Southover and South Malling were on the platform. On this occasion, however, few could hear the words of the principal speaker, the rector of Barcombe, because of the hissing and booing and the loud cries of 'No, No'. But the Nonconformists remained the most vigorous opponents of the 'drink trade', which now became effectively an Anglican monopoly. No longer were brewers and innkeepers to be found among the worshippers at Westgate, the Tabernacle or the Friends' Meeting House. By the 1880s, Henry Wingham, the proprietor of the Crown Hotel and the last Nonconformist in Victorian Lewes to be involved with the sale of alcohol, had withdrawn from Westgate and joined the Church of England.[29]

Differences between Anglicans and Nonconformists were also reflected in their politics. Colin Brent's study of voting patterns in Lewes in the general elections of 1865 and 1868 has shown that, while most Anglicans were Conservative, the overwhelming majority of Nonconformists were Liberal. Except at Jireh, which remained the principal bastion of political and theological conservatism, a Tory Nonconformist was virtually a contradiction in terms. In 1865, when there were two seats and each party fielded two candidates, the Conservative William Christie was nominated by Ebenezer Morris of Jireh and the Liberal Henry Brand by the Quaker Burwood Godlee. In 1868, when (following the Second Reform Bill) there was only one seat, Christie was again nominated by Morris, while the Liberal Lord Pelham's nomination was seconded (as it had been in 1855) by Charles Parsons of the Tabernacle. The Tabernacle, the main stronghold of Liberalism in Lewes, was the place where some of the wealthiest and most influential local employers worshipped. The builders John and Charles Parsons, the timber merchant Charles Wille and the candle-maker James Broad were all great supporters of Gladstone – and so, unsurprisingly, were most of their employees. The pattern was repeated on a smaller scale at Westgate, where Liberal voters included the ironfounder John Every, a 'model' employer who was to concede the 54-hour week in 1871, and the drapers William and Robert Crosskey, whose firm of Browne and Crosskey was in 'the front rank of county trade'. At Eastgate the congregation was solidly behind J. B. Pike, minister there from 1864 to 1867, who said that

'the scruples that made him a Dissenter also made him a Liberal'. Although
they included the master builder Benjamin Thorpe and the wholesale grocer
Henry Moore, most Baptist voters seem to have been small self-employed
tradesmen. The Wesleyan Methodists, who generally belonged to the same
social stratum, were now also predominantly Liberal: Jabez Blaber, foreman
of the Southover tanyard, was sufficiently independent-minded to diverge
politically (and, because there was not yet a ballot, publicly) from his
Conservative employer, the Anglican William Baxter. In Lewes as elsewhere
the Nonconformists were indeed 'the Liberal party at prayer' and it is a
reflection of their strength that the party triumphed in the 1865 and 1868
elections.[30]

As in many English towns at this time the split between Anglicans and
Nonconformists was accentuated by the introduction of denominational
day schools. In pre-Victorian times Lewes children, irrespective of their
parents' religious affiliations, had been educated at the non-denominational
Lancasterian school established in 1809. In 1840, however, a new school
was opened in Southover Road under the auspices of the National Society
for the Education of the Poor in the Principles of the Established Church.
Nonconformists saw this initiative, which was later followed by the
establishment of additional National schools in the parishes of St Anne
(1867), St John sub Castro (1871) and Southover (1872), as representing
a determined bid on the part of the Anglicans to gain control of the town's
educational system. Most of them, however, probably continued to send
their children to the British School in Lancaster Street, whose buildings
were enlarged in 1863 and which, until its closure in 1897, remained a
major focus of Nonconformity in the town. On a number of occasions it
served as a venue for their united prayer meetings.[31]

Although divided over a number of major issues Anglicans and
Nonconformists nonetheless worked closely together in local government.
For most of the Victorian era the town administration remained in the hands
of a self-perpetuating oligarchy, who annually appointed two of its number
as high constables. Although it may not have been intentional, it often
happened that one constable was a churchgoer and the other a chapelgoer.
This confessional balance seems to have been preserved after the borough
was formally incorporated in 1881; of the town's first four mayors two
(Wynne Baxter and Joseph Thorne) were Anglicans and two (Walter
Crosskey and Caleb Kemp) were Nonconformists. Crosskey, a popular local
doctor who had topped the poll in the first borough council election,
belonged to an old General Baptist family who had linked up with the
Westgate congregation in 1825. The Crosskeys were public-spirited people.
Walter took an active part in the work of the town's Sanitary and District
Hospital Committees. His brother Robert, a JP who had twice served as
high constable, was an early supporter of the Lewes Co-operative Society,

which held its first general meeting in the Westgate schoolroom in 1865. A third brother, Henry William, became a Unitarian minister in Birmingham, where his 'Christian citizenship' preaching inspired Joseph Chamberlain (also descended from a Westgate Chapel family) to transform it into 'the best governed city in England'. [32]

The spirit of co-operation that enabled Anglicans and Nonconformists to forget their differences was particularly noticeable in times of crisis, when all offered up prayers to the one God. Charles Wille recorded that all places of worship in the town were well attended on 26 September 1849, a day 'set apart for Humiliation in Lewes and Hastings to bewail our sins and to seek for a blessing that cholera might be stayed and that God's judgments might be turned away'. Again, on 26 April 1853, a day 'set apart as a Fast and Humiliation on account of the war between Turkey and Russia' was recorded as being 'a very quiet day in Lewes, the congregations very good as to number – double services in churches and chapels'. The last such entry was on 12 May 1875, after a typhoid epidemic, when the evening was 'devoted to Thanksgiving in all churches and chapels for recovery of sickness'. The subsequent improvements in the town's water supply, which helped to remove the threat of such epidemics, may have caused people in Lewes to give thanks not only to God but to the members of the new borough council, in which Anglicans and Nonconformists worked together for the common good. [33]

There is no doubt that the greatest display of ecclesiastical unity in Victorian Lewes was occasioned by the Queen's Diamond Jubilee in 1897, when for the first time ever there was a united service of thanksgiving. It was held at All Saints' in the afternoon of Sunday, 20 June and was attended by all the town's Anglican clergy, the ministers of almost all the Nonconformist chapels and a representative of the Society of Friends. Charles Nolloth, the distinguished scholar who was currently rector of All Saints', gave a special welcome to the Nonconformists and offered up a prayer for Christian unity, imploring the Almighty to 'take away all hatred and prejudice and whatsoever else may hinder us from godly union and concord'. In his sermon he urged his hearers to give practical expression to their religion by uniting in works of charity and announced that at the close of the service the collection would go to help fund a nursing home for the Lewes district. The occasion, of course, did not mark the end of ecclesiastical disunity, as is shown by the absence from the service of representatives from Jireh and Providence and (at the other end of the spectrum) the Roman Catholics. The only man present with even the remotest papal connections was Thomas Alphonsus Gorton, a former Roman Catholic priest then ministering at Westgate Chapel. But Gorton's conspicuous absence from a second thanksgiving service – held that evening at the Tabernacle under the auspices of the Lewes Free Church Council –

is a reminder that at the close of the Victorian era sectarianism, if less pronounced than at its beginning, continued to be a cause of division in the town.[34]

It is likely, however, that most lay people did not take the divisions very seriously. An account of a 'Lewes childhood in the Eighteen Eighties' by one whose father belonged to Jireh and whose mother to the Church of England, accepts that 'there was a seriousness about doctrine, leading sometimes to bigotry', but suggests that this was not widespread:

> When as a child I heard Mr Welland praying that we might be delivered from Socinianism, Erastianism and Arianism, I laboriously looked up their meanings. . . . My little cousins went to the Unitarian chapel, so they were wrong. My special friend was brought up in the Established Church, so she was wrong. My aunt, who was a Methodist, thought that all could be saved, so she was wrong. But I came to the conclusion that neither my father nor my mother worried much about it, nor did the rest of the folks who did not attend Jireh Chapel, so I gave the problem up.

At the close of Queen Victoria's reign most Lewes people may still have gone regularly to a church or chapel but many of them were evidently ceasing to believe all that was said there.[35]

VIII. From Conflict to Cooperation

The news of the death of Queen Victoria reached Lewes on the evening of 22 January 1901 and, according to the corporation records, 'created a visibly sorrowful impression upon all who were in the streets waiting in expectation of some message from Osborne'. Almost immediately the solemn notes of the town bell 'Gabriel' and those of numerous churches 'broke upon the night air, carrying the message of grief to all parts of the borough'. The bells tolled again on 2 February, the day of the royal funeral, and signs of mourning were everywhere. 'It is safe to say', states the official record, 'that never have so many or so great manifestations of grief been seen in Lewes.' That day special services were held in the parish churches, including a particularly memorable one at Southover. Here, after its muffled bells had rung a complete peal of Grandsire Triples, comprising 5,040 changes and lasting for over three hours, an 'immense congregation' crammed into the church, where 'a spirit of deep solemnity and intense fervour prevailed'. There was also a united Free Church service at the Wesleyans, where the Tabernacle's minister Burgess Wilkinson preached. And then there was the town's official memorial service in the afternoon at St John sub Castro, where 1000 people assembled in a building said to have seating for only 850 and Arthur Perfect, rector of the parish and rural dean of Lewes, read special prayers.[1]

Although temporarily united by their common sorrow the people of Lewes at this time were still deeply divided religiously. It is clear from the reports of what happened on the day of the funeral that the community was in fact split three times over. The oldest and deepest division remained that between Catholics and Protestants or, as Anglicans who now called themselves Catholics might have preferred to put it, between Romanists and the rest of Christendom. The absence of any report of a Roman Catholic memorial service suggests that 'papists' were still not regarded as loyal subjects of the Queen. That certainly continued to be a common view in Lewes, where an organisation called the Protestant Alliance waxed strong. In March 1900 the Alliance put on a lantern lecture at the Ragged School, which was clearly intended to keep old conflicts alive. The subject was the Reformation: slides were shown of the 'tortures to which Protestants were put' and an exhibition was mounted of some of the 'instruments of torture' employed and of some of the 'hair shirts used by Romanists and ritualists'. At this time members of the Alliance were busy collecting money for a memorial to the Protestants burned at the stake in Lewes under Mary. Having failed to persuade the borough council to attach one to the outer wall of the Town Hall (near the place where the martyrs suffered) they decided to erect a monument in a prominent position on high ground overlooking the town. The site chosen was on land belonging to the Ragged School proprietor and leading Jireh member, Isaac Vinall, who had named it Cuilfail after the Scottish village where his family spent their summer holidays. By the spring of 1901 over 800 people (including Francis Chavasse, the evangelical bishop of Liverpool, and many others without any connection with Lewes) had subscribed to the memorial fund. 210 tons of stone – principally Aberdeen granite – went into the making of the obelisk, standing 35 ft 9 in high. The unveiling ceremony took place on 8 May and to mark the great occasion the evangelical publishers Morgan and Scott brought out an introductory booklet, *Turn or Burn*, written in language clearly designed to fan the flames of controversy. 'This noble granite memorial', it said, 'stands and will stand as an object lesson for succeeding generations to gaze upon and a lasting sermon in stone preaching silently but eloquently of the tyranny and persecuting character of Romanism.'[2]

On the Sunday before the unveiling ceremony special services were held at Jireh, at the Baptist, Congregational, Methodist and Presbyterian churches, and also in the parish churches of Southover and South Malling. Representatives from all these congregations were among the crowd that assembled at Cuilfail to watch the countess of Portsmouth unveil the memorial. Isaac Vinall and his staff stood at the gates to count them in and the tally came to 5,812 – possibly the largest number of people ever to come together in one place in the whole history of Lewes. Although the weather was unexpectedly bad the *Sussex Express* reported that 'the showers, which were heavy and almost continuous, failed to damp the enthusiasm' of the spectators. In his welcoming speech the mayor George Holman, who may have lifted a few phrases from Horsfield's *History of Lewes*, said that 'the foundation of religious liberty and thought was laid by those martyrs'. Added poignancy to the occasion was given by the presence of one Richard Woodman, a Brighton man 'who attends Lewes market' and was said to be a direct descendant of the most famous of the 17 martyrs named on the memorial. The afternoon ceremony was followed by an evening meeting in the Town Hall at which Arthur Morris, the Lewes postmaster who claimed kinship with two of the martyrs, made an inflammatory speech. Morris, the secretary of the memorial fund, pointed out that the project had been supported 'not by the elite of the town but by a few plain, blunt men'. The 'elite' that he had in mind probably included the Quaker Caleb R. Kemp, who had opposed the erection of the memorial out of consideration for the feelings of local Roman Catholics, for whom it would be 'a slap in the face'. Another opponent was the biggest employer and the richest man in Lewes, the Unitarian John H. Every, for whom religious toleration was a major article of faith. It is interesting to note that on this issue the two leading representatives of historic Dissent in Lewes found themselves standing shoulder to shoulder with people who were furthest removed from them theologically and ecclesiastically; for the most vociferous opponent of the memorial project was Henry Belcher, the Anglo-Catholic rector of St Michael's. This suggests that, although it was still very much in evidence in Lewes, the oldest line of religious demarcation – that between Protestants and Catholics – had lost some of its sharpness.[3]

Beating the Free Church Drum

As yet, however, there had been little blurring of the second oldest line of demarcation – that between those inside and outside the established Church. Although Nonconformists now liked to call their chapels 'churches' and to adorn them in gothic style, the old distinction between Church and Chapel still persisted. In fact the new custom of referring to themselves as 'Free Churches' (with the implication that Anglicans were somehow 'unfree') may have done something to widen the gap. Certainly, with the founding of the Lewes and District Free Church Council in 1897, the Nonconformists acquired a clearer identity in the town. Local press reports suggest that there was now much beating of the 'Free Church' drum. In January 1900 Joseph Compton Rickett, a Liberal MP and future cabinet minister, currently serving as President of the National Federation of Free Church Councils, came to the Tabernacle to address the annual general meeting of the local council. He said that the Free Church movement was 'a forward movement' and one 'that was bound to make headway'; although himself a prominent Congregationalist, he hoped to see the end of denominationalism and the creation of 'one great Evangelical Church'. Two weeks later Burgess Wilkinson, the outgoing chairman of the Lewes Free Church Council, struck an equally optimistic note in a lecture at Eastgate. Here he contended that Nonconformity, 'one of the mightiest forces of the age', would continue to benefit the nation by 'preserving and promoting the idea of the spiritual power of Christ's kingdom'. He returned to this theme in the following year when he gave the address at the united Free Church memorial service for Queen Victoria. He observed that, because the Queen had probably never entered a Nonconformist place of worship, she 'did not know much about our inner life and doings'. But he suggested, to the evident satisfaction of his hearers, that there was no doubt that 'the Free Churches of England had helped very largely to render such a reign as Queen Victoria's possible'.[4]

In Lewes the continuing division between Anglicans and Nonconformists manifested itself most openly in the rivalry between their respective Sunday schools. Every year each school had its own individual outing on a Saturday in June or July. In 1900, the summer being fine, they seem to have been particularly well supported. On 20 June the Jireh scholars marched through the streets to the Dripping Pan, where they played games, consumed a large tea and afterwards walked to the top of the Mount: over 500 children were said to have been present. On the same day about 100 children from the Wesleyan Sunday school marched to the railway station, caught the train to Falmer and walked on to Stanmer Park, where tea was served by Mrs and Miss Hogsflesh and their helpers. On 4 July the Tabernacle children took the same route and 'about 200' sat down to tea, and on the 18th 'considerably over 200' from Eastgate enjoyed games and tea at the Dripping Pan. The outings came to a grand climax on 25 July when 400 scholars from the Ragged School marched up to their superintendent's grounds at Cuilfail, where they were joined by 100 more scholars. The total number present, including teachers and visitors, was reported to be 1000, who between them consumed 600lbs of cake, 750 buns and 105 gallons of lemonade. No Anglican Sunday school could compete with such statistics. That summer, when the scholars from All Saints' and St Thomas's went on their outings, it was reported that they had marched through the streets with a band at their head but, significantly, no indication was given of their numbers. Later, in the autumn, the Nonconformist ascendancy in the field of religious education was further demonstrated when Compton Rickett returned to lay the foundation-stone of the Tabernacle's new Sunday School down by the riverside, the largest building of its kind in Lewes and designed to accommodate 340.[5]

Although Nonconformists may have felt themselves to be in the ascendant there is no doubt that some Anglicans thought them socially inferior. Kathleen Vinall once described an incident from her childhood in Lewes before the World War 1. One Sunday morning when she was walking along the High Street with her father, a prominent Jireh member, they met a well-dressed woman walking in the opposite direction. He raised his hat and bade her good morning, but the woman passed by, ignoring him completely. When Kathleen asked, 'Papa, why was that lady so rude?', he replied: 'Well, my dear, she is Church and we are Chapel.' In the countryside, where chapel folk frequently came from a lower social class than churchpeople, the persistence of such attitudes is perhaps understandable but it is surprising to find them in Lewes. Hugh Vinall, a respected local solicitor and the son of Isaac Vinall, owner of the Cuilfail estate, was probably no less prosperous (or, for that matter, less cultured) than the woman who sought to snub him. At this time it was demonstrable by any yardstick that Lewes Nonconformists, such as the Kemps of Bedford House (now Rotten Row House) and the Crosskeys of Castlegate House, were firmly entrenched within the town's elite.[6]

Although individual prejudices persisted there is evidence that in the early years of the twentieth century relations between Church and Chapel as institutions were beginning to improve. For this much credit should go to Burgess Wilkinson, who was sometimes jokingly referred to as 'the Bishop of Nonconformity'. It was probably due largely to his statesmanship that Lewes escaped the troubles experienced in other towns following the 1902 Education Act which, because it failed to abolish Anglican day schools, displeased many Nonconformists. Wilkinson was the Free Church representative on the Lewes Education Committee set up in 1902 and for twenty years took a prominent part in its proceedings, serving as vice-chairman in 1912-13. In 1906 one of his Anglican colleagues on the committee, John Miles, then the town's mayor, clearly had him in mind when he voiced his appreciation of the services that his 'good friends', the Nonconformists, had rendered to the town. He praised 'the way in which they had joined with all the other bodies that took an interest in education with a view to doing their very best for the people'.[7]

In addition to the old Church-Chapel cleavage there were newer ones on each side of that divide. Within the Church of England the nineteenth century had seen the opening of a breach between the High and the Low, and in the next century it continued to widen. What has been referred to irreverently as 'London, Brighton and South Coast Religion' had reached Lewes at about the same time as the railway and, although it had only become firmly rooted at St Michael's, its impact on the town had been considerable. By the close of the Victorian period, while evangelicals had become less aggressively anti-Puseyite than they had been in Scobell's day, they had nevertheless remained on their guard. Scobell's successor at Southover, William Richardson, had supported the bonfire societies' stand against Catholicism both Roman and Anglican – as had David Lee Elliot, who succeeded him as rector in 1900. Elliot, who was the sole official representative of Lewes Anglicans at the unveiling of the martyrs' memorial in 1901, evidently made no secret of his sympathy with the Protestant Alliance's views about Romanism and ritualism. But the presence of apparently non-partisan clergy at St John sub Castro, St Anne's, All Saints' and St Thomas's meant that there was never any danger of the High-Low divide splitting the town asunder.

Orthodoxy *versus* Unorthodoxy

If the Anglicans were divided, so too were the Nonconformists, but in their case the division was threefold. Two groups of people remained outside the Free Church Council: one to the right and one to the left. On the right

stood the strict Calvinists at Jireh Chapel, who found any body of people
not subscribing to the 1643 Westminster Confession too liberal to be
associated with. On the left stood the congregation of Westgate Chapel
whom the evangelical Free Churches, in their turn, looked upon as being
theologically beyond the pale. While for people at Jireh not belonging to
the Council may have been a matter of some satisfaction, for those at
Westgate their exclusion was a cause of sadness and regret. They thought
of themselves less as Unitarians than as 'Free Christians', that is, Christians
who were free not only from the fetters of established religion but from
the 'bonds of creed and dogma'.

    Among the town's 'orthodox' Nonconformists, however, there were some
whose attitude towards the Unitarians – 'the awkward squad of Christendom'
– appears to have been at best ambivalent. One such was J. P. Morris
(younger brother of Arthur Morris, the anti-papal postmaster) who had a
distinguished ministry at Eastgate Baptist church from 1895 to 1920.
Preaching at his church anniversary in October 1900 he said that his
congregation, founded in 1784, was 'the oldest organised Nonconformist
church which had had a continued existence in the town'. Whatever made him
make such an extraordinary claim? The most likely explanation is that he
genuinely believed that the Westgate congregation, dating from 1662 and to
which his own ancestors had once belonged, had not had a 'continued existence'.
To his way of thinking it had ceased to be a proper 'Nonconformist church'
when it lapsed into Unitarianism at the beginning of the 19th century. But
although he disliked Westgate's theology he seems to have enjoyed good
relations with its people. In fact one Sunday evening in November 1900 he
devoted an entire sermon to a eulogy of John Every, the chairman of the
Westgate congregation, who had recently died. He commended his 'sturdy
active life and upright character' and his support for the cause of Temperance.
He also said that he had been 'a valued friend to the Baptist church'. Because
he had so appreciated what the Eastgate congregation had been doing on
behalf of the children in its locality Every had sold them a site for their
Sunday school at a nominal price and had contributed generously to the
cost of its building. Perhaps to allay the anxieties of anyone present who
might have been shocked to hear him heaping such praise on a heretic,
Morris concluded by speaking of 'the veneration and affection which Mr
Every always manifested for the person and work of Christ'.[8]

    One who was much more open in his acceptance of the Unitarians was
Burgess Wilkinson, whose theological stance was more liberal than that of
most Nonconformists. A Fellow of the Geological Society and a regular
reader of the avant garde *Hibbert Journal*, he had no fear that his faith
would be undermined by biblical criticism or the writings of Darwin or
Huxley. So it was that in October 1906, when the Unitarian Provincial
Assembly held its annual meeting in Lewes, Wilkinson accepted an

invitation to attend and, in the course of a long speech, explained why he and the Baptist, Presbyterian and Wesleyan ministers had decided to do so. There were, he said, four considerations. One was their respect for Westgate's chairman, Alderman John H. Every, 'a splendid representative of Unitarianism at its best', who had 'entered so fully and sympathetically and brightly into all that affected the welfare of the town'. Another was their affection for the chapel's minister, John Felstead, 'a high-minded, sweet-hearted, noble-spirited man'. A third was their recognition of 'the debt they owed to many brilliant preachers and writers of the Unitarian community', including L.P. Jacks, the founder-editor of the *Hibbert Journal*, who had conducted the service at Westgate that morning and whom Wilkinson had later sat next to at lunch. The final consideration was their respect for 'the truths and the principles which the Unitarian churches had stood for in many a stormy day in the history of religious opinion and service'. He concluded by saying that 'he trusted, as the years rolled by, they would not be afraid and not be ashamed to work together as harmoniously and unitedly as they could socially, educationally, morally and religiously'. Seven years later, speaking at the re-opening of Westgate Chapel after its refurbishment, Wilkinson returned to the same theme. As the *East Sussex News* reported:

> He was pleased to recognise the increasing unity amongst Free Church ministers in face of the many social and moral problems which were pressing for solution. This was not a time to accentuate those things whereon they differed; rather they should concentrate attention upon those things whereon they agreed. He rejoiced that there was a more brotherly feeling among the Free Churches of the town now than when he began his ministry in the town 25 years ago.[9]

The common enemy of Apathy

Wilkinson might have added that there was now more brotherly feeling among *all* the churches in the town, who were coming to realise that what united them was more important than what divided them. At a time when most churches were suffering from declining attendances Christians of differing persuasions felt a need to stand together against the common enemy of apathy. Among the parish churches numbers were spectacularly low at All Saints', where the small size of offertories was the main item on the agenda at the annual parochial church meeting in April 1914. In the course of an acrimonious discussion Cecil Morris, one of the churchwardens, said that Sunday attendances had declined so drastically that 'the whole congregation could be seated in the transept'. A former churchwarden Montague Blaker complained that 'people do not come to church as they used to' and put most of the blame for this on the rector,

Mackay Clarke, since whose arrival 'the congregations have drifted away'. In the end Morris, who said that the time had come to close the church, resigned as a churchwarden and, since no-one could be persuaded to take his place, the meeting was adjourned in confusion. Shortly afterwards the rector wrote an explanatory letter to his parishioners, which was published in full in the local press. He pointed out that since his arrival in 1901 the population of the parish had fallen from 1,801 to 1,528 because, as people had died or moved away, their houses had been turned into shops and offices. As a consequence All Saints' was now like a City parish, full by day and empty by night. He also said that on his coming to Lewes the congregation had included many people from St Anne's, who then had good reason to prefer another church to their own, but who (when that reason 'disappeared') went back to their own parish church. This was a veiled reference to the departure from St Anne's in 1902 of an evidently unpopular rector and his replacement by a more acceptable one, in whose time the congregation grew considerably: in 1914 Easter communicants at St Anne's, who in 1900 had numbered 199, had increased to 358.[10]

A further reason the rector put forward for the decline of All Saints' was the presence within (or close to) the parish of no fewer than eight Nonconformist places of worship. Besides Baptists, Congregationalists, Presbyterians, Wesleyans and Quakers, there were Plymouth Brethren, the 'Reformed Episcopal Church' and 'Gospel Temperance' – a reference to those then congregating in the former British Workmen's Institute in Little East Street. This explanation, however, was perhaps a little disingenuous, since these congregations drew their support not only from the vicinity of All Saints' but from all over the town. If Nonconformist advance was a factor in Anglican decline it was one that would have affected other parishes as well as All Saints'. Moreover, with the exception of the last three on the list (which were numerically insignificant), the Nonconformist congregations that Clarke specified had all been established long before his arrival at All Saints' and there is no evidence that they were currently expanding. In the Edwardian era even the Congregationalists at the Tabernacle do not seem to have been making progress. There were reports of dwindling attendances at weekday services and prayer meetings and, at the annual general meeting of the congregation in February 1910, several references were made to 'the need for united and increased endeavours on the part of the church and congregation for the deepening of spiritual life and the adequate maintenance of the funds'. Nor were things any better at Jireh, whose records show that the numbers joining the congregation were now consistently lower than those lost by death and removal.[11]

Why was this happening? Michael Watts has recently suggested that a major cause of falling church attendances in England from the 1880s onwards, particularly among Nonconformists, was the abandonment of 'hell-fire preaching'. If it was the fear of hell- fire that had filled the chapels in the first place it may have been the loss of such fear that was now emptying them. This could well have applied to the Calvinists at Jireh, Eastgate and elsewhere but it cannot explain declining attendances among the Unitarians, whose creed (it was sometimes said) had always been 'One God, No Hell and Twenty Shillings in the Pound'. At Westgate Chapel congregations were clearly dwindling in the 1890s and, although conscious efforts were made to attract more people to services, these were clearly unsuccessful. Eventually, in 1913, recognising the logic of the situation, the chapel was divided in two, one half being retained for worship and the other half being made into a lecture hall and vestibule. As a result there was now seating for only about 80 worshippers in a meeting-house that had once accommodated more than three times that number.[12]

After the 1914-18 war Lewes churches found themselves contending with an even sharper decline in attendances. Addressing a Tabernacle meeting in 1925 Charles Morrish, a deacon who had been a member there for 40 years, said that the 'decadence of public worship' was mainly due to 'the demoralising effects of the war'. He did not think that there had been a loss of faith: he questioned the view, currently in vogue, that people were abandoning public worship because the church was regarded as 'the repository of old and exploded methods and beliefs'. He put the blame on the social and economic consequences of the war. He suggested that the high wages paid to women munition workers had produced in many of them 'that desire for pleasure and extravagance which left them spiritually weaker, with little or no taste for spiritual matters or church attendance'. But there were in fact much more obvious reasons for the decline. In pre-war years people in Lewes, as in other English towns, had gone to church in their leisure hours because there was often nothing else to do. Strong institutional churches had offered a wide range of attractions. At the Tabernacle the Sunday school classes had provided instruction and entertainment for adults as well as children. In addition there had been a regular programme of activities organised by the Social and Literary Society, the Christian Endeavour Society or one or other of the organisations connected with the church. But by 1919 the situation had changed. Neither lantern lectures nor anything else available at the Tabernacle could compete with the films being shown at the cinema, as the church meeting recognised when in October that year it condemned the 'objectionable cinema posters displayed in the town and their baneful effect, particularly on boys and girls'. As with entertainment, so with adult education: no congregational adult school could offer the range of educational opportunities provided by such organisations as the WEA, founded in 1903. In almost every department of life secular institutions were beginning to occupy what had once been the special preserve of the churches.[13]

'The War that has not Ended'

It is also possible that people were being put off religion by the behaviour of some of its practitioners. At this period throughout England, as David Edwards has suggested, 'congregations were often not a very attractive advertisement for the gospel of love' – and this may have been especially true of Lewes. Now that there was no longer an external outlet for men's aggressive energies there was a resumption of the conflicts that in pre-war Lewes had been such a prominent feature of the religious scene. In October 1919 a meeting was held in the Town Hall under the auspices of the Protestant Reformation Society, to which Jireh Chapel was affiliated, on the subject of 'the war that has not ended'. The chairman, Hugh Vinall, said that England now had 'a subtle foe to contend with'; an 'atmosphere of idolatry' was spreading fast and Protestants had to be on their guard. The warnings were repeated a week or so later when a large congregation, including numerous ex-servicemen, gathered at Jireh on the Sunday before Bonfire Night to hear a visiting preacher declare that Rome was 'a paganised apostate system, the masterpiece of Satan'. A borough councillor, wearing his Orange Lodge sash, read the roll of the Sussex martyrs while the congregation stood in respectful silence. This year, however, the Guy Fawkes Night festivities, held for the first time since 1913, witnessed no burning of the Pope's effigy, since DORA (the Defence of the Realm Act) 'prohibited the religious element in the Lewes Bonfire celebrations'. The prohibition was still in force in 1920 when, addressing his congregation on the Sunday before Bonfire Night, B. Harvey-Jellie, the newly appointed Presbyterian minister, expressed the hope that 'the celebration had lost its religious significance'. 'It was quite time', he said, 'that this thing was relegated to oblivion and forgotten, as the anniversary was largely nothing but a reminder of the old jealousies, hostilities, bitterness and unrighteous antagonisms which once rent the great church of God.'[14]

Members of the Cliffe Bonfire Society disagreed strongly and in November 1921 they commemorated the repeal of the hated DORA in their tableau, burned Pope Paul V in effigy and arranged for their mock 'Bishop of Lewes' to deliver a virulently anti-Catholic speech. At the service held at Jireh on the previous Sunday Leonard Atherton, a former missionary with the Protestant Truth Society who had become minister there in 1921, forcefully attacked the enemies of Bonfire: 'Let them remember the martyr fires that burned in Lewes and in other places.' In June 1925, to commemorate the anniversary of the burnings, Atherton arranged a public meeting in the Town Hall. Harvey--Jellie, who appears to have swallowed some of his previous scruples, was on the platform but, as one speaker was at pains to point out, no Anglican clergy were present. 'I am disgusted with the Lewes clergy', he said. 'If they had been living at the time of the

Reformation I am afraid we should never have had a Reformation.' He thought it disgraceful that in a town like Lewes, 'where such splendid testimony was given in the past for the truth', none of the town's clergymen was on the platform.[15]

The issue of the *East Sussex News* that carried this report also published a strongly worded letter from Kenneth Rawlings, the recently instituted rector of St Michael's. Rawlings, whose churchmanship was so 'high' that some townspeople would soon be describing him as 'no better than a Roman Catholic', expressed horror at what he had heard at the Town Hall meeting, saying that 'this sort of Protestantism is incompatible with the religion of Christ'. Consequently Atherton challenged him to a public debate in the Town Hall, which duly took place on 21 July on the motion 'that the recent Protestant demonstration at Lewes was opposed to Christian charity and misrepresented the faith of Catholics'. At the end of a heated debate Rawlings, insisting that 'they were all agreed that Christ was the hope of the world', called for a 'truce' and the motion was not put to the meeting. But the debate did not end there. Four sermons by Rawlings on 'The Church of England: Protestant or Catholic?' were followed by a series of public lectures by Atherton on 'The Church of England, Catholic and Protestant'. On 5 November that year the Cliffe Bonfire Society's tableau represented a 'High Church' with the title of 'The Road to Rome'. No one was left in any doubt that the church so depicted was St Michael's. It was in response to such junketings that Alice Dudeney, a St Michael's parishioner who shared her rector's Anglo-Catholicism, was moved to pen a limerick:

There once was a parson called Rawlings
Whose church was the scene of sad brawlings
For the Protestants stated
That they were quite sated
With the Catholics' creepings and crawlings.

Strictly speaking of course it was now the street, and not (as it had been 300 years earlier) the church, that was the scene of the 'brawlings'.[16]

Through the later 1920s and on into the 1930s the Protestant-Catholic conflict continued to be a prominent feature of the religious life of Lewes. Although Atherton had left in 1927 to prepare for ordination in the Church of England, leaving the chapel without a pastor for six years, Jireh retained its strongly anti-Romanist stance. On 4 November 1928 the speaker at the chapel's annual thanksgiving service (attended by nearly 1000 people) was Major Richard Rigg, Grand Master of the Loyal Orange Institution of England and (as he proudly informed his hearers) President of the 'Imperial Grand Orange Council of the World'. His affirmation that 'in no place did the lamp of Protestantism burn more brightly than it did in Protestant Lewes in Protestant Sussex' was greeted by loud applause. Those who knew that in Elizabethan times the town had played an important part in the defence of the Sussex coast would doubtless also have appreciated his reference to the Spanish Armada as part of 'a plot to destroy the liberties of England'. A similar historical note was struck at another pre-Bonfire Night service six years later when Herbert Moore, the newly appointed pastor at Jireh, wearing the collar of the Orange Order, addressed another bumper congregation. He said that he was glad that Lewes people were not forgetting their Protestant history 'in days when great parts of England seemed to be drifting back almost to pre-Reformation days with regard to religion'.[17]

Peace and Disharmony

In the next decade, with the rise of Nazi Germany, the churches were united by their concern to rid the world of war. Here the lead was taken by Kenneth Rawlings, who had served in the army as a combatant officer from 1914 to 1918. He had come to believe that war was the greatest evil because 'it depends for its very existence upon the deliberate fostering of the vilest passions of which human nature is capable'. On Armistice Day 1934, addressing a congregation of between 800 and 900 assembled in the Town Hall, he said that 'our debt to the dead' was 'to resolve that there shall be no more precious lives sacrificed to the god of war' and in conclusion made this passionate personal affirmation:

> I declare that as long as I live I will hate and denounce and oppose war. . . . And I pledge myself to do all I can to root out of my own heart and out of the hearts of others all those evil passions that lead to war – national pride and jealousy and false patriotism. And I most solemnly declare that if war comes again in my time I will have neither part nor lot in it. I will denounce it and oppose it until my mouth is stopped, so help me God!

He then invited all those present who felt they could make the same pledge to rise in their seats. 'The response', according to the report in the *Sussex Express*, 'was instantaneous. With one or two exceptions the assembled hundreds rose in their places.'[18]

Later that month, when the Lewes branch of the League of Nations Association held a public debate about war at the Corn Exchange, between 400 and 500 people attended. John Newton Holder, who had recently become minister at the Tabernacle and who described himself as a pacifist, proposed the motion that 'the League of Nations must be prepared, if necessary, to employ military measures' and Rawlings opposed it. The main speaker from the floor was the rector of St Anne's, Charles Ensell, who before coming to Lewes in 1923 had served for over 20 years as an army chaplain. He had been present at the Armistice Day service in the Town Hall and had been appalled by what Rawlings had said. He now took the opportunity to protest against 'the asphyxiating gas poured upon my head on Sunday last week by my friend Mr Rawlings'. At this point he was interrupted by a voice from the audience asking, 'Are you a minister of religion?' 'Yes', he replied. 'I am a minister of religion. I believe Christianity cannot accept evil: it exists to fight against evil of every sort.' Another speaker, who said he was a friend of Ensell and had a great deal of respect for him, commented: 'I have never heard a more un-Christian speech in my life.' At the end of the evening an overwhelming majority followed Rawlings in voting against the motion, but a minority evidently thought he had gone off his head. After the meeting he was amused to overhear one member of the audience say to another, 'What do you think of that man Rawlings?'; to which came the answer, 'I think he ought to be put in a lunatic asylum.' But Rawlings was undeterred and a few weeks later called a meeting in St Michael's church hall to consider the formation of a Christian Pacifist Fellowship. About 250 people attended the meeting, which was presided over by the mayor of Lewes, J. C. Kenward, a prominent Tabernacle member who was in sympathy with the rector's views. At the conclusion Rawlings proposed the formation of a Lewes branch of the Fellowship of Reconciliation and was seconded by Holder who, having renounced the position he had adopted in the Corn Exchange debate, said that he had a duty to a 'Higher Power than the King of England'. The motion was put to the meeting and carried, with only seven voting against.[19]

The Quest for Catholicity

Most things that Rawlings did were controversial. Some even disapproved of his plans, comparable to those of another turbulent Anglo-Catholic priest, Conrad Noel of Thaxted, to bring back drama into the life of the church and the community. From 1932 onwards he produced Passion plays at Easter and Nativity plays at Christmas, staged in the church hall in Watergate Lane. Originally the players were drawn almost exclusively from the St Michael's congregation but in due course, as secular drama was added to the programme, the performers came from a wider constituency. In 1937 the drama group, now known as the Lewes Players and in need of better accommodation acquired the former Providence Chapel in Lancaster Street. In 1939 the move to this 'little theatre' was finally accomplished and the Lewes Theatre Club was born. To those who disapproved of his theatricals Rawlings responded: 'Can we not see all the fruits of human genius – great art, great poetry, great music and great drama are as truly inspired by the Holy Spirit of God as the writings of the prophets?' Although the outbreak of World War 2 severely curtailed its activities the club managed to stage 'St Simeon Stylites' in 1940 and a few other plays thereafter; but apart from 'Everyman' all Rawlings's productions were secular. In the end nothing came of his dream of restoring sacred drama to the place it had occupied in the Middle Ages.[20]

Rawlings's desire to restore to the church what it had lost at the Reformation was reflected in other ways. In 1928 he revived the Confraternity of the Blessed Sacrament at St Michael's and, wishing to emphasise the importance of the sacrament of penance, pronounced that the number of confessions rather then the number of communicants was the true indicator of 'the spiritual tone of the life of the parish'. But if the parishioners of St Michael's accepted their rector's innovations without demur it was a different story up at St Anne's. In May 1928 it was reported that 'upwards of 100 parishioners' were opposed to Ensell's plan to introduce choral communion on the first Sunday of the month as part of the normal morning service. Their main objection was that this would deter those who had made their communion earlier in the day from attending mattins. But the rector declined to be 'dictated to' by the laity and, adopting language more redolent of the Navy than of his beloved Army, declared: 'There can only be one captain of a ship and I must be captain in these matters.'[21]

Rather surprisingly there was a similar clash of opinions at Westgate Chapel, where J.M. Connell was then introducing liturgical changes. In 1926 he replaced *Common Prayer for Christian Worship*, which had long been in use, by a new book of his own compilation, *Common Prayer in Nine Services*, which included not only prayers already known to the congregation but others drawn from 'a wide variety of sources of Christian devotion'. But although the book aroused 'a variety of criticisms' from the congregation and two prominent members resigned, Connell was undeterred. He believed that he was maintaining what he termed Westgate's 'fine traditions of a free and Catholic Christianity'. Like the seventeenth-century English Presbyterians he was strongly unsectarian in outlook, disapproving of 'gathered churches of the elect' and seeing himself as a parish minister, serving a church commensurate with the community. His ideal was a kind of Anglicanism without creeds. After the alterations made to the building in 1913, which were largely inspired by Connell, the ethos of Westgate was distinctly Anglican: facing east and fitted with choir stalls, off-centre pulpit and raised communion table, it had a close resemblance to an Oxford or Cambridge college chapel. And after 1922, when John H. Every, encouraged by his minister, had installed a stained glass east window depicting Christ as the Good Shepherd of the sheep (designed by Clayton & Bell of Cambridge) the transformation was complete. Like his mentor James Martineau, whose portrait hung in his vestry, Connell believed that a theological term should never be used as an ecclesiastical label and even banned the word 'Unitarian' from the chapel notice-board. To his mind the only acceptable designation was 'Free Christian'. His catholicity made it possible for liberal Anglicans like Sir George and Lady Boughey of Malling

House to become regular members of the congregation. Connell was thoroughly ecumenical in outlook, enjoying excellent relations with clergy and ministers of all denominations. He was closest of all to Wilkinson, but was also on good terms with Morris, who left Eastgate in 1920 but returned to Lewes in 1928 to share with him in the conduct of Wilkinson's funeral. Seven years later Connell helped to organise the first week-long ecumenical Mission to Lewes, himself conducting its concluding service at Westgate, when (as the *East Sussex News* reported) the chapel 'was filled to overflowing with one of the most representative gatherings within its walls since its opening in 1700'.[22]

That Anglican and Nonconformist congregations were prepared to co-operate in the Mission to Lewes is a clear indication of the presence of an ecumenical spirit in the town. In 1934 the Presbyterian Harvey-Jellie had noted approvingly that, although 'there were more churches in Lewes than there were in some towns of similar size', they were not 'warring or competing with one another'. Much of the credit for this was due to Wilkinson and later to Rawlings who, soon after his arrival at St Michael's, inaugurated Good Friday processions through the town, at first just for Anglicans and after 1928 for all the churches. Another ecumenically minded Anglican was Evan Griffiths, who from 1932 was rector of All Saints' and St Thomas's (and from 1930 rural dean of Lewes). He was even prepared to attend services in Nonconformist chapels – probably something that no rural dean had ever done before. In 1933, when Holder was inducted at the Tabernacle, Griffiths spoke at the welcome meeting. He said that, walking into the hall with 'my friend Mr Connell', he had immediately felt himself to be 'among friends'; and he spoke affectionately of Wilkinson, 'one of the first people to extend the right hand of fellowship to him' on his arrival in Lewes 25 years before.[23]

This decrease in confessional strife, a cynic might argue, was a sign that the churches had become too weak to indulge in it. By this time nearly all the town's congregations were in decline. Indeed the only church in Lewes that seems to have been going from strength to strength was the Roman Catholic church of St Pancras. Its congregation had been greatly increased by the efforts of William McAuliffe, whose 35-year ministry ended with his death at the age of 86 in 1924. This venerable priest, who 70 years after his death was described by one of his former altar boys as 'a living saint', was greatly respected and loved not only at St Pancras but throughout Lewes. Wilkinson, who sat with him for many years on the local education committee, called him 'the gentlest of all gentlemen'. The stories of McAuliffe's kindness and generosity are legion. On one occasion he gave away his shoes to a beggar and walked back to his presbytery barefoot. On another, when a Bonfire Boy was injured by a firework, he headed the list of those subscribing to his relief. On the day of his funeral the whole

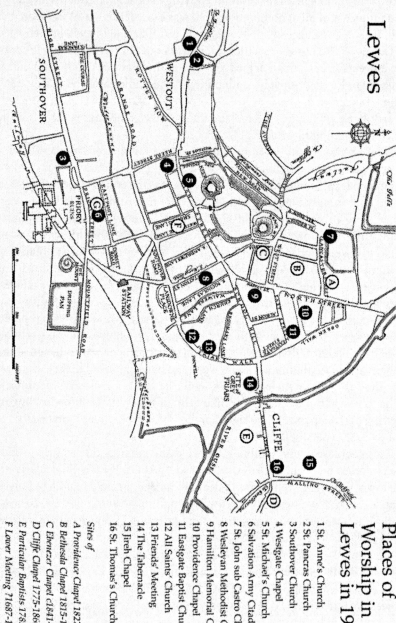

Lewes

Places of Worship in Lewes in 1935

1 St. Anne's Church
2 St. Pancras Church
3 Southover Church
4 Westgate Chapel
5 St. Michael's Church
6 Salvation Army Citadel
7 St. John sub Castro Church
8 Wesleyan Methodist Church
9 Hamilton Memorial Church
10 Providence Chapel
11 Eastgate Baptist Church
12 All Saints' Church
13 Friends' Meeting
14 The Tabernacle
15 Jireh Chapel
16 St. Thomas's Church

Sites of

A Providence Chapel 1827-1919
B Bethesda Chapel 1815-1929
C Ebenezer Chapel c1841-1877
D Cliffe Chapel 1775-1860
E Particular Baptists 1785-1819
F Lower Meeting 1687-1759
G General Baptists 1741-1825

borough council walked in procession behind his hearse and the blinds of many shops were drawn. Even the fervently anti-Catholic Atherton, speaking at a meeting to commemorate the Lewes martyrs in the Town Hall, paid tribute to him – while at the same time pointing out that, since Rome was still persecuting Protestants, 'they must not allow sentiment to rule them in this great matter'.[24]

The Second World War and its Aftermath

The mood in Lewes at the outbreak of war in 1939 was very different from that which had prevailed in 1914. Then the great mass of churchgoers had been united in their patriotic stand; but now opinions were divided, even within the established Church. At St Michael's, Rawlings continued to proclaim that war was the greatest evil in the world, saying that he 'intended to go on teaching the absolute necessity for Christ's love of charity in war-time as at other times'. He kept the church open day and night for those wishing to pray for an end to war and held a special mass for peace every Friday. Meanwhile up at St Anne's his old adversary Ensell was saying that he 'believed from the bottom of his heart that it was God's war' and that England was fighting 'on the side of right against the forces of evil'. His views were evidently shared by Griffiths at All Saints' and St Thomas's. In March 1941 the rector, who had six sons serving in the forces, was the preacher at a civic service at All Saints' to mark a National Day of Prayer. Taking his text from a prayer of Sir Francis Drake he compared the Battle of Britain to the defeat of the Spanish Armada. His words echoed those of Austin Atkins, minister of Providence Chapel (now Strict Baptist and occupying the former Temperance Hall in Little East Street), who had recently given a series of talks on 'God and the War'. In 1940, as in 1588, he declared, 'God was on the side of right' and in both instances Englishmen 'could see the divine hand in the preservation of their nation'.[25]

Such a stance, however, became less appropriate as the war progressed and England, no longer on the defensive, went over to the attack. In 1944 when his diocesan bishop, George Bell, protested in the House of Lords about the mass bombing of Germany, Rawlings sent him a 'petition' in support, calling the RAF's action 'cruel and barbarous'. This so angered one Conservative MP that he asked the Home Secretary to order the controversial priest to be interned as a traitor to his country under Regulation 18B. Rawlings's stand also upset some people in Lewes. An anonymous resident wrote to the *Sussex Express* to say that 'clergy should stick to their pulpits and leave politics to those who are best fitted to deal with them'. The writer of the letter may have been Alice Dudeney, who approved of her rector's churchmanship but disliked both his pacifism and his passion for drama. Her diary for 1944 records her disgust at a sermon in which

Rawlings had 'raved and ranted about the evil of bombing Germany'. 'He cares nothing for St Michael's', she wrote, 'nor for the views of his congregation. He has emptied the church, he never visits, he cares for nothing but play acting and (but we mustn't be malicious!) *I've no use for him* – except in the Sacraments of the Church when he becomes impersonal.'[26]

After peace was concluded in 1945 Rawlings continued to warn people about the dangers of war which, following the invention of the hydrogen bomb, had become potentially more destructive then ever. If war were to break out again, he told his annual parochial church meeting in 1950, 'it would certainly mean the end of our own nation, if not of the world'. In the face of such a situation, he contended, there was only one thing that Christians had to do: to practise the teachings of Christ. He recognised, as he had done in pre-war years, that preaching about the Kingdom of God would make him unpopular. But he said that he had never sought to be a 'popular preacher', for this would mean telling people what they wanted rather than what they ought to hear. In 1965, at the age of 80 and after 40 years in the parish, Rawlings finally retired from the fray and was succeeded by Ambrose Reeves. As was to be expected, the former bishop of Johannesburg and president of the Anti-Apartheid Movement maintained much of his predecessor's reputation for political radicalism. Reeves emphasised the importance of 'making full use of the strategic position of St Michael's church in the service of the community' and arranged for the showing of lunch-hour films dealing with contemporary problems. He said that the congregation should be more concerned about national and international issues. He had no doubts about the answer to the question that Rawlings had continually put to his congregation. Was it Christ's purpose 'to save individual souls one by one' or 'to save the world and to establish his kingdom on earth'.[27]

After the war numbers attending St Michael's seem to have remained fairly stable because it was very much 'a gathered church', drawing in Anglo-Catholics from all over the town and also from places further afield. But at another town centre church, All Saints', where many had been leaving the parish to settle in the suburbs, the situation was much more serious. Numbers on the electoral roll shrank from 104 in 1946 to 63 in 1966, when consideration was given to a proposal that the building should be divided in two, with the congregation worshipping in the chancel and the nave being occupied by a 'House of Friendship'. But after that plan had fallen through and the electoral roll revised to include 'only members of the parish or regular attenders at church' (who numbered 15) it was eventually decided in 1972 to declare the building redundant and merge the parish with St Thomas's. This church, although older than All Saints', was smaller and less costly to maintain and its parish had not suffered as

much from depopulation. It continued to play an important role in the life
of the community in Cliffe and in due course, in a notable ecumenical
gesture, agreed to share the use of its premises with a Russian Orthodox
congregation.[28]

On the outskirts of the town the outlook for Anglican churches was
generally brighter. Although St John sub Castro derived little benefit from
the creation of a new council estate down by the marshes of Landport, the
building of new owner-occupied houses on the sunny slopes of the Downs
brought a great accession of strength to St Anne's. Between 1952 and 1955
numbers on the electoral roll rose from 208 to 286. Similar progress was
to be reported at Southover, where in the period 1964-1970 numbers rose
from 211 to 300. In this parish, where there was little new housing, success
seems to have been largely due to the efforts of Arthur Hurd, who in 1963
had come to Sussex from East Africa with a great sense of mission. On his
retirement in 1976 what was described as 'the decided evangelical tradition
of the parish' was well and truly maintained with the appointment of Peter
Markby who, like his seventeenth century predecessors Alexander Reason
and Edward Newton, was an alumnus of that renowned 'puritan seminary',
Emmanuel College, Cambridge. Another parish with a decided evangelical
tradition was South Malling, where the living was in the gift of the Martyrs'
Memorial Trust. Only brought within the borough boundaries at the
beginning of the century, the parish remained predominantly rural until the
coming of new housing estates in the 1950s and 1960s, when the population
expanded rapidly. Responding to the challenge, the congregation turned
their church into a dual-purpose building and so put themselves in a position
to play a fuller part in the life of the local community.[29]

How were the Lewes Nonconformist congregations faring at this time
of rapid social and demographic change? Two of them remained in their
old 'down town' locations and by all accounts continued to flourish. The
Quakers, who drew their members and attenders from a wide area, may in
fact have benefited from the greater mobility afforded by the car – which
had become the only means of travel in most of Sussex on a Sunday.
Increasing numbers and expanding activities necessitated the enlargement
of their Friars' Walk meeting-house in 1978. And there was a similar success
story along the road in Eastgate Street, where in the 1960s so many children
were attending the Baptist church that the congregation was obliged to build
a new Sunday school room. Another thriving evangelical cause, which began
as an offshoot of the Baptist church in nearby Barcombe, was 'King's
Church'. From 1985 onwards the congregation, affiliated to a family of
charismatic churches known as 'New Frontiers International', held Sunday
services in the assembly hall of the Priory Comprehensive School. Not
having an expensive building to maintain, the members were able to devote
their energy to other things. In conjunction with other evangelical

congregations in the town they helped to organise a highly successful series of 'Alpha' courses, which aimed to bring the good news of the Gospel to those outside the churches.

Elsewhere in Lewes, however, the picture was not so rosy. Several old-established Nonconformist congregations were in decline, one or two of them terminally. On the instructions of the regional presbytery the Presbyterian Church in Market Street had been closed abruptly 'in consequence of decreased membership and financial difficulties' on the day war began, 3 September 1939. In due course its premises were turned – appropriately enough in view of its Scottish origins – into a kilt factory. Providence Chapel in Little East Street shut its doors for the last time in 1968, when its premises were converted into flats. Two years later the Salvation Army finally abandoned the citadel in St John Street which it had occupied since its removal from the Eastport Lane meeting-house in 1939. Jireh Chapel, with enough seats for 850 but only a handful to sit on them, had fallen into such a bad state of repair that in 1985 the congregation had to abandon it and meet in temporary accommodation elsewhere in the town. But since the building was listed Grade I its trustees were able to repair it with the help of a maximum grant from English Heritage. After its restoration the original box-pews, the deacons' grand pew, the clerk's desk and the 'wine glass' pulpit were put back in good order, and the magnificent structure was re-opened for worship in 1996. Two years later, after linking up with Ian Paisley's Free Presbyterians, a cause that had appeared to be dying was revived by a last-minute transfusion of blood from across the Irish Sea.[30]

The difficulty of maintaining over-large premises also pre-occupied the congregation of the Tabernacle down at the bottom of the High Street. In 1946, having re-opened the negotiations for the sale of their building that had been interrupted by the war, they planned to 'rebuild in the part of the town where there is greater need'. These proposals were strenuously resisted by a small group within the congregation who urged that 'the need for a Congregational church in its present form was no longer there, since there were other Nonconformist and evangelical Anglican churches available'. But the majority opposed this suggestion and, noting 'the need for more members if our church is to survive', continued to search for another building in a better location. Eventually in September 1954 they abandoned their historic porticoed Tabernacle – soon, to the consternation of many, to be pulled down – and moved to smaller, newly-built premises in a suburban setting in Prince Edward's Road. Here, with much the same catchment area as St Anne's, attendances soon increased. In 1972 the congregation became part of the newly-established United Reformed Church, leading them to embrace some of the Scottish Presbyterian traditions not represented in Lewes since the closure of the Hamilton

Memorial Church in Market Street.[31]

The Congregationalists' move to Prince Edward's Road was noted with interest (and probably some envy) by the Methodists, who also had a town centre church that was too large and too expensive for them to maintain. In 1954, observing that 'the population is gradually moving to the outskirts of the town and people do not come into the centre of the town for purposes of worship', they too would have liked to move out. However, the Congregationalists' relocation seems to have pre-empted this and so they decided to stay on in Station Street. Eventually the decision was made to sell and in 1970 they were offered hospitality at Westgate Chapel. Sharing a building with Unitarians was clearly not thought to be an ideal solution but, having been assured that there was 'no question of compromise over doctrine', the offer was accepted. The Methodists continued to worship at Westgate for fifteen years and, in spite of the doctrinal dangers, were occasionally permitted to hold joint services with the residents. One of the most memorable of these took place in March 1983, when the two congregations came together to commemorate the 250th anniversary of the death of George Herbert, whose hymns they both cherished. At the deepest level, which perhaps only great poetry could plumb, there was no division between them. By this time, however, the Methodists were running out of steam and in 1985 the congregation was dispersed, the circuit directing that the remaining members should join the United Reformed Church. The coming together of these two important strands of Lewes Nonconformity was formally recognised in June 1999 when a joint URC-Methodist congregation came into being under the umbrella name of 'Christ Church'.[32]

After the departure of the Methodists the tiny congregation of Westgate Chapel, without anyone to share the cost of maintaining their great pile of a building, faced an uncertain future. But soon help was at hand from an unexpected quarter. For some time moves had been afoot among peace movements, environmental groups and others in the town to set up a 'One World Centre', where people might come together to work for justice, peace, international understanding and responsible stewardship of the Earth. Now it was suggested that Westgate, with its central location and underused accommodation, might be just the place in which to house it. Although not everyone in the congregation was delighted with the idea – especially since there was at first no question of any rent being paid for the hire of the old 'lecture hall' – the suggestion was eventually accepted and in the summer of 1987 the Westgate One World Centre was opened. The first affiliated groups included the local branches of the World Disarmament Campaign, Oxfam, Amnesty International and Friends of the Earth – and the Lewes Peace Library, which had formerly been housed in rather cramped quarters at the Friends' Meeting House. From these groups and from other local sympathisers were drawn the volunteers who staffed the One World Shop, open on three mornings a week for the sale of fairly traded goods marketed by Traidcraft and Oxfam. Although many were Anglicans, Roman Catholics or Nonconformists of one sort or another a high proportion of the helpers were (and have continued to be) people without any connection with institutional religion. Their spirituality, it seems, finds a secular expression – in their commitment to justice, peace and the care of the environment. Where once those hoping for a 'better world' looked to the churches they now look to charitable organisations and protest groups. In fact it could be said that much of the spiritual energy that once animated religious bodies is now flowing through other, broader and less restricted channels.[33]

No more 'No Popery'?

While the fortunes of Anglicans and Nonconformists waxed and waned those of the town's Roman Catholics took an upward turn when in 1957 Leonard O'Donnell took over as parish priest of St Pancras. In his time the numbers on the church roll increased so rapidly that two assistant priests had to be appointed to serve the parish. He cultivated good relations with other churches in the town: he was particularly friendly with Rawlings at St Michael's and also, less predictably, with Basil Viney, minister at Westgate Chapel from 1958 to 1965, who shared his passion for Beethoven. O'Donnell died in harness in 1972 at the early age of 67, deeply mourned by all who knew him. The memory of this 'kind and gentle pastor', whose 'calm and quiet sincerity shone through to the end', is perpetuated by the Canon O'Donnell Centre, established in the former St Anne's church hall.[34]

The year of O'Donnell's arrival saw the inauguration of Lewes & District Council of Churches (later renamed Churches Together in Lewes & District), embracing almost all the congregations in the town and the surrounding villages. The first chairmen were drawn from the Anglican, Baptist, Congregationalist and Methodist churches, since Roman Catholics, Quakers and Unitarians, not being members of the World Council of Churches, officially attended only as 'observers'. In practice, however, their 'second class' status made little difference. When it came to practical Christianity all the local churches worked well together, whatever their doctrinal disagreements. When Christian Aid Week was inaugurated in1960 they divided up the town between them and co-operated closely in the street collections ably superintended that year, and for over 30 years thereafter, by Pamela Hollins of St Anne's. In 1972, at the instigation of a Westgate Chapel member Mildred Geering, the Council organised the first of the Christmas Day parties for lonely old people that have since continued to be an important event in its calendar. There were, however, serious divisions within the Council. Not everyone welcomed the presence of Roman

Catholics. In October 1975, soon after Denis Hayes (O'Donnell's successor at St Pancras) had been nominated as chairman of the Council, the new Eastgate minister, David Tucker, wrote to say that his congregation no longer wished to belong to it. But any anti-Catholic feelings there may have been among the Baptists were almost certainly confined to the men. The St Pancras women's league continued to enjoy the best of relations with their opposite numbers at Eastgate who, moreover, were largely instrumental in establishing the ecumenical Women's World Day of Prayer services in Lewes.[35]

Anti-papalism in the town was now an almost exclusively masculine phenomenon, limited to a few worshippers at Eastgate and Jireh and a handful of militant Cliffe Bonfire Society supporters. In November 1945, when the annual Guy Fawkes Night celebrations were revived after a seven year gap, members of the Cliffe society once more paraded with their 'No Popery' banners and proceeded to burn Pope Paul V in effigy. Their leading member, attired as the 'Archbishop of Cliffe', made an anti-Romanist oration in which he 'condemned the attitude of the Vatican during the war and gave examples of what Protestantism had done for the country'. But there was nothing to parallel the great resurgence of anti-Catholic feelings that had followed the conclusion of World War 1. From now onwards it was only when someone publicly condemned the continuing practice of pope-burning that there were any expressions of anti-papal feeling. In 1980 there were strong protests when Denis Hayes wrote to the *Evening Argus* criticising the Cliffe Bonfire Society. 'The fact that they still keep alive those anti-Catholic sentiments, even if they are not meant seriously,' he said, 'is both offensive and shocking to many people'. In 1981 the priest himself was burned in effigy as an 'enemy of bonfire'.[36]

1981 was the year when Ian Paisley, the militantly Protestant MP from Ulster, came to Lewes on Bonfire Night and tried to fan the flames of conflict by distributing anti-Catholic leaflets in the town. But his intervention backfired badly, for in the following year he himself was burned in effigy. This, like the subsequent burning of a large, life-like representation of Margaret Thatcher, suggests that by this time the Cliffe Bonfire Society was motivated not so much by anti-Catholicism as by a wish to ridicule pompous public figures. Nevertheless its 'No Popery' banners naturally continued to give offence to Catholics and the LDCC was constantly trying to get the local authority to remove the huge one suspended above Cliffe High Street which, they said, 'besmirched the reputation of Lewes'. The besmirching, however, continued unabated and in 1984 it was decided to tackle the problem at the highest level. On 12 October that year Sussex church leaders were invited to Lewes to consider the question of Catholic-Protestant relations. Those present included Eric Kemp (bishop of Chichester), Peter Ball (bishop of Lewes), Cormac

Murphy-O'Connor (Roman Catholic bishop of Arundel and Brighton) and their opposite numbers in the Baptist, Methodist and United Reformed churches. After the formal meeting the church leaders and a few others who had joined them walked up to the Martyrs' Memorial and, standing in a circle in front of it, prayed for peace and reconciliation. Taking place only hours after the IRA's attempt to blow up the Grand Hotel in Brighton, it was a historic gesture, but it was not appreciated by the owners of the memorial garden, a body of trustees associated with Jireh Chapel, who threatened to sue the intruders for trespass. The survival of archaic anti-Catholic feelings, confined though they were to a few fundamentalists, eventually persuaded the LDCC to make religious toleration the theme of the BBC 'Songs of Praise' TV programme produced in Lewes and put out, with a great fanfare of fireworks, on 5 November 1989.[37]

Seven years later there was a slight resurgence of confessional strife in Lewes when the annual pre-Bonfire services, which had been discontinued from 1984 because Jireh had fallen into disrepair, were revived after the chapel's re-opening. In 1996, on the Sunday before 5 November, nearly 150 bonfire supporters attended a thanksgiving service at which the visiting preacher was a man from Brighton, wearing the distinctive sash of the Orange Order. He claimed that, although not wanting to stir up anti-Catholic feelings, he felt obliged to warn that 'ecumenicalism would lead to one unified church with the Pope as leader'. The subsequent Guy Fawkes night celebrations saw the usual anti-papal rituals, which led Eric Flood, the newly appointed parish priest of St Pancras, to say that the burning of crosses and effigies reminded him of the Nazi practices of the 1930s. 'The ethos', he said, 'was not good and certainly not pleasurable; it felt very far from any spirit of love or universal brotherhood.' The absence of such a spirit was also commented upon by some who attended the special service held at Jireh in April 1998 to mark the congregation's decision to affiliate to the Free Presbyterian Church of Northern Ireland and to induct an Ulsterman as minister. About 800 people, many of whom had come over from Ulster for the occasion, attended and the special preacher was the church's moderator Ian Paisley. He treated his hearers to a tirade against Romanists, ecumenists, modernists, charismatics and anyone else who departed from the letter of the King James Bible or the strictly Calvinistic doctrine of the Thirty Nine Articles. In the middle of the sermon a man was evicted by the police for shouting out: 'Why are you so full of hate? What do you believe?' He was probably expressing the feelings of many of the Lewes people present.[38]

In the following year, as Christians were preparing to celebrate the 2000th anniversary of the birth of their founder, positive measures were taken to ease the old Catholic-Protestant tension. Although, at the pre-Bonfire service at Jireh on 31 October, the old prayers of thanksgiving for deliverance from 'Popish tyranny' were repeated, the language of Kyle

Paisley's sermon was less inflammatory than that of his father. For the first time ever the parish priest of St Pancras was in the congregation. He too stood in prayerful silence while the names of the seventeen Protestant martyrs were read out and, in a notable gesture of reconciliation, took the printed list away with him so that he could include the names in his prayers at mass on All Souls' Day. Also present that afternoon was a group of local people who, concerned about the perpetuation of anti-Catholic sentiments, had long been preparing a 'celebration of religious tolerance and unity-in-diversity' for the afternoon of 5 November. Calling themselves 'Humanity United' they proposed to lead a procession round Lewes, 'encircling the town with love, joy and peace'. But the 'march for peace', prominently featured as such in the local press, met with objections from opposite ends of the ecclesiastical spectrum. Jireh members saw it as a betrayal of the memory of the Lewes martyrs. Less predictably some Roman Catholics protested that they found nothing offensive in burning the effigy of a dead pope or displaying 'No Popery' banners: in their view there was no longer any religious bigotry in Lewes. But the truth of this was quickly belied by a letter from Noel Shields, the pastor of Jireh Chapel, who declared that the Bonfire Night celebrations served as a reminder that the Pope is 'an anti-Christ, a man of sin, a deceiver of the souls of many people'.[39]

As it transpired, Guy Fawkes Day 1999 was excessively wet and windy, but 22 people braved the elements to gather under a great oak in the Priory grounds. At 3 pm there was a flash of lightning and a single clap of thunder and the procession, preceded by a rainbow banner proclaiming 'We are One', moved off to circumnavigate the town in a clockwise direction, eventually returning (drenched to the skin) to the Priory ruins. The party included one Roman Catholic and two members of the Lewes Baha'i community but, although all the churches in the town had been invited to participate, the majority of the marchers had no formal religious affiliation. Some in fact affirmed that the spectacle of Christians in conflict, in the present and in the past, had put them off institutional religion for ever.

In October 2000 the rains fell even more persistently and the people of Lewes experienced a great natural disaster, the news of which made headlines in the national press and on television throughout the world. The Ouse overflowed its banks, causing hundreds to be evacuated from their homes and many millions of pounds' worth of damage to property. The event led one native of the town, now prudently non-resident, to proclaim that the floods had been sent by God as a punishment for sin. His proclamation, carried under banner headlines on the front page of the *Sussex Express* and featured on bill-boards throughout the town, caused one of the biggest postbags of protest in the paper's history. People were angry not only with the maker of the pronouncement but with the paper for deciding to publish it. Few took up the theological issues, but one writer was led to ask: 'If the recent floods were sent to punish the sinners of Lewes, how come the Jireh Chapel was flooded?' The question was clearly rhetorical and probably jocular, but James North, Jireh's former pastor, took it seriously. God, he replied reassuringly, 'sendeth rain on the just and the unjust'.[40]

To some it may have seemed that there was an element of divine judgment in the flood, which occurred just in time to frustrate preparations for the biggest event in Jireh Chapel's year – the annual anti-Catholic service held on the Sunday before Bonfire Night. This year, because the Fifth fell on a Sunday, Guy Fawkes Night was put back to Saturday and the actual day was marked instead by a very different kind of event. On the Sunday afternoon the congregation of Westgate Chapel celebrated the anniversary of the opening of the building for public worship exactly 300 years earlier – on 5 November 1700. It was an ecumenical occasion, attended by civic dignitaries, the local MP, the rector of St Michael's and representatives of other churches in the town. Charles Goring, an Anglican clergyman descended from three ministers ejected in 1662 and a distant kinsman of James Martineau, conducted the service. There were three lessons. Eric Flood, parish priest of St Pancras, read from the Epistle to the Ephesians (Jerusalem Bible), with its ringing exhortation to Christians to 'preserve the unity of the Spirit by the peace that binds you together'. Maurice Burge, a member of Lewes Friends' meeting, read a passage from the writings of William Penn urging all to worship the one Universal Father 'in spirit and in truth'. Hilary Bowes, a Methodist who had stayed on at Westgate after the 1985 exodus and had eventually become lay leader of the congregation, read from a sermon of John Wesley's that Connell had included in his extra-biblical lectionary:

> Although a difference in opinion or modes of worship may prevent
> an entire external union, need it prevent our union in affection?
> Though we cannot think alike, may we not love alike? Without all
> doubt we may. Herein all the children of God may unite,
> notwithstanding these smaller differences. . . . My only question
> at present is, Is thine heart right as my heart is with thy heart? If it
> be, give me thine hand.

The readings set the tone for the address that followed on 'the healing of ancient divisions'. In fact the whole event sent out a clear signal that the old animosities that once divided Lewes –- Anglicans from Dissenters, Protestants from Catholics, 'orthodox' from 'unorthodox' – were now dead and buried. It was fitting that at the close of the service everyone should rise to sing Frederick Lucian Hosmer's great anniversary hymn, whose last verse begins, 'Burn, holy fire and shine more wide!'[41]

Conclusion

The religious history of Lewes is, in many respects, far from being unique. Countless other towns also felt the full impact of the Reformation and of subsequent attempts to extend or counter its influence. In later years they too experienced the ebbs and flows of spiritual energy, with periods of change and upheaval being succeeded by epochs of calm, sometimes even stagnation. They also witnessed outbreaks of the sectarian strife to which the self-confessed disciples of the Prince of Peace have always been so prone. And at the end of the twentieth century churchpeople in every town in England, as in Lewes, have sought to atone for their former divisiveness by promoting interdenominational co-operation. In Holy Week 2000, when Lewes congregations came together to perform a grand succession of Passion plays to mark the Millennium, they gave dramatic expression to a commitment to ecumenism that has now almost everywhere become the norm.

Yet although the religious history of Lewes is in some ways similar to that of other towns it does have a number of distinctive features. For one thing the town experienced a burgeoning of Nonconformity that was probably without equal in south-eastern England. Was there anywhere in this region to compare with Lewes where, if the census figures are to be believed, nearly half the population attended a Nonconformist place of worship in 1851? There are a number of possible explanations for this notable Nonconformist ascendancy. There is the town's geographical location, far from the western bastion of Anglicanism at Chichester but close to the pockets of radicalism in the eastern Sussex Weald. There is the particular composition of its population: no other town in Sussex and few in southern England had such a high proportion of the 'middling sort' of people – the independent-minded artisans and tradesmen who have traditionally formed the backbone of Protestant Dissent. The town was also well provided with prosperous merchants and manufacturers with sufficient surplus wealth to maintain the Dissenting causes virtually out of their own pockets, as the Morrises did at Jireh and the Everys at Westgate. But no such socio-economic explanations are ever entirely satisfactory: as Geoffrey Elton put it, Sussex – and he clearly had *east* Sussex in mind – has always been 'a shire given to its own secret ways'. East Sussex, the last region in England to be converted to Christianity, has a long tradition of independency and its people continue to protest (as the old Sussex saying goes) that, come what may, they 'won't be druv'.[1]

There are several other things that serve to make Lewes distinctive. Geographical and economic factors have restricted immigration, so that its recent religious life has not been affected by large influxes of Irish Catholics or Afro-Caribbean Pentecostalists, let alone Jews, Muslims, Sikhs or Hindus. But throughout its history, partly because it is such an attractive town, numerous individuals have come to reside here and some of them have played a significant part in its social and cultural life. In this way immigrants from other parts of the United Kingdom have continuously leavened the 'lump' of Lewes. 'There is no doubt that the spiritual life of this quiet southern town has been greatly invigorated by the arrival of people from the peripheries of the realm, especially from the Celtic regions where Christianity has always been most vibrant. It has been said of eighteenth and nineteenth century Wales that one of its principal exports was Nonconformist ministers: certainly the frequency with which Welsh names crop up in this book shows how much Lewes has been affected by this 'sacred trade'. Things might have turned out very differently had not that disputatious divine Jenkin Jenkins come to Lewes as a 'Welsh Ambassador' to stir up the congregation of Cliffe Chapel. The great secession of 1805 might never have taken place and the cause at Jireh might never have been founded. In addition to the Welsh there have been incomers from Scotland and Ireland, some of whom have had a great influence on the religious life of Lewes. Few men made a greater impact on the town than Ebenezer Johnston, the Scotsman whose 40 year ministry at Westgate helped to heal divisions within the Old Dissent, or William McAuliffe, the Irishman whose benign presence at St Pancras over a lengthy span of years did so much to improve relations between Roman Catholics and the rest of the population.

Perhaps the most distinctive – and least attractive – feature of the public religious life of Lewes has been the persistence of an unusually pronounced antipathy towards Roman Catholics. The town that for many years had a flourishing Orange Lodge and provided the setting for some turbulent anti-Romanist demonstrations is still notorious for the 'No Popery' banners paraded through its streets on Guy Fawkes night. Although other English towns, such as Edenbridge and Bridgwater, have great street processions on 5 November, they do not burn the Pope in effigy or recite militantly Protestant 'bonfire prayers'. Why does this only happen in Lewes? The usual answer, trotted out every year in newspaper articles and TV programmes, is that townsmen have never forgotten the Protestants who were burned alive here in Mary Tudor's time. But although their names are displayed on banners strung across the street and their number is represented by 17 flaming crosses carried in procession through the town, the commemoration of the martyrs is not an ancient practice. It is in fact a nineteenth-century innovation – an example of the 'invention of tradition' for which the Victorians are famed. The custom dates only from 1850 when a local newspaper, alarmed by the extension of rights and privileges to Roman Catholics and searching for a stick with which to beat them, decided to revive the memory of those who had long ago perished for their Protestantism. Ironically, it was an account of the martyrdoms taken from the *History and Antiquities of Lewes*, the work of that great champion of Catholic Emancipation, Thomas Walker Horsfield, that provided the Bonfire Boys with the justification for their anti-papal activities.[2]

Contrary to popular belief, Lewes's famed anti-Catholicism does not have a long history behind it. Hostility towards the Church of Rome, strong in the town in the immediate post-Reformation years, had virtually died out by the beginning of the eighteenth century. Then reason and tolerance were the order of the day and, when it came to religion, it became the rule to keep things cool. But the heat was turned on again at the time of the Evangelical Revival. The first Methodists to preach in Lewes were Calvinists, whose view of the world tended to be 'paranoid-schizoid'. They posited a sharp polarity between good and evil, God and the Devil, Christ and Antichrist. Not acknowledging their own 'shadow side', they projected it on to others, who then became legitimate targets for their hostility. At that period the natural recipients of such negative projections were the Roman Catholics, whose worship was then becoming tolerated in England. So it was that in 1825, when petitions against Catholic Emancipation were sent up to Westminster, more came out of Lewes than any other town in southern England. They did not emanate from the old-established Protestant Dissenters, who generally favoured toleration, but from the newly formed Calvinist congregations; and in 1850, when the flames of anti-Catholicism were rekindled, it was to the prejudices of such people that the local press pandered. To make matters worse anti-Romanist feelings were then also being aroused by the activities of High Anglicans like Frederick Teed at St. Michael's, who was endeavouring to re-introduce practices that to many townsmen smacked of 'popery'. To try to plant Puseyism anywhere at this date was almost certain to provoke opposition but to do so in such a hotbed of Protestantism as Lewes was to court hostility on a grand scale. It is arguable that, were it not for the Oxford Movement, the memory of the Marian martyrs might not have been revived with such enthusiasm and Lewes Bonfire Night would not have acquired quite such a strongly anti-Catholic character. Had not High Churchmen first sought to glorify and romanticise the past it is possible that their opponents would not have been tempted to do likewise. In this instance the invention of one tradition seems to have led directly to the invention of another.[3]

Today, however, anti-Catholic attitudes are rare. The tolerant religious stance that was once largely confined to Quakers and Unitarians is now more or less universal. Militant Calvinism may be alive and well in Ulster but it is all but extinct in Lewes, and not even the huffing and puffing of Ian Paisley has been able to bring its dying embers to life. Although the Ulsterman whom he appointed pastor of Jireh Chapel continues to refer to the Pope as 'Antichrist' and denounces him (in the words of the preface to the King James Bible) as a 'man of sin', hardly anyone in Lewes takes him seriously. In spite of the 'No Popery' banners the Lewes November the Fifth processions, in which Catholics as well as Protestants now participate, have little in common with the summer parades on the streets of Derry or Belfast. In fact they bear more resemblance to those that once took place throughout western Europe at the time of carnival, when the 'lord of misrule' held sway for a day and the established order was turned upside down. According to Ladurie the carnival was 'intended as a protest against a ruling caste', in which 'the prime satirical instrument was the carnival dummy or effigy made up to look like the enemy of the day', who might be the Pope, Martin Luther or some other prominent person that the crowd wished to single out for punishment or ridicule. There is a similarity here with the situation in Lewes, where the Bonfire Boys are known to have burned Methodists as well as Papists in effigy. Today there is still an element of carnival in the Bonfire Night festivities, when people who for the rest of the year keep a low profile come out into the open, dress up as bishops or Red Indian chiefs, reclaim the streets of their town and register their protest against whatever to them represents oppression: a cabinet minister, a prominent local government official or the tyrannical ruler of a foreign land. Unlike Idi Amin, Saddam Hussein or Slobodan Milosevic (all burned in effigy in recent years) the Pope no longer has the power or the will to be a tyrant and so the incineration of the image of a distant predecessor, while understandably distressing to some Catholics, has no contemporary political or religious significance. The practice of burning the effigy of Paul V, a peaceable man who happened to become Pope in 1605 and who cannot properly be held responsible for the Gunpowder Plot, shows how strong is the influence of folklore. Linking the Pope to the Plot and the Plot to the persecution of Marian Protestants is a good example of the way in which people's thoughts and actions can be affected by a misunderstanding of the past.[4]

It is arguable that the churches, supposedly the principal repositories of religious truth, are in part to blame for these misunderstandings. Although it is not their intention to do so, they do sometimes mislead the historical enquirer. Any visitor to Westgate Chapel, seeing a mural tablet erected in 1887 to commemorate its opening 200 years earlier, would naturally (but wrongly) assume that this was the building in which the congregation first worshipped after the 1687 Declaration of Indulgence. And although J.M. Connell, having made a systematic study of the chapel archives, corrected the error in his *Story of an Old Meeting House*, the wrong one survives on a tablet of stone and continues to mislead the unwary. Similar confusion is occasionally caused by the lists of incumbents displayed in parish churches. What visitor to St Michael's, looking at the names of the rectors which (with technical accuracy) excludes all those not episcopally instituted, would know that here, in the aftermath of the Civil War, Walter Postlethwaite had proclaimed the imminent establishment of the Fifth Monarchy of Christ? And what visitor to St Anne's would be aware that the notable puritan Thomas Underdowne (disguised on the list of rectors as 'Puderdowne') had ministered here in Elizabeth's reign or that the eminent seventeenth century divines Benjamin Pickering and Edward Newton had regularly preached from its fine Jacobean pulpit? Neither is listed among its rectors, although for some inexplicable reason Postlethwaite of St Michael's is.

It seems that there is sometimes a conscious or unconscious wish to construct a past consistent with the present and to see continuity where there has been change. There is, for instance, a common assumption that the Church of England, like the Gospel, is 'the same yesterday, today and forever'. It is often imagined that the currently prevailing pattern of Anglican worship, emphasising the Sacrament rather than the Word, has always been the norm. How could any visitor to St Michael's, impressed by the fine furnishings and the lingering smell of incense, ever imagine that this was once the principal bastion of Protestantism in the town? What is there to show that in the sixteenth century this was one of the first churches in Sussex to be purged of 'popery' and, in the seventeenth, one of the first to resist Laud's High Church reforms? But the notion that there has been no break in the continuity of belief and practice in the Church of England is dispelled by the discovery that for nearly two centuries most Lewes chancels lay in ruins and that at St Michael's (and probably other churches also) the rarely used communion table was hidden away behind a dominant central pulpit.

However, if Anglicans sometimes maximise continuity and minimise change, so also do Nonconformists. There is, for example, a widely held view that the United Reformed Church represents a union between two historic Dissenting denominations – the Presbyterians and the Congregationalists. The truth, however, is rather different. Most of the old English Presbyterian congregations that survived into the nineteenth century eventually became affiliated to the General Assembly of Unitarian and Free Christian Churches. Only a handful in the far north of England joined the

Scottish-based Presbyterian Church of England, which linked up with the Congregationalists to form the United Reformed Church in 1972. Moreover, although many of the constituent Congregationalist churches had their origins in seventeenth-century Independency, a substantial proportion of them stemmed, as was the case with the Tabernacle, from eighteenth century Calvinistic Methodism. In Lewes the only 'united reformed' congregation to combine the two major elements of English Protestant Dissent was the one that came into being in 1742, when Presbyterians and Independents united to call a 'Middle Way man' to be minister of Westgate Meeting.

If some have emphasised continuity where there has been change, others have done the opposite. When in 1900 the minister of Eastgate Baptist church claimed that his congregation, founded in 1784, was the oldest Nonconformist one in Lewes he was doubtless ruling out Westgate because in his view the Unitarians were intruders, occupying a building formerly belonging to another set of people called 'Presbyterians'. Like the people who in 1844 had tried to deprive Unitarians of buildings originally belonging to 'Trinitarians', he mistook a change of name and a shift in doctrine for a complete break in tradition. In 1844 members of old-established congregations such as Westgate were able to prove that, although their beliefs might have changed, successive generations of the same families had maintained their membership over the years; and so the Dissenters' Chapels Act, which confirmed the Unitarians' rights of ownership, was passed. Families such as the Ridges, prominent in the affairs of Westgate since its foundation, provided incontrovertible evidence of continuity in times of change. When it comes to delineating a tradition the focus, it seems, has always to be on people rather than ideas.[5]

Unitarians, however, perhaps because of an excessive fondness for ideas, have themselves sometimes inadvertently contributed to historical misunderstanding. Defining Unitarianism as a body of ideas rather than as a body of people, they have tended to adopt as a 'forbear' anyone who appeared to share their belief in the 'trinity' of Freedom, Reason and Tolerance; and in so doing have lost touch with their real roots. For them 'tradition' is often a pejorative word, standing for something to be broken with in the onward march towards Truth. Horsfield, Westgate's first avowedly Unitarian minister, appears to have had such a negative attitude towards tradition. His decision, on his first arrival at Westgate, to introduce 'doctrinal preaching' gave offence to those who wished to maintain the congregation's traditional non-sectarian stance. Nor was everyone happy with his designation of Westgate as 'the Unitarian meeting'. Like other pioneering English Unitarians he came from right outside the ranks of Protestant Dissent and knew little of its history. His account of his congregation in the *History of Lewes*, which gives the erroneous information that the building was opened for worship in 1687, suggests that he had not spent any time exploring the Westgate archives. The first person to do so was his twentieth-century successor J.M. Connell who, although also a newcomer to the English Dissenting tradition, had a great love and respect for it. His *Story of an Old Meeting House,* thoroughly researched, enabled his congregation to become properly re-connected to its past.[6]

It was therefore fitting that, at the tercentenary service of thanksgiving held at Westgate Chapel on 5 November 2000, all the prayers should have come from the pen of Connell's mentor James Martineau, a staunch upholder of the traditions of Protestant Dissent. Martineau, a direct descendant (in the female line) from a minister ejected in 1662, was very conscious of his Presbyterian heritage. In fact one of the prayers had been specially composed for a collection published in 1862 to mark the bicentenary of the Great Ejection:

> O God, who art and wast and art to come, before whose face the generations rise and pass away; age after age the living seek thee and find that of thy faithfulness there is no end. Our fathers in their pilgrimage walked by thy guidance and rested on thy compassion: still to their children be thou the cloud by day, the fire by night. . . .

It is Martineau's best known prayer: recited at Westgate down the generations, it speaks of a spiritual continuity that transcends time.[7]

Establishing the truth of a tradition – discovering 'what really happened' in the past – is especially difficult in the realm of religion, where objectivity is hard to achieve and records are often unreliable. That the religious history of Lewes since the Reformation consists so largely of accounts of conflict, both within groups and between them, is due in part to the nature of the sources. The records of church courts, parochial church councils, congregational committees or (in the case of the Quakers) 'meetings for sufferings' often give the impression that disputes and disagreements were the dominant feature of the religious scene. Even such correspondence as survives frequently consists largely of letters of protest and complaint, while diaries such as Charles Wille's tend to devote an inordinate amount of attention to divisions and dissensions. And as for the newspapers it goes without saying that the reports of controversy and contention comprise a large part of their stock in trade. This book has provided innumerable examples of what Stephen Sykes has called 'the media's fascination with rows and the tendency to present church history as a chronic succession of disputes'. Nevertheless, the prevalence of religious conflict in the records of Lewes cannot be blamed entirely on the preoccupations of the record-keepers. The records are full of it because there was clearly a great deal of it. And it is arguable that one reason for this was the influence of militant Calvinism.[8]

The Calvinism that came to Lewes in Elizabethan times and inspired the first puritans had many positive aspects. Their insistence on 'godly discipline' did much to promote morality, orderliness and good governance in the town. Their faith in the Sovereignty of God and their trust in Divine Providence strengthened them in their stand against oppression and, after their eventual ejection from the established Church, sustained them during the long years of persecution. But the 'shadow side' of the belief that they were peculiarly predestined to salvation was the conviction that those not so 'elected' were damned. This led them to establish a strident polarity between the 'godly' and the 'ungodly'. The 'godly exercises' to which a pious Elizabethan Lewes merchant requested that his children be brought up were contrasted sharply with the 'devil's dances' enjoyed by the great mass of the people but condemned by Calvinistic moralists such as William Perkins. Such a 'holier than thou' attitude later led local puritans to rejoice that a fire started on a Sunday by a bunch of delinquent youths had destroyed the 'most profane' houses but had left unscathed one described as 'very famous for religion'. With the resurgence of Calvinism in the later years of the eighteenth century a similarly divisive spirit manifested itself once again in Lewes. It was most clearly exemplified in the ministry of Jenkin Jenkins who, not long after he came to Cliffe Chapel, was reported to have upset people with his 'censorious, ill-natured and condemning mode of preaching'. Yet behind the aggressive exterior, as his surviving letters show, there was a deeply troubled man. 'My life is warfare, a continual conflict', he once wrote to a friend. The conflict to which he was referring was evidently an inward one, but at times it became dramatically externalised – causing him to turn what he called the 'artillery of heaven' upon people opposed to him. It was such 'paranoid-schizoid' positioning that, for many years after Jenkins's death, lay behind not only the animosity of Protestants toward Catholics but also the conflicts among Calvinists. The most bitter disputes can occur when disturbed personalities clash, with each side claiming divine justification for their stance.[9]

The marked reduction in religious conflict in the twentieth century, some might say, was due to the decline not only of Calvinism but of all institutional religion – which had the effect of leaving Christians far too weak to fight each other. A more positive interpretation is that the change had to do with a refreshingly new spirit of ecumenism. In Lewes this spirit was most fully embodied in the person of Burgess Wilkinson, minister of the town's largest congregation, who during his 40 years in Lewes had a more profound influence upon the local community's religious life than perhaps anyone else in its history. Just as in the eighteenth century, when Calvinists and Arminians were in dispute over doctrine, Ebenezer Johnston had sought to follow a 'middle way' between the two extremes, so too in the nineteenth and on into the twentieth century Wilkinson strove to reconcile the differences between the town's evangelical and liberal Nonconformists. He did much, for example, to bring together the congregations at Eastgate and Westgate, which were as far apart theologically as they were geographically. After his death the representatives of both congregations spoke very warmly of him. J.P. Morris referred to Wilkinson's 'readiness to assist everybody and everything', while J.M. Connell commended his contribution to 'the breaking down of old misunderstandings and prejudices and the bringing of the various denominations into closer sympathy and co-operation'. It was a cause of great pleasure – and some amusement – to Wilkinson that, when in his retirement he went as a visiting preacher to both 'liberal' and 'orthodox' congregations, he was able to get away with preaching the same sermons to both. So long as the Gospel of Love lay at the heart of his message none of his hearers dared raise an objection. His liberalism had a lasting influence upon the Tabernacle congregation. Some years after his death, when the Baptists proposed that local Nonconformists should become affiliated to the national Free Church Federal Council, the Congregationalists passed a resolution deeply regretting that its constitution 'does not allow the membership of their local Unitarian friends'.[10]

It may be that the marked decrease in confessional strife in recent years has had something to do with the increasingly important role of women, who are generally less disputatious than men. Now that women are able to occupy the offices previously reserved for men and to serve their churches as committee members, churchwardens, elders, deacons, ministers and priests, the whole ethos of the enterprise has changed. The success of the Lewes and District Council of Churches – subsequently re-named Churches Together in Lewes and District – has owed much to the work of women. Although the chairmen have usually been drawn from the ranks of the (exclusively male) clergy and ministers, most of whom have come and gone with great rapidity, those who have done most to sustain the council's activities down the years have been lay women. There is no doubt that from the 1950s until her death in 1992 the guiding spirit of the ecumenical movement in Lewes was Pamela Hollins, a large-minded Anglican with deep roots in Protestant Dissent.

In previous centuries, although women have almost invariably constituted the majority of any congregation, their contribution to the religious life of the community has almost always been overlooked. Calamy wrote his famous *Account* in order 'to revive the memory of some excellent men', but he ignored the equally excellent women, whose role in the maintenance of the ministry was simply taken for granted. But how would the ministers ejected in 1662 have survived without the support of the womenfolk? How would John Earl have managed without his long-suffering wife or William Wallace without that bevy of women 'big with child' who stood around him and concealed him from his persecutors? Calamy's neglect of the role of women was perpetuated by Connell, who recorded the subsequent exploits of the Lewes Dissenters in his *Story of an Old Meeting House.* Of all the hundreds of women who had occupied the pews at Westgate during the previous two and a half centuries only one got a mention in his book – and then only because she happened to have married one of the men whose doings dominate the story. One who might well have been included was Mary Ridge, who died in 1858 at the advanced age of 93, when a notice of her death appeared in the *Christian Reformer.* The magazine, which was ahead of its time in including obituaries of women, recorded that as a child Mary had been so sickly that she had not been expected to reach adulthood. Her subsequent longevity was attributed to her 'serene, quiet temper' and 'placid amiable disposition', which were 'conjoined with and sustained by a fervent, gentle piety'. All her life, in spite of the radical changes that had taken place there, she had continued to be a 'zealous member' of the Westgate congregation: 'Always, when strength permitted, it was her delight to be in her accustomed pew.' After her death she was fondly remembered, especially by the poor of her neighbourhood, to whom she had shown much generosity.[11]

Another Lewes woman of exemplary piety who lived to a great age and left a fragrant memory behind her was Ellen Hogsflesh, who died in her 99th year in 1939, when she was said to be the town's oldest inhabitant. The widow of Amos Hogsflesh, whose family had lived in Lewes 'for generations' and who was sprung from the same stock as the 'famous heretic' of Henry VIII's day, she was one who (like Mary Ridge) provided an important element of continuity in a period of great social and religious change. Since the 1870s she had been a regular worshipper at the Methodist Church in Station Street and, as one who 'never believed in being idle', had participated fully in its activities. Apart from a passing reference to her and her daughter Rose in the report of the Sunday school's summer outing in 1900 her name was hardly ever in the news, but it is clear from the obituary notice in the local paper that, like the virtuous woman praised in Proverbs, 'her price was far above rubies'. The spiritual influence of one woman sitting quietly in her pew may have been greater than that of a succession of men pounding away in the pulpit, particularly in a denomination where there was such a swift turnover of ministers. If continuity and change are the weft and warp of the historical process, it seems to be – in religion as in other spheres of life – the women who provide the continuity and the men who produce the change. While the men debate and argue it is often the women who, in less spectacular fashion, pave the way for peace. In Lewes, as in Belfast, in situations where Catholics and Protestants have been at loggerheads, it is the women who have crossed the confessional divides to sit and talk and drink tea together.[12]

The most remarkable examples of the contribution of women to the religious life of Lewes come from the Friends, who have long been renowned for their work for peace and reconciliation. From the beginning Quaker women have been free not only to speak in meetings but also to join the select group set apart as 'ministers', and at times it has been a woman who has come to embody the very 'soul' of a congregation. One such among the Lewes Friends was Elizabeth Harland, who died at the age of 80 in 1995. Brought up a Methodist she became a Quaker by 'convincement' while a young woman and, following faithfully in the footsteps of her great exemplar St Francis of Assisi, devoted her life to being an 'instrument of peace' – in the family, the local community and the wider world. Quick to respond to a cry for help, she gave unstintingly of her time and money to anyone in need, and her giving was done in such secrecy that it was only after her death that the full extent of it was revealed. She was a valued friend and counsellor to many people: devoid of self-regard she had the gift of making the other person the whole centre of her attention, so that to be in her company was always a healing experience. She was an active member of CND, Amnesty International and other movements for peace and justice and, strongly ecumenical in outlook, she was from the outset an enthusiastic supporter of the local council of churches and of the Westgate One World Centre. Although, in common with many deeply sensitive people, she was at times troubled by depression and experienced what the mystics call 'the dark night of the soul', she invariably found her faith restored in the quiet meetings of the Lewes Friends. Like William Penn, who also once worshipped with them, she believed that, when the heart grew cold, 'fire must come from heaven, life and power from God, to enable the soul to pour out itself acceptably before him'.[13]

> Burn, holy fire, and shine more wide!
> While systems rise and fall,
> Faith, hope and charity abide –
> The heart and soul of all.

The 'holy fire' of Hosmer's hymn, which provides the title of this book, does not refer to the one in which his forebear suffered death in Mary Tudor's time. Nor has it any connection with the flames to which, in later years, the effigies of popes have regularly been consigned on Lewes Bonfire Night. And it certainly has nothing to do with the fiery Hell that has featured in many a stirring Calvinist sermon. Like Penn, Hosmer was referring to the Pentecostal fire of the Spirit. He believed that throughout history the upholders of religious 'systems' had often sought to quench this fire. Standing as he did in the tradition of the New England Transcendentalists –

Emerson, Thoreau, Longfellow – he was convinced that in due course all such systems, having outlived their usefulness, would disappear. He looked for the coming of the Kingdom of God, that 'reign of light and love' that would render all religious institutions redundant. He believed that the Kingdom, for which (as he expressed it in his best known hymn) 'the passing ages pray', would bring with it a new outpouring of the Holy Spirit that would transform the world.[14]

This book has plotted the rise and fall of some of the 'systems' to which Hosmer referred. It has shown how the ecclesiastical system swept away by the Reformation was in its turn replaced by an even more oppressive one, reinforced by the coercive power of the state. Temporarily dismantled by the puritans, this regime was re-established at the Restoration and for long remained in the ascendancy – although never totally so in Lewes, where those outside the established Church were often more numerous than those within it. In due course, however, Nonconformity created its own 'systems', some of them more systematic than the Catholic or Anglican ones. Can anything compare with the efficiency and effectiveness of the ecclesiastical machinery of Wesleyan Methodism, Scottish-based Presbyterianism or the Salvation Army? Is it significant that none was able to establish a permanent foothold in Lewes, where the spirit of congregational independency has always been strong?

Today, in Lewes as elsewhere in England, *all* ecclesiastical systems have become gravely weakened. With only 10% of the population attending church regularly, organised religion has experienced the decline that Tom Paine long ago predicted. With so many of their former functions now being fulfilled by the social and educational services, secular charities or the entertainments industry, churches have lost their central place in the community and the main stream of life now flows in other channels. As long ago as 1931 J.M. Connell, in concluding his *Lewes: Its Religious History*, observed that 'all over the country the tale is told of dwindling congregations, of Sundays given up to games and motoring'. In Lewes, as everywhere else in England, he was aware of a 'generation growing up that has no use for religion'. But even the prospect of the total disappearance of the Christian church did not alarm him, because he believed that 'the Divine Spirit, which has hitherto functioned through the church, may be finding other institutions and means, better fitted for its purposes'. It was not for him, as he looked forward into a future that he knew he would not see, to speculate about the long purposes of God. Though man-made 'systems' might crumble Connell, like Hosmer, believed that faith, hope and love – 'the heart and soul of all' – would never fail. It was his conviction that there would come a time when the 'holy fire' of the Spirit, far from being extinguished, would 'shine more wide' than ever.[15]

GLOSSARY

Anabaptist: The original name (meaning 'twice baptisers') given to those who practised adult (or believers') baptism by total immersion.

Arian: One who affirmed, with Arius of Alexandria (d. 336), that the Son was subordinate to the Father. In 18th-century England the name was given (usually inaccurately) to anyone who denied the doctrine of the Trinity.

Arminian: One who believed with the Dutch Reformed theologian Jacobus Arminius (1564-1609) that Christ had died for all and not only (as Calvin held) for the 'elect'. The name was given: 1. in the early 17th century to High Church Anglicans who followed William Laud; 2. in the early 18th century to liberal Dissenters who broke with orthodox Calvinism; 3. in the late 18th and early 19th centuries to the Methodists who followed John Wesley in rejecting the Calvinism of George Whitefield.

Baptist: Originally known as 'Anabaptists' (q.v.), the English Baptists were of three kinds: **General Baptists**, who were Arminian and (by the late 18th century) usually Unitarian in theology; **Particular Baptists**, who were Calvinist and Trinitarian in theology; **Strict Baptists**, who were even more particular in that they restricted admission to communion to baptised believers.

Calvinist: One who followed John Calvin (1509-64), the French theologian who reformed the church in Geneva and affirmed that the 'elect' were predestined to salvation.

Classis: A meeting of ministers seeking to set up an alternative form of ecclesiastical government on the model of that established by Calvin in Geneva. The word was later translated into English as 'presbytery'.

Deist: An upholder of 'Natural Religion', who believed that God created the world but did not intervene in its affairs thereafter, thus denying the Revelation of God in Christ. In 18th-century England Protestant Dissenters were generally united in their opposition to Deism.

Erastian: One who followed the Swiss theologian Thomas Erastus (1524-83) in asserting the ascendancy of the State over the Church in ecclesiastical affairs.

Independent: One who upheld the independence or autonomy of each local congregation. It is often, but not always, synonymous with 'Congregationalist'. Independents were the second largest body of Protestant Dissenters in England for about a century after 1662.

Lollard: One who believed, with John Wycliffe (c.1330-84), that the Bible was the sole authority in religion and that people had the right to read and interpret it for themselves. In the late 15th and early 16th centuries Lollards, who were especially numerous in the Weald of Sussex and Kent, were sometimes referred to as 'Anabaptists'.

Predestination: The action of God in decreeing that some people were fore-ordained to salvation. It became the most distinctive doctrine of the Calvinists.

Presbyterian: One who adhered to a form of ecclesiastical polity in which the church was governed by groups of 'presbyters' (or 'elders') rather than by bishops. The 'presbyteries' established in 17th-century England were usually composed only of ordained ministers, whereas in Scotland they always embraced lay elders as well. The Presbyterians constituted the largest and most influential body of Protestant Dissenters in England for about a century after 1662. By the mid-19th century most of the surviving congregations had become Unitarian.

Puseyite: A pejorative term for Anglicans in sympathy with Edward Pusey (1800-82), one of the founders of the High Church 'Oxford Movement'.

Socinian: One who followed the Italian theologian Faustus Socinus (1539-1604) in denying the doctrine of the Trinity. In 18th-century England the name was used loosely of people who were more strongly antitrinitarian than those dubbed 'Arians' (q.v). It later became virtually synonymous with 'Unitarian' (q.v.).

Test and Corporation Acts: The **Corporation Act (1661)** stated that all municipal officers were to take the oaths of allegiance, supremacy and non- resistance, and also to receive communion according to the rites of the Church of England. It was primarily designed to destroy the political power of Dissenters in corporate towns and in Parliament. Annual Indemnity Acts were passed from 1727 and the Act was finally repealed in 1828. The **Test Act (1673}** stated that all holders of civil and military offices had to be Anglican communicants, repudiate transubstantiation and take the oaths of allegiance and supremacy. It was primarily directed against Roman Catholics, but also affected Dissenters. The Act was in force until the passing of the Catholic Relief Act (1829) and was not finally repealed until 1863.

Thirty Nine Articles: The Articles drawn up in 1563 in an attempt to define the doctrinal position of the Church of England and distinguish it from the Church of Rome. Prior to 1865 all clergymen were required to subscribe to the Articles, but since then they have merely had to undertake not to preach against them.

Transubstantiation: The doctrine, condemned in the Thirty Nine Articles, that in the communion the whole substance of the bread and wine is converted into the whole substance of the body and blood of Christ.

Unitarian: One who denies the doctrine of the Trinity and affirms the full humanity of Christ. In the 19th century the name became attached to those English Presbyterian and General Baptist congregations that were eventually (in 1928) to become affiliated to the General Assembly of Unitarian and Free Christian Churches.

Westminster Confession: The Calvinistic (q.v.) profession of faith set forth by the Westminster Assembly of Divines, the synod appointed by Parliament in 1643 to reform the Church of England.

Abbreviations

Al. Cant.	*Alumni Cantabrigiensis*, pt. 1 (Cambridge, 1922-7)
Al. Ox.	*Alumni Oxoniensis 1500-1714* (Oxford, 1891-2)
APC	*Acts of the Privy Council*
BL	British Library
Bolam	C.G. Bolam, J.J. Goring, H.L. Short and R. Thomas, *The English Presbyterians: From Elizabethan Puritanism to Modern Unitarianism* (1968)
Brent (1980)	C.E. Brent, 'The immediate impact of the Second Reform Act on a southern county town: voting patterns at Lewes Borough in 1865 and 1868', *Southern History*, **2** (1980), 129-77.
Brent (1983)	C.E. Brent, 'The neutering of the Fellowship and the emergence of a Tory party in Lewes 1663-1688', *SAC*, **121** (1983), 95-107.
Brent (1985)	C.E. Brent, 'Lewes Dissenters outside the Law', *SAC*, **123** (1985), 195-214.
Brent (1993)	C.E. Brent, *Georgian Lewes* (Lewes, 1993)
Brent (1995)	C.E. Brent, *Historic Lewes and its Buildings* (Lewes Town Council Guide, revised edn, 1995)
Calamy	E. Calamy, *An Account of the Ministers . . . who were Ejected or Silenced after the Restoration* (2nd edn, 1713)
Cal. Rev.	A.G. Matthews, *Calamy Revised: Being a Revision of Edmund Calamy's Account of the Ministers and Others Ejected and Silenced, 1660-2* (Oxford, 1934)
Connell (1931)	J.M. Connell, *Lewes: Its Religious History* (Lewes, 1931)
Connell (1935)	J.M. Connell, *The Story of an Old Meeting House* (2nd edn, 1935)
CSPD	*Calendar of State Papers Domestic*
Davey	C.R. Davey, 'The Church of St Michael-in-Lewes and the Oxford Movement' (1983), typescript in ESRO
Diocesan Surveys	*Chichester Diocesan Surveys 1686 and 1724*, ed. W.K. Ford (SRS, **78**)
DNB	*Dictionary of National Biography*
DWL	Dr Williams's Library
ESN	*East Sussex News*
ESRO	East Sussex Record Office
Etherington	J. Etherington, *Lewes Bonfire Night* (Seaford, 1993)
Fletcher	A. Fletcher, *A County Community in Peace and War: Sussex 1600-1660* (1975)

Foxe   J. Foxe, *Acts and Monuments*, ed. S.R. Cattley and G. Townsend (1837-42)

Godfrey   W.H.Godfrey, *The Official Guide to Lewes* (Lewes, 1977)

Goring (1981)   J.J. Goring, 'The Fellowship of the Twelve in Elizabethan Lewes', *SAC*, **119** (1981), 157-72.

Goring (1983)   J.J. Goring, 'The Reformation of the ministry in Elizabethan Sussex', *JEH*, **34** (1983), 345-66.

Goring (1991)   J.J. Goring, 'A Sussex Dissenting family: the Ridges of Westgate Chapel, Lewes', *SAC*, **129** (1991), 195-215.

Goring (1996)   J.J. Goring, 'Reformation and Reaction in Sussex, 1534-1559', *SAC*, **134** (1996), 141-54.

Haakonssen   D.K. Haakonssen, ed, *Enlightenment and Religion* (Cambridge, 1996)

Hitchin   D. Hitchin, *Quakers in Lewes: An Informal History* (Lewes, 1984)

Holman   G. Holman, *Some Lewes Men of Note* (2nd edn, Lewes, 1922)

Horsfield   T.W. Horsfield, *The History . . . of Lewes and its Vicinity* (**1**, 1824; **2**, 1827)

JEH   *Journal of Ecclesiastical History*

Keeble   E.B. Keeble, *The Story of the Lewes Baptists* (Lewes, n.d.)

Kitch   M.J. Kitch, ed., *Studies in Sussex Church History* (1981)

Lewes Diary   Mrs Henry Dudeney, *A Lewes Diary 1916-1944*, ed. D. Crook (Heathfield, 1998)

LJ   *The Lewes Journal and Sussex Weekly Advertiser*

Lower   M.A. Lower, *The Worthies of Sussex* (Lewes, 1865)

LP   *Letters and Papers of Henry VIII*

Manning   R.B. Manning, *Religion and Society in Elizabethan Sussex* (Leicester, 1969)

Marten   *Selections from the Diary . . . of the late William Marten of Lewes* (1828)

PRO   Public Record Office

SAC   *Sussex Archaeologlical Collections*

SAS   Sussex Archaeological Society

SCM   *Sussex County Magazine*

SE   *Sussex Express* (formerly *Sussex Agricultural Express*)

SRS   Sussex Record Society

Sussex Wills   *Transcripts of Sussex Wills*, ed. R.G. Rice, vol. 3 (SRS, **43**)

TBL, **1**   *The Town Book of Lewes 1542-1701*, ed. L.F. Salzman (SRS, **48**)

TBL, **2**   *The Town Book of Lewes 1702-1837*, ed. V. Smith (SRS, **69**)

TBL, **3**   *The Town Book of Lewes 1837-1901*, ed. V. Smith (SRS, **70**)

TUHS   *Transactions of the Unitarian Historical Society*

VCHS   *The Victoria History of the Counties of England: Sussex*

Wal. Rev.   A.G. Matthews, *Walker Revised: Being a Revision of John Walker's Sufferings of the Clergy during the Grand Rebellion 1642-60* (Oxford, 1948)

Whitley   H.M. Whitley, ed., 'The churchwarden's accounts of St Andrew's and St Michael's, Lewes from 1522 to 1601', *SAC*, **45** (1902), 40-61.

WSRO   West Sussex Record Office

References

INTRODUCTION

1. E.L. Ladurie, *Carnival in Romans* (Penguin edn, 1981), xv.
2. The following account of the history of Lewes is largely based on Godfrey, 9-22 and Brent (1995), 1-15.
3. A.M. Everitt, *Landscape and Community in England* (1985), 93-107.
4. G.J. Copley, ed., *Camden's Britannia: Surrey and Sussex* (1977), 38-9, 46, 49.
5. Brent (1993), *passim*.
6. *Lewes Diary*, 9.
7. *SE*, 26 Jun 1981; A. Thomas, *Streets of Fire* (Seaford, 1999), 62-6.
8. *ESN*, 11 Apr 1919.
9. Brent (1993), 108; Connell (1931), 88, 159-60.
10. Connell (1931), 5-6.

I. RELIGION BEFORE THE REFORMATION

1. H. Mayr-Harting, 'St Wilfrid in Sussex' in Kitch, 1-17; J. Bleach, 'A Romano-British (?) barrow cemetery and the origins of Lewes', *SAC*, **135** (1997), 131-42.
2. *VCHS*, **2**, 66.
3. E.B. Poland, *The Friars in Sussex* (Hove, 1928), 87-91.
4. *Saint Richard of Chichester: the Sources for his Life*, ed. D. Jones (SRS, **79**), 189, 204; *Chartulary of Lewes Priory* (1), ed. L.F. Salzman (SRS, **38**), 104.
5. *Cf.* E. Kemp, 'The Mediaeval Bishops of Chichester' in Kitch, 21; J.A.F. Thomson, *The Later Lollards 1414-1520* (Oxford, 1965), 1-2, 182, 186-9; Goring (1996), 145.
6. *VCHS*, **7**, 40-1; J. Houghton, *Unknown Lewes* (Heathfield, 1997), 83-101.
7. *Sussex Wills*, 116; *VCHS*, **7**, 38, 40.
8. *Sussex Wills*, 129-30.
9. D. Park, 'The "Lewes Group" of wall paintings in Sussex', *Anglo-Norman Studies*, **6** (1983), 201-35; *Sussex Wills*, 107-8.

II. REFORMATION, REACTION AND THE ROOTS OF CONFLICT

1. *TBL*, **1**, 1; *LP*, **9**, 1066; Poland, *Friars in Sussex*, 92-3.
2. C.E. Welch, 'Three Sussex heresy trials', *SAC*, **95** (1957), 60-3.
3. Whitley, 47; G.J. Mayhew, *Tudor Rye* (Brighton, 1987), 60-1; Goring (1996), 145; *Lay Subsidy Rolls 1524-5*, ed. J. Cornwall (SRS, **56**), 96-101; see above, p. 22.

4. W.H.S. Hope, 'The Cluniac Priory of St Pancras, Lewes', *SAC*, **49** (1906), 73-82; L.F. Salzman, 'The last Prior of Lewes', *SAC*, **76** (1935), 178-82.
5. Goring (1996), 143.
6. *Ibid*; *LP*, 13 (1), 383; *Sussex Wills*, 140-44, 147-50; Poland, *Friars in Sussex*, 94.
7. L.F. Salzman, 'Sussex religious at the Dissolution', *SAC*, **92** (1954), 32-4.
8. *VCHS*, **7**, 41; Whitley, 50-2.
9. Goring (1996), 147.
10. *Ibid*, 148.
11. *Sussex Wills*, 115, 134.
12. *Ibid.*, 112.
13. G.J. Mayhew, 'The progress of the Reformation in East Sussex', *Southern History*, **5** (1983), 46; ESRO, W/A 3/256, 269.
14. ESRO, W/C 4/106; *Sussex Wills*, 100.
15. *Sussex Wills*, 113, 122, 126; *cf*. W.K. Jordan, *Philanthropy in England* (1959), *passim*.
16. F.W. Steer, *The Grey Friars in Chichester*, Chichester Papers, **2** (Chichester, 1955); *VCHS*, **3**, 92-3; *cf*. R. Tittler, *The Reformation and the Towns in England* (Oxford, 1998), 89-92, 113.
17. Whitley, 56; Goring (1996), 153, n.72; *Sussex Wills*, 109, 112.
18. Foxe, **7**, 321-6; *cf*. P. Collinson, 'Truth and Legend: the Veracity of John Foxe's Book of Martyrs' in his *Elizabethan Essays* (1994), 151-77.
19. Foxe, **8**, 151, 332-3; M.A. Lower, *The Sussex Martyrs* (Lewes, 1851), 10; R. Davey, 'Three Lewes martyrs of 1557', *SAC*, **138** (2000), 231-3.
20. *TBL*, **1**, 11; *Sussex Wills*, 97, 126
21. Whitley, 56-7; *SAC*, **48** (1905), 22-3.
22. SAS, Clergy index; *SAC*, **61** (1920), 114.
23. T.J. McCann, 'The Clergy and the Elizabethan Settlement in the diocese of Chichester' in Kitch, 100-02.
24. BL, Add. 39, 330, ff.91-2; *APC*, **9**, 94; *cf*. C.W. Marsh, *The Family of Love in English Society* (Cambridge, 1994), 103-4.
25. *SAC*, **100** (1962), 119-20; SAS, Clergy index; PRO, SP12/159/14, 16; Manning, 192-9; Goring (1983), 345-51.
26. Manning, 195-8, 213; WSRO, Ep II/9/5, ff.39, 43.
27. WSRO, Ep II/5/1, ff. 45-50; Goring (1981), 166-7; *cf*. Mayhew, *Tudor Rye*, 77-9.
28. WSRO, Ep II/5/2, ff.163-4; Manning, 264; PRO, PROB 11/62/46.
29. Manning, 198n; J.J. Goring, *Sussex and the Spanish Armada* (Lewes, 1988), 3, 9.
30. WSRO, Ep II/9/5, ff.156, 238*v*, 272*v*, 274*v*; Manning, 213-14; *SAC*, **12** (1860), 258.
31. WSRO, Ep II/9/3, f.42*v*; ESRO, PAR 414/9/la; *VCHS*, **7**, 37.
32. Whitley, 59; *SAC*, **48**, 28-9; **49**, 52; WSRO, Ep II/9/3, f.5*v*.
33. SAS, Clergy index; WSRO, Ep II/5/4, ff.71-3; 9/3, f.35*v*.
34. *TBL*, **1**, 130-4; WSRO, Ep II/9/7, ff.101, 109*v*; Mayhew, *Tudor Rye*, 77-8; *cf*. P. Collinson and J. Craig, ed., *The Reformation in English Towns 1500-1640* (1998), 10.
35. Mayhew, *Tudor Rye*, 55; *cf*. Manning, 205-7.

III. PURITANS, LAUDIANS AND THE GREAT CIVIL WAR

1. Hatfield House, MS 103, f.64.
2. P. Collinson, *The Elizabethan Puritan Movement* (1967), 456; Manning, 216; ESRO, W/A 28/28; Goring (1983), 365.
3. SAS, Clergy index; *Al. Cant.*, **1**, 255; **2**, 450; **3**, 435; **4**, 144; Fletcher, 71-2, 111;

R. Baxter, *Catholic Communion Defended Against Both Extremes* (1684), **2**, 32-3. (I am grateful to William Lamont for the Baxter reference.)

4. Lower, 299-300; *Wal. Rev.*, 358; WSRO, Ep II/5/11, f.7; *SAC*, **50** (1907), 43, 44.
5. WSRO, Ep V/3/1, ff.44*v*, 46; Ep II/9/11, f.173.
6. P. Collinson, *The Religion of Protestants* (Oxford, 1982), 197; ESRO, W/A 18/ 125, 20/73; PAR 414/9/1/lc; *TBL*, **1**, 56, 71.
7. *Calendar of Assize Records: Sussex Indictments, Elizabeth I,* no.1924; *James I*, no.2; SRS, **4**, 12; Fletcher, 102.
8. D. Cressy, *Bonfires and Bells* (1989), 30, 142; A. Fraser, *The Gunpowder Plot* (1996), 290; Etherington, 13; ESRO, PAR 414/9/1/lc, 415/9/la; *cf.* D. Underdown, *Fire from Heaven* (1992), 93.
9. Collinson, *Religion of Protestants*, 19, 82; *DNB, s.v.* Edward Sackville, 4th earl of Dorset; SAS, Clergy index; *Al. Ox.*, 1292, 1469; WSRO, Ep II/15/1, p.4.
10. Fletcher, 90; *SAC*, **49**, 64; ESRO, PAR 415/9/la.
11. *SAC*, **49**, 63; ESRO, PAR 414/9/1/lc; WSRO, Ep II/15/1, p.50. 12.
12. *VCH*, **2**, 33; *CSPD, 1635*, xliii; WSRO, Ep II/15/1, p.49.
13. ESRO, PAR 414/9/1/lc;*Wal. Rev*, 353.
14. *Wal. Rev*, 358; Lower, 299; WSRO, Ep II/5/11, f. 7.
15. ESRO, PAR 415/9/1a; *SAC*, **50**, 43.
16. Fletcher, 63-4, 326; Holman, 18.
17. ESRO, PAR 414/9/1/1c; 415/9/la.
18. BL, Add. 15, 671, f. 94; 39,328, f. 240; *SAC*, **36** (1888), 137, 145; Fletcher, 73, 106; SAS, Clergy index; PRO, PROB 11/267/323.
19. Calamy, 673-4; *Cal. Rev.*, 364.
20. Calamy, 675; *Cal. Rev.*, 396; Fletcher, 120.
21. Horsfield, **1**, 199-200; Brent (1985), 199.
22. *SAC*, **16** (1864), 71-7; Hitchin, 3, 6.
23. *TBL*, **1**, 74, 82; Brent (1983), 104; Brent (1985), 207-11; Fletcher, 111-13; C. Durston and J. Eales, ed., *The Culture of English Puritanism 1560-1700* (1996), 30, 219; *SAC*, **5** (1852), 100.

IV. EJECTION, SCHISM AND THE LONG PERSECUTION

1. J.J. Goring, 'Some neglected aspects of the Ejection of 1662', *TUHS*, **13** (1962), 1-8.
2. D.L. Wykes, *'To revive the memory of some excellent men': Edmund Calamy and the early historians of nonconformity* (Friends of Dr Williams's Library 50th lecture, 1997), 5, 19-20; *Cal. Rev.*, xliv.
3. Calamy, 674-5.
4. *Cal. Rev.*, 45, 71, 73, 150-1, 176-7, 225, 459; Calamy, 686-7; Brent (1985), 208-11.
5. Calamy, 689, 693; *Cal. Rev.*, 465; Brent (1985), 210.
6. Brent (1985), 195-6, 198, 200.
7. *Ibid.*, 206-7.
8. *Ibid.*, 201, 206.
9. Brent (1983), 95-107; Brent (1985), 196
10. Brent (1985), 199; Horsfield, **1**, Appendix, xxv-xxxii.
11. *SAC*, **51** (1908), 10, 11; *Cal. Rev.*, 396; Brent (1985), 195-6.
12. Hitchin, 14, 18, 31; W. Penn, *The Peace of Europe, the Fruits of Solitude and Other Writings* (Everyman Library, n.d.), 182.
13. PRO, SP 29/86, f. 87; SAS, Clergy index; ESRO, Q1/EW3, f. 35*v*.
14. Hitchin, 9, 27; *SAC*, **46** (1903), 108, 111; J.D. Ramsbottom, 'Presbyterians and

"Partial Conformity" in the Restoration Church of England', *JEH*, **43** (1992), 268; Brent (1983), 103; SAS, Clergy index.

15. Brent (1985), 198, 199, 201.
16. *Churchwardens' Presentments: Archdeaconry of Lewes*, ed. H. Johnstone (SRS, **50**), 59; ESRO, PAR 415/9/la.
17. Brent (1983), 103-4.
18. Godfrey, 18; Hitchin, 9.
19. Connell (1935), 22; *Cal. Rev.*, 524; Goring (1991), 198.

V. DISSENSIONS WITHIN DISSENT

1. L.E. Whatmore, 'The birthplace and parentage of Bishop Challenor: an enquiry', *Recusant History,* **12** (1973), 254-60.
2. WSRO, Ep I/88/39; *Diocesan Surveys*, 123, 125, 132, 146-9, 163, 184, 229, 230; *A Memorandum Book for the use of the Church of our Lord Jesus Christ meeting in and about Ditcheling*, ed, L.J. Maguire (1976), *passim; ex inf.* Judith Brent.
3. *The General Baptist Advocate*, **72** (1836), 177-79.
4. Connell (1935), 33-7.
5. Hitchin, 31-2.
6. ESRO, SOF 5/l, pp. 293, 328, 330, 354; Hitchin, 33; *Diocesan Surveys*, 121, 147, 148, 182, 229; *cf.* A. Davies, *The Quakers in English Society, 1655-1725* (Oxford, 2000), 158, 163-5.
7. Connell {1935), 28-33; ESRO, NU 1/1/l, ff.2-7.
8. Connell (1935), 26, 37-9; ESRO, NU 1/1/1 (at rear in reverse), ff.1-3.
9. Connell (1935), 40-3; ESRO, NU 1/1/1 (a/r/r), ff.2-3; Calamy, 674.
10. ESRO, NU 1/1/1 (a/r/r), f.5; W/A 38/98; Connell (1935), 19-20.
11. Connell (1935), 23-5, 43-4.
12. ESRO, NU 1/1/1 (a/r/r), ff.5-6; Goring (1991), 198.
13. *Diocesan Surveys*, 229, 230, 250; D. Ridge, *A Sussex Family: the Family of Ridge from 1500 to the Present Day* (Chichester, 1975), 29-30, 45.
14. ESRO, NU 1/9/l, 2; W/A 52/94; Connell (1935), 48-9; Brent (1993), 48, 54-5, 89, 123-4, 152; *TBL*, **1**, 114; **2**, 5, 13, 15, 18, 25, 26, 29, 30, 87.
15. J.J. Goring, 'The Break-up of the Old Dissent' in Bolam, 175-6; *SAC*, **51**, 184; ESRO, PAR 411/9/l; 414/9/l/2; 'An Account of those persons who were contributors to the support of the ministry' (MS. in possession of Richard Philcox of Lewes).
16. Connell (1935), 48-9; *cf.* R. Thomas, 'Presbyterians in Transition' in Bolam, 155-63.
17. *SAC*, **51**, 184-6.
18. D.L. Wykes, 'After the Happy Union', *Studies in Church History,* **32** (1996), 288-9, 295; *SAC*, **51**, 184-6.
19. *SAC*, **51**, 184-6; Connell (1935), 52, 55, 63.
20. ESRO, AMS 6235/l, f.17r; Connell (1935), 55-6, 63; M.R. Watts, *The Dissenters*, **1** (Oxford, 1978), 369.
21. Connell (1935), 57-9; ESRO, AMS 6235/2; R. Thomas, 'Presbyterians in Transition', 115-16; Goring, 'Break-up of Old Dissent', 178.
22. *SAC*, **51**, 184-6.
23. Goring, 'Break-up of Old Dissent', 201-2.
24. *Ibid.*, 186-8, 194-5; D.L. Wykes, 'The Dissenting Academy and Rational Dissent' in Haakonssen, 118-20, 128.

25. Goring, 'Break-up of Old Dissent', 203; R.K. Webb, 'The Emergence of Rational Dissent' in Haakonssen, 36; 'Rational Piety' in *ibid.*, 289; ESRO, AMS 6235/l, f. 11*r*.
26. Connell (1935), 63-4.
27. ESRO, AMS 6235/l, ff.57*r*, 61*v*; Brent (1993), 52-5.
28. Brent (1993), 149, 152; *Diocesan Surveys*,121, 146-9, 229.
29. *Diocesan Surveys*, 146-9; ESRO, PAR 411/9/1, 18 Jul 1750; *SCM*, **15** (1941), 250; Holman, 78-81.
30. *Diocesan Surveys*, 121, 146-9.
31. *Ibid.*, 121, 132, 146, 252, 274, n. 65; ESRO, SOF 5/l, p.330.
32. Brent (1993), 150-l; ESRO, SOF 5/l, pp.345, 354; W/A 58/144.
33. *Diocesan Surveys*, 121, 147; BL, Add. 32,703, f. 17*v*; Brent (1993), 150.
34. Brent (1993), 124, 150; D. Vaisey, ed, *The Diary of Thomas Turner 1754-1765* (Oxford, 1984), 251; ESRO, XA 4l, 27 Jun 1762.
35. *Cf.* H.L. Short, 'From Presbyterian to Unitarian' in Bolam, 221; W. Whitaker, *One Line of the Puritan Tradition in Hull* (1910), 116f.

VI. EVANGELICAL REVIVAL AND SECTARIAN STRIFE

1. *LJ*, 15 Sep 1760; A.H.C. Seymour, *The Life and Times of Selina, Countess of Huntingdon* (1839), **1**, 363-4, 381.
2. *LJ*, 6 Nov 1769, 29 Jan 1770, 6 Aug 1771; ESRO, NI 1/27/1/2; Keeble, 4.
3. *Sussex Notes and Queries,* **1** (1926-7), 123-4; Keeble, 4-6; Brent (1993), 158.
4. Keeble, 6-11.
5. *Ibid*, 11-13; ESRO, NB 1/1/lA, 258, 261, 290; *LJ*, 15 Jul 1816; Brent (1993), 159.
6. Brent (1993), 159-61; J.E. North, *A History of Jireh Chapel, Lewes* (Huntingtonian Press, n.d.), 3-5; *The Letters of Jenkin Jenkins*, ed. G. Miller (Huntingtonian Press, 1996), 4-5.
7. *The Life and Experience of, and some traces of the Lord's gracious dealings towards the author John Gibbs* (1827), 85-9, 100-6, 123-4; Brent (1993), 163.
8. Brent (1993), 163-4; WSRO, Ep I/88/39.
9. ESRO, AMS 5569/65.
10. *LJ*, 15 Jul, 9 Sep, 2 Dec 1816; Brent (1993), 165-6.
11. *LJ*, 13 Apr 1847; Brent (1993), 165; SAS, Dudeney's diary, 23, 26, 28 Jun, 12 Nov 1821.
12. Brent (1993), 165; *LJ*, 31 May 1824, 17 Nov 1828.
13. *Transactions of the Congregational Historical Society*, **5** (1911-12), 374; Goring (1991), 199; ESRO, NU1/9/11-12; Brent (1993), 161; *ex inf.* Susan Haines.
14. Connell (1935), 64-6, 76-7; J. Keane, *Tom Paine: A Political Life* (1995), 62-75; J.J. Goring, 'Young Tom Paine: Wesleyan Methodist or Rational Dissenter?', *TUHS*, **23** (2003), 472-8.
15. Goring (1991), 198-201; Connell (1935), 78-8l; S. Parker, *The Old Testament Illustrated* (1805), list of subscribers.
16. D.P. Waley and J.J. Goring, 'Lewes Library Society: the early years, 1785-1831', *SAC*, **138** (2000), 154-5; ESRO, R/L 11/1/2, 2 Feb, 4 May 1791; Brent (1993), 189.
17. Waley and Goring; 155; see above, p.92.
18. Connell (1935), 81-94; ESRO, NB 1/6/2, 24 Aug 1817.
19. Hitchin, 35-8, 47-9, 56-7.
20. *Ibid.*, 43-5.
21. *LJ*, 18 Dec 1815, 16 Dec 1816.
22. Marten, 16-17, 38-9, 46-7.

23. *DNB, s.v.* Richard Cecil (1748-1810); *LJ*, 5, 12 Jan, 15 Jun 1778.
24. *DNB, s.v.* Richard Cecil; Marten, 6.
25. *LJ*, 15, 29 Jun, 6 Jul, 7 Sep 1807; G.A. Mantell, *A Day's Ramble in Lewes* (1846), 28; Brent (1993), 150-1.
26. WSRO, Ep II/27/25.
27. E.B. Ellman, *Recollections of a Sussex Parson* (1912), 18, 55-6, 155.
28. E.C. Curwen, ed, *The Journal of Gideon Mantell* (1940), 71, 95, 96.
29. Brent (1993), 97-100, 128; ESRO, AMS 6006/1/l; ESC 113.
30. Brent (1993), 196-7.
31. *Ibid,*, 200-2; J.J. Goring, 'Why did Horsfield leave Lewes?', *SAC*, **138** (2000), 234-5.
32. *TBL*, **2**, 273, 277.
33. WSRO, Ep II/27/48; *SE*, 6 Jun 1840.

VII. PROTESTANTS, PAPISTS AND PUSEYITES

1. *Religious Census*, xvii-xviii, 80-5. See Appendix.
2. M.R. Watts, *The Dissenters*, 2{Oxford, 1995), 27.
3. Horsfield, **1**, 305-8; Keeble, 17-18; North, *Jireh Chapel*, 16; *ESN*, 22 Jun 1877; *ex inf.* Kathleen Vinall.
4. *Religious Census*, xxiii.
5. Keeble, 18-25; W.O. Chadwick, *The Victorian Church*, **2** (2nd edn, 1972), 472.
6. *The Life of John Vinall* (Huntingtonian Press, n.d.), *passim*; North, *Jireh Chapel*, 17-21; ESRO, AMS 5581/2-4.
7. ESRO, NC 2/9/22, pp. 1-10; ESRO, AMS 5569/27; DWL, Surman card index.
8. ESRO, AMS 5569/29, 32, 35, 36.
9. *Ibid.*, 27, 29, 31; *Religious Census*, 82; DWL, Surman card index.
10. W.R. Ward, *Early Victorian Methodism* (1976), 193-5.
11. *Religious Census*, 82; ESRO, NMA 12/1/l, 2; 12/4/l; *ESN*, 17 May, 1 Nov 1867.
12. *ESN*, 3 Jan, 26 Jun 1868; *SE*, 20 Mar 1877.
13. Goring (1991), 201-2.
14. Connell (1935), 102-16; *ESN*, 17, 24 Nov; l, 8, 15 Dec 1865; *cf.* D.L. Edwards, *Christian England* (1989), **3**, 247-8.
15. Hitchin, 59-64, 67-8.
16. *Ibid.*, 76-8; ESRO, ACC 778311; *Lewes Directory* (1887).
17. A. Briggs, 'The Salvation Army in Sussex 1883-1892' in Kitch, 189-208; *ESN*, 15, 22 May 1891.
18. *ESN*, 24 Jul; 7, 14 Aug 1891; 26 Jan 1900; *SE*, 5, 9 May 1891.
19. *ESN*, 11, 18 Sep 1891; ESRO, ACC 778311.
20. *ESN*, 11 Feb 1910.
21. *SE*, 26 May 1866; I. Nairn and N. Pevsner, *The Buildings of England: Sussex* (1965), 551-3.
22. The following account of events at St Michael's is based on Davey, 1-11 and N. Victor and M. Smythe, *Some Notes on the History of S. Michael-in-Lewes* (Hove, 1940), 12-23.
23. Davey, 4; J. Scobell, *A Reply to the Postscript of the Rev. John M. Neale* (1858), 11-13.
24. Brent (1993), 202; Goring, 'Why did Horsfield leave Lewes?', 234; C.J. Barnes, *East Sussex Census: 1851 Index*, **22** (1993); Etherington, 20-21; *TBL*, **3**, 70; *SE*, 9 Nov 1850, 8 Nov 1851.

25. *SE*, 10 Nov 1849, 9 Nov 1850; Horsfield, **1**, 184-6; Lower, *Sussex Martyrs*, iii-iv.
26. Lower, *Sussex Martyrs*, iii-iv; Etherington, 28-31; Brent (1980), 165; *ESN*, 6 Nov 1868.
27. *Lewes Catholic Quarterly*, May 1962.
28. Brent (1980), 165; *SCM*, **3**, 66.
29. R.C. Swift, 'Methodism in Sussex and its influence on the life of the community, 1756-1900' (M.Phil. thesis, Univ. of Sussex, 1984), 135, 137, 141; *ESN*, 3 Jul 1868, 5 Jul 1879; Hitchin, 78-9; Brent (1980), 159.
30. Brent (1980), 140-3, 167.
31. ESRO, ESC 113; AMS 5569/32, 9 Feb 1860.
32. *TBL* **3**, *passim*; Brent (1980), 141; R.V. Holt, *The Unitarian Contribution to Social Progress in England* (1938), 231-5; A. Briggs, *Victorian Cities* (Penguin edn, 1990), 198, 202.
33. *SCM*, **3**, 758, 759, 765.
34. *SE*, 22 Jun 1897.
35. *SCM*, **27**, 426-7.

VIII. FROM CONFLICT TO COOPERATION

1. *TBL*, **3**, 452-4; *ESN*, 8 Feb 1901.
2. *ESN*, 30 Mar 1900, 26 Mar 1901; *SE*, 7, 11 May 1901.
3. *SE*, 11 May 1901; *ESN*, 6 Mar 1896; Etherington, 33.
4. ESRO, NC 2/9/3, 20 May 1897; *ESN*, 9 Jan, 2 Feb 1900; 8 Feb 1901.
5. *ESN*, 22 Jun; 6, 13, 20, 27 Jul 1900.
6. *Ex inf.* Kathleen Vinall.
7. *ESN*, 5 Oct 1906, 10 Aug 1928.
8. *Ibid.*, 23 Nov 1900; *cf.* J.J. and R.J. Goring, *The Unitarians* (Christian Denominations Series, RMEP, 1984), 59.
9. *Ibid.*, 5 Oct 1906, 19 Dec 1913.
10. *Ibid.*, 20 Apr 1900; 17, 24 Apr, 1 May 1914.
11. ESRO, NC 2/9/3; NI 1/3/3/1.
12. M.R. Watts, *Why did the English stop going to church?* (Friends of Dr Williams's Library 48th lecture, 1995), 10; ESRO, NU 1/11/1/4, p.38; Connell (1935), 118.
13. *ESN*, 27 Feb 1925; ESRO, NC 2/9/5, 2 Oct 1919.
14. *ESN*, 24 Oct, 7 Nov 1919; 5 Nov 1920; D.L. Edwards, *A Concise History of English Christianity* (1998), 166.
15. *ESN*, 4, 11 Nov 1921; 26 Jun 1925.
16. *Ibid.*, 26 Jun, 24 Jul, 11 Sep, 6 Nov 1925; *Lewes Diary*, 134.
17. *ESN*, 9 Nov 1928, 9 Nov 1934.
18. K. Rawlings, *Our Debt to the Dead* (Lewes Press, 1934), 4, 7; *SE*, 16 Nov 1934.
19. *ESN*, 23 Nov, 14 Dec 1934.
20. *ESN*, 31 Mar 1939; *ex inf.* Rowena Bingham.
21. *ESN*, 27 Apr, 4 May 1928.
22. ESRO, NU 1/11/1/4, p. 153; Connell (1935), 133.
23. *ESN*, 27 Apr 1928, 13 Oct 1933, 28 Jul 1934.
24. *Ibid.*, 20, 27 Jun 1924; *Lewes Catholic Quarterly*, Winter 1969/70; *ex inf.* Laurence Keogh.
25. *ESN*, 17 Nov 1939; 14 Feb, 28 Mar, 2 May 1941.
26. *SE*, 3 Mar 1944; *Lewes Diary*, 238, 239.

27. ESRO, PAR 414/14/1/3, 13 Mar 1947, 20 Apr 1950; 14/1/4, p. 98; 14/1/5, pp.62, 140-l.
28. ESRO, PAR 410/14/l, pp. 64, 137, 358-9, 366, 390, 395.
29. ESRO, PAR 411/14/1/4, 3 Apr 1952, 19 Apr 1955; 413/14/3, pp.74, 149; 14/4, 3 Nov 1976; 419/16/3.
30. *ESN*, 1, 8 Sep 1939; North, *Jireh Chapel*, 23.
31. ESRO, NC 2/9/6, 7 Feb 1946, 3 Feb 1947, 3 Jan 1952.
32. ESRO, NMA 1/1/7, 16 Feb 1954, 3 Sep 1969, 9 Sep 1970.
33. See p. 172.
34. *SE*, 23, 30 Jun 1972; B. Viney, *I Am Sure* (1975), 148.
35. ESRO, ACC 4508, 31 Jan 1964; 6 Apr 1970; 16 Mar, 1 Dec 1972; 25 Nov 1975.
36. S. Mansfield, 'Lewes Bonfire Societies: a continuing manifestation of anti-Catholicism in East Sussex' (B.Ed. dissertation, 1990/1, SAS Library), 15-2l.
37. ESRO, ACC 4508, 29 Jun 1973; *SE*, 19 Oct 1984; *The Inquirer*, 10 Nov 1984.
38. *SE*, 8, 15 Nov 1996; l May 1998.
39. *Ibid.*, 17, 24 Sep; 1 Oct 1999.
40. *Ibid.*, 20, 27 Oct; 3, 10 Nov 2000; *Evening Argus*, 3 Nov 2000.
41. J.M. Connell, ed., *A Book of Devotional Readings from the Literature of Christendom* (1913), 191-2.   •

CONCLUSION

1. G.R. Elton, *Policy and Police* (Cambridge, 1972), 84.
2. See above, pp. 128-9.
3. R.W. Davis, *Dissent in Politics 1780-1830* (1971), 225-6.
4. Ladurie, *Carnival in Romans*, 295.
5. Goring (1991), 204; see above, p. 140.
6. J.J. Goring, 'Unitarianism: history, myth or make-believe', *TUHS*, **19** (1990), 213-27; Horsfield, **1**, 302-3.
7. J.J. Goring, 'The Dissenting Tradition', *Faith and Freedom*, **39** (1986), 130-6; *Common Prayer for Christian Worship* (1862).
8. S. Sykes, article in *Church Times*, 22 Feb 2002,
9. *The Letters of Jenkin Jenkins*, 16, 24; *cf.* J.J. Goring, *Godly exercises or the devil's dance?: puritanism and popular culture in pre-Civil War England* (Friends of Dr Williams's Library 37th lecture, 1983), 6, 21-3; see above, p. 38.
10. *ESN*, 17 Aug 1928; ESRO, NC 2/9/6, 4 Sep 1941.
11. Goring (1991), 203; see above, p.
12. *ESN*, 13 Jan 1939.
13. *Ex inf.* David Hitchin; W. Penn, cited in V. Gollancz, *From Darkness to Light* {1956), 249.
14. *Songs of Praise* (1931), nos. 192, 680.
15. Connell (1931), 174-5.

Index of Persons

General Index

Cynthia

cuttng geen

Printed in the United Kingdom
by Lightning Source UK Ltd.
9720500001B/66-420